PUBLICATIONS OF THE DEPARTMENT OF
ROMANCE LANGUAGES
UNIVERSITY OF NORTH CAROLINA

General Editor: ALDO SCAGLIONE

Editorial Board: JUAN BAUTISTA AVALLE-ARCE, PABLO GIL CASADO, FRED M. CLARK, GEORGE BERNARD DANIEL, JANET W. DÍAZ, ALVA V. EBERSOLE, AUGUSTIN MAISSEN, EDWARD D. MONTGOMERY, FREDERICK W. VOGLER

NORTH CAROLINA STUDIES IN THE
ROMANCE LANGUAGES AND LITÉRATURES

ESSAYS; TEXTS, TEXTUAL STUDIES AND TRANSLATIONS; SYMPOSIA

Founder: URBAN TIGNER HOLMES

Editor: JUAN BAUTISTA AVALLE-ARCE
Associate Editor: FREDERICK W. VOGLER

Other publications of the Department: *Estudios de Hispanófila, Hispanófila, Romance Notes, Studia Raeto-Romanica*

Distributed by:

INTERNATIONAL SCHOLARLY BOOK SERVICE, INC.
P. O. BOX 4347
Portland, Oregon   97208
U. S. A.

NORTH CAROLINA STUDIES IN THE
ROMANCE LANGUAGES AND LITERATURES
Number 138

DON QUIJOTE *(1894-1970)*:
A SELECTIVE ANNOTATED BIBLIOGRAPHY

VOLUME ONE

DON QUIJOTE *(1894-1970)*:

A SELECTIVE ANNOTATED BIBLIOGRAPHY

VOLUME ONE

BY
DANA B. DRAKE

CHAPEL HILL

NORTH CAROLINA STUDIES IN THE
ROMANCE LANGUAGES AND LITERATURES
U.N.C. DEPARTMENT OF ROMANCE LANGUAGES
1974

Library of Congress Cataloging in Publication Data

Drake, Dana B

Don Quijote (1894-1970): a selective annotated bibliography.

(North Carolina studies in the Romance languages and literatures, no. 138) (Publications of the Dept. of Romance Languages, University of North Carolina)
1. Cervantes Saavedra, Miguel de, 1547-1616 — Bibliography. I. Title.
II. Series: North Carolina studies in the Romance languages and literatures, no. 138.

Z8158.D69   016.863'3   74-8503
ISBN 978-0-8078-9138-4

DEPÓSITO LEGAL: V. 3.351 - 1974

ARTES GRÁFICAS SOLER, S. A. - JÁVEA, 28 - VALENCIA (8) - 1974

DEDICATION

Deep appreciation is expressed to Professor Sterling A. Stoudemire for his helpful words of advice and for his continued encouragement. Gratitude is also expressed to those who were kind enough to assist in this project. The kind support of Virginia Polytechnic Institute and State University is respectfully acknowledged.

EXPLANATORY NOTE

The style and arrangement of the following summaries is somewhat unusual. Matter *not* in brackets is a rephrasing of the particular critic's observations from *his* point of view. A great deal of the *un*bracketed material consists of direct quotes even though quotation marks may not be used. This procedure was used, wherever possible, to simplify the summaries and to avoid the appearance that that critic was quoting another. Some works selected do not lend themselves to this form of summary, and brackets have been used when we are summarizing a work from *our* point of view. Brackets are also used to furnish citations and cross-references and to give credit to those who have assisted in this project.

FOREWORD

This is our second effort at an annotated or critical bibliography, the first being our work on the *Novelas ejemplares* published at Virginia Polytechnic Institute in 1968. Since that time Tilbert Diego Stegmann's fine treatise on the *Persiles* has appeared, which work contains an excellent commentated bibliography on Cervantes' posthumous adventure novel. Thus this type of practical Cervantine study is progressing bit by bit, and it is our hope that in the near future similar annotated bibliographies will appear on the *comedias* and *entremeses*, and other of Cervantes' *obras*.

The purpose of this present study to select and summarize leading books and articles on the *Quijote*, published between 1894 and 1970. This period is chosen because Leopoldo Rius' great three-volume bibliography contains excerpts from critical works on the *Quijote* up to the end of the nineteenth century. It is true that Rius' work is not complete, and hence it would be logical to start at the beginning of *Quijote* criticism. However, Daniel Quilter (241) has most ably dealt with the *Quijote* in the seventeenth century. Similar studies of the eighteenth and nineteenth centuries would be appropriate subjects for dissertations and would be most helpful to students of Cervantes' masterpiece. Such studies would bring to light the content of numerous earlier works and lead to the preparation of various types of practical bibliographical studies, including an up-to-date bibliography based on categories, such as the work of J. D. M. Ford and Ruth Lansing in 1931.

We are well aware of the short-comings of the chronological approach which we are following here, but feel that this selective work on recent criticism will be of some value to the reader, if for the sole reason that it calls to his attention certain recorded thoughts of the past seventy-five years on the subject of Cervantes' masterpiece.

As stated above, this volume is selective, and in some cases the process of inclusion was vexing. It seemed best to us, on the whole, to limit ourselves here to *leading* works dealing extensively with the *Quijote*, its meaning, its composition, style and structure, its principal characters, or its overall criticism over the years. Certain leading collections of articles on the *Quijote* are also included for the reader's benefit. There are many general studies on Cervantes' life and works, but only a comparatively few are included. Those selected were chosen on the basis of their quality and informativeness. It was felt best to postpone until the following volume several categories of studies: works on Cervantes' vocabulary and grammar; studies dealing with the meaning of a particular word or phrase such as *duelos y quebrantos;* indexes and bibliographies; studies on the influence of the *Quijote* on the literature of a given country or author; articles which discuss the sources or meaning of a particular episode or intercalated tale; studies of minor figures; histories of literature; works dealing with the adaptations of the *Quijote;* studies of the Avellaneda *Quijote* of 1614; technical though highly informative articles on such matters as coins and clothing in *Don Quijote*.

In some cases the above *criteria* will be stretched, if not ignored. For example, we have included Ludwig Pfandl's history of Golden Age literature (235) because it contains that writer's often-quoted concept of Cervantes as an non-baroque writer. Similarly, we have dealt with Fitzmaurice-Kelly's (109) history of Spanish literature because of the renown of that critic and because many of his ideas on the *Quijote* are found in that work. Serrano-Plaja's (283) work deals with similarities between Twain, Dostoyevski and Cervantes and would ordinarily be found in the following volume. But because Serrano-Plaja's study presents basic questions as to be interpretation of Cervantes' novel it is included. While articles dealing with the interpretation of a particular phrase are not generally dealt with here, a few works on the opening line of the *Quijote* are included: those of Joaquín Casalduero (56) and María Rosa Lida (174). As pointed out above, works on the false *Quijote* are not considered here, for that novel is worthy of a separate study. However, Stephen Gilman's (128) work on Avellaneda is summarized because of its meaningful comments on Cervantes' novel.

As the reader well knows, there have, through the centuries, been many approaches to the *Quijote*. We do not believe it expedient or appropriate to give a lengthy summary of those approaches here, and will keep our remarks to a minimum. In the seventeenth century in Spain readers generally regarded the *Quijote* as merely a funny book full of satirical remarks about prior literature. This approach to the novel is found today in the so-called "hard school." Early readers also sought to identify the characters with specific persons; and this approach continues through the centuries, the Knight being identified with the Duke of Lerma, Saint Ignatius of Loyola and many others. In the twentieth century this approach is found in the works of Rodríguez Marín (258), Astrana Marín (11), and Doña Blanca de los Ríos (251).

In the eighteenth century certain readers, particularly in France, looked upon Cervantes' novel as a satirical-activistic work. That is, it was viewed as having been written to satirize a particular Spanish institution or custom, such as honor, if not the Spanish nation as a whole. This approach to the *Quijote* is found in the lecture of A. Morel-Fatio (210) who views the novel as a satire on *hidalguismo*. Certain Socialist critics, such as Novitsky (221), take a similar attitude.

England of the eighteenth century begins, with Motteux in 1700, to take a sympathetic view of the Knight and to identify with him. Samuel Johnson and Henry Fielding adopt this view. With the German Friedrich Schiller the Don becomes a tragic figure. The German Romantics, following the sympathetic approach of the English and of Schiller, convert the Knight into a symbol: the idealist struggling in an unworthy society. In the mind-nineteenth century he becomes an activistic-idealistic symbol, the champion of political freedom and personal liberty. This idealistic approach is used by numerous critics writing in the period covered here.

An idea which appears to develop in the late eighteenth century is that the *Quijote* is basically a vivid picture of its times, a study of the customs of the day. This thought is found A. Morel-Fatio's

(210) lecture and in other works summarized here, such as that of Arco y Garay (7).

There is a strong tendency at the time of this writing to examine the *Quijote* from a structural or esthetic viewpoint. This approach, according to Harri Meier (195), goes back to the early Romantics such as the Schlegel brothers and Ludwig Tieck, who sought to explain the function of the *Curioso impertinente* (and other intercalated material) in the overall novel. This approach becomes intense after World War I, and many today seek to find a thematic or other unity in Cervantes' masterpiece: A. A. Parker (231), Joaquín Casalduero (58), Helmut Hatzfeld (141). There is also a tendency to study the author's style and to seek to categorize it as either classical, renaissance or baroque.

With the increased interest in psychology at the end of the nineteenth century, several critics examine the personalities of the protagonists from a medical point-of-view. José Goyanes (131) and Helene Deutsch (92) psychoanalyze the Knight and Squire. With the rise of Existentialism certain critics seek to portray the Knight as a man seeking to develop his personality to the fullest. There is a good bit of this attitude in Unamuno's works [(308), (309)] and others summarized in this volume.

One question about the author of *Don Quijote* which has concerned the critics for centuries is his cultural level. Some in the seventeenth century appear to have regarded him as untutored. In the late nineteenth century Menéndez y Pelayo (198) reexamines this idea and finds Cervantes to be generally well-read. Américo Castro (63), in 1925, studies Cervantes' general cultural level in detail and concludes that he is steeped in renaissance writings.

The true attitude in which the *Quijote* was written will probably never be ascertained. It has been debated for years. Some find the author a jocular optimist, others a bitter pessimist. Still others seek a happy compromise and conclude that he is merely a realist. A related question, the attitude of the author toward his hero, has been studied in some detail by John J. Allen (1) and many others, who find that Cervantes fluctuates in his feelings toward the Knight.

Another approach is the historical-philosophical one. This school seeks to categorize Cervantes' outlook as either medieval, renaissance, baroque, or modern. This form of analysis appears to have begun with the German Romantics in the early nineteenth century, and is still very much present in our survey period.

Another troublesome question in *Quijote* criticism is the matter of the Knight's relative sanity. Most regard him as insane only on the question of chivalry. Others find him mad at all times, even during his so-called lucid intervals. Still others, including Unamuno (309) and Serrano-Plaja (283), consider him more an accomplished actor than a lunatic.

These are only some of the major points that have been raised about Cervantes and the *Quijote*, and our above remarks are intended as only a brief summary, not a complete outline of *Quijote* criticism.

In preparing this work we have made use of Leopoldo Rius' three-volume study at the turn of the century. Raymond L. Grismer's two-volume bibliography, 1946-1963, was repeatedly consulted, as was the bibliography of J. D. M. Ford and Ruth Lansing in 1931. The work of Victor R. B. Oeslchläger, "More Cervantine Bibliography" [*Hispania* XXXIII (1950), 144-150.] was closely examined, as were Alberto Sánchez' annual bibliographies in *Anales Cervantinos*. For current material heavy reliance was placed on the annual bibliographies of the *Modern Language Association* and of *Studies in Philology*. There is a great deal more bibliographical material available to the *cervantista*, such as Suñé Benages' and Suñé Fonbuena's study of the editions of the *Quijote*, which extends up to 1937. The Library of Congress, the Hispanic Society and British Museum catalogues provide valuable assistance. Francisco Aguilera, in 1960, published a helpful list of Cervantes holdings in the Library of Congress. Also of aid is Antonio Palau y Dulcet's *Bibliografía de Don Miguel de Cervantes Saavedra*, Vol. III. For Latin American Cervantes criticism the work of Rafael Heliodoro Valle and Emilia Romero [*Bibliografía cervantina en la América española*, (1950)] can be rewarding. Also available for study are *Cervantes: Bibliografía fundamental* (1900-1959), published in Madrid in 1961, and Miguel Herrero García's *Repertorio analítico de estudios cervantinos*, in *Revista de Filología Española*, XXXII (1948), 39-106. For a most complete list of bibliographical material available to the student of Cervantes the reader is urged to consult pages 209-273 of Tilbert Diego Stegmann's recent work, *Cervantes'*

Musterroman "Persiles", published in Hamburg in 1971 by Hartmut Lüdke Verlag.

In conclusion, we feel compelled to re-emphasize the fact that this current volume is selective and is intended to give the reader a general understanding of the varying approaches to the *Quijote* over the past seventy-five years. Leading works which have been omitted will be included in the following volume.

DANA B. DRAKE

Virginia Polytechnic Institute and State University
Department of Foreign Languages
Blacksburg, Virginia 24061

INDEX OF WORKS SUMMARIZED

1. Allen, John Jay. *Don Quijote: Hero or Fool? A Study in Narrative Technique.*
2. Alonso, Amado. "Don Quijote no asceta..."
3. Alonso, Dámaso. "El hidalgo Camilote y el hidalgo Don Quijote."
4. Alonso, Dámaso. "La novela cervantina."
5. Alonso, Dámaso. "Sancho-Quijote, Sancho-Sancho."
6. Arbó, Sebastián Juan. *Cervantes.*
7. Arco y Garay, Ricardo del. *La sociedad española en las obras de Cervantes.*
8. Armas y Cárdenas, José de. *El Quijote y su época.*
9. Asensio y Toledo, José. "Interpretaciones del *Quijote*."
10. Astrana Marín, Luis. *Cervantinas y otros ensayos.*
11. Astrana Marín, Luis. *Vida ejemplar y heroica de Miguel de Cervantes Saavedra...*
12. Aubier, Dominique. *Don Quichotte Prophète d'Israël.*
13. Auden, W. H. "The Ironic Hero: Some Reflections on Don Quixote."
14. Auerbach, Erich. "The Enchanted Dulcinea."
15. Avalle-Arce, Juan Bautista. *Deslindes Cervantinos.*
16. Avalle-Arce, Juan Bautista. "Don Quijote, o la vida como obra de arte."
17. Avalle-Arce, Juan Bautista. "Tres comienzos de novela."
18. Avery, William. "Elementos dantescos del *Quijote*."
19. Ayala, Francisco. "La invención del *Quijote* como problema técnico-literario."
20. Ayala, Francisco. "Nota sobre la creación del Quijote."
21. Ayala, Francisco. *La invención del Quijote.*
22. Ayala, Francisco. "Nota sobre la novelística cervantina."
23. Ayala, Francisco. "Experiencia viva y creación literaria."
24. Azaña, Manuel. *Cervantes y la invención del Quijote.*
25. Azorín [Martínez Ruiz, José]. *La ruta de Don Quijote.*
26. Azorín [Martínez Ruiz, José]. *Con Cervantes.*
27. Azorín [Martínez Ruiz, José]. *Con permiso de los cervantistas.*
28. Basave Fernández del Valle, Agustín. *Filosofía del Quijote.*
29. Bataillon, Marcel. *Érasme et l'Espagne: Recherches sur l'histoire spirituelle de XVIe siècle.*
30. Bataillon, Marcel. "Publications cervantines récentes."
31. Bell, Aubrey F. G. *Cervantes.*

32. Bell, Aubrey F. G. "The Wisdom of Don Quijote."
33. Bell, Michael. "The Structure of *Don Quixote*."
34. Benardete, M. J. "Los galeotes..."
35. Benardete, M. J. and Flores, Angel, ed. *The Anatomy of Don Quixote: a symposium.*
36. Bergson, Henri [Louis]. *Laughter: An Essay on the Meaning of the Comic.*
37. Bertrand, J.-J. A. "La naissance du chef-d'œuvre."
38. Bickermann, Joseph. *Don Quijote y Fausto, los héroes y las obras.*
39. Blanco Aguinaga, Carlos. "Cervantes y la picaresca: Notas sobre dos tipos de realismo."
40. Blasco Ibáñez, Vicente. "The Greatest Novel."
41. Bodensieck, Annemarie. "The Comic of Expression."
42. *Boletín de la Real Academia Española.* Número especial para conmemorar el cuarto centenario del nacimiento de Cervantes. XXVII (Oct., 1947-Abr., 1948).
43. Bonilla y San Martín, Adolfo. *Don Quijote y el pensamiento español.*
44. Bonilla y San Martín, Adolfo. *Cervantes y su obra.*
45. Bonilla y San Martín, Adolfo. *De crítica cervantina.*
46. Booth, Wayne C. "The Self-Conscious Narrator in Comic Fiction Before *Tristam Shandy*."
47. Borges, Jorge Luis. "Nota sobre el *Quijote*."
48. Borges, Jorge Luis. "Magies partielles du *Quichotte*."
49. Borges, Jorge Luis. "Análisis del último capítulo del *Quijote*."
50. Brenan, Gerald. "Cervantes."
51. Brenes, Dalai. "The Sanity of Don Quixote."
52. Buchanan, Milton A. "Extraneous Matter in the First Part of Cervantes's *Don Quijote*."
53. Camón Aznar, José. *Don Quijote en la teoría de los estilos.*
54. Cannavagio, Jean François. "Alonso López Pinciano y la estética literaria de Cervantes en el *Quijote*."
55. Carbonell y Basset, Delfín. "*Don Quijote* desde un punto de vista existencio-fenomenológico."
56. Casalduero, Joaquín. "Explicando la primera frase del *Quijote*."
57. Casalduero, Joaquín. El desarrollo de la obra de Cervantes."
58. Casalduero, Joaquín. *Sentido y forma del Quijote.*
59. Casares, Julio. "Las tres edades del *Quijote*."
60. Casella, Mario. *Cervantes. Il Chisciotte.*
61. Cassou, Jean. *Cervantes.*
62. Castro, Américo. "Cervantes y Pirandello."
63. Castro, Américo. *El pensamiento de Cervantes.*
64. Castro, Américo. "¿Cervantes, inconsciente?"
65. Castro, Américo. "Cervantes y la Inquisición."
66. Castro, Américo. *Cervantes.*
67. Castro, Américo. "Erasmo en tiempos de Cervantes."
68. Castro, Américo. "Los prólogos al *Quijote*."
69. Castro, Américo. "Incarnation in *Don Quixote*."
70. Castro, Américo. "La estructura del *Quijote*."
71. Castro, Américo. "El cómo y el por qué de Cide Hamete Benengeli."
72. Castro, Américo. "Cervantes y el *Quijote* a nueva luz."
73. Castro, Américo. "La palabra escrita y el *Quijote*."
74. Castro, Américo. "*El Quijote*, taller de la existencialidad."

75. Castro, Carmen. "Personajes femeninos de Cervantes: las mujeres del *Quijote*."
76. Castro Silva, José Vicente. *Epílogo de Don Quijote*.
77. Cernuda, Luis. "Cervantes."
78. Chambers, Leland. "Structure and the Search for Truth in the *Quijote*: Notes Toward a Comprehensive View."
79. Chasca, Edmund de. "Algunos aspectos del ritmo y del movimiento del *Quijote*."
80. Chesterton, G. K. "The Divine Parody of *Don Quixote*."
81. Corley, Ames Haven. "Word-Play in the *Don Quijote*."
82. Cotarelo y Mori, Emilio. *Efemérides cervantinas...*
83. Cotarelo y Mori, Emilio. *Últimos estudios cervantinos*.
84. Criado de Val, M. "*Don Quijote*, como diálogo."
85. Croce, Benedetto. "The 'Simpatía' of Don Quixote."
86. Crocker, L. G. "*Hamlet, Don Quixote, La vida es sueño*: The Quest for Values."
87. Croft-Cooke, Rupert. *Through Spain with Don Quixote*. (First published as *The Quest for Quixote*).
88. *Cuadernos de Literatura*, III, núms. 8-9.
89. Darío, Rubén. "Un soneto a Cervantes" and "Letanía de Nuestro Señor Don Quijote."
90. Descouzis, Paul Marcel. "Don Quijote y la generación del 98."
91. Descouzis, Paul Marcel. *Cervantes, a nueva luz. I. El Quijote y el Concilio de Trento*.
92. Deutsch, Helene. "Don Quijote und Don Quijotismo."
93. Díaz-Plaja, Guillermo. "La técnica narrativa de Cervantes."
94. Durán, Manuel. "Cervantes y el realismo fluido."
95. Durán, Manuel. *La ambigüedad en el Quijote*.
96. Efron, Arthur. "Satire Denied: A Critical History of English and American Quixote Criticism."
97. Eguía Ruiz, Constancio. "Cervantes, Calderón, Lope, Gracián: Nuevos temas crítico-biográficos."
98. El Saffar, Ruth Snodgrass. "The Function of the Fictional Narrator in *Don Quijote*."
99. Ellis, Havelock. "Don Quixote," in *The Soul of Spain*.
100. Entwistle, William J. *Cervantes*.
101. Farinelli, Arturo. *Cervantes zur 300 jährigen Feier des "Don Quijote"*.
102. Farinelli, Arturo. "Cervantes con ocasión del cuarto centenario de su nacimiento."
103. Farinelli, Arturo. "Cervantes," in *Aufsätze, Reden und Charakteristiken zur Weltliteratur*.
104. Faure, Élie. "Cervantes."
105. Fernández Suárez, Álvaro. *Los mitos del Quijote*.
106. Fichter, William L. "Estudios cervantinos recientes."
107. Fitzmaurice-Kelly, James. "Introduction to *The History of Don Quixote of the Mancha*.
108. Fitzmaurice-Kelly, James. *The Life of Miguel de Cervantes Saavedra...*
109. Fitzmaurice-Kelly, James. *A History of Spanish Literature*.
110. Fitzmaurice-Kelly, James. *Cervantes and Shakespeare*.

111. Flecniakoska, Jean-Louis. "Reflexions sur la parodie pastorale dans le *Quichotte*."
112. Flores, Ángel and Benardete, M. J., ed. *Cervantes Across the Centuries*.
113. Forcione, Alban K. *Cervantes, Aristotle and the Persiles*.
114. Ford, J. D. M. "Plot, Tale, and Episode in *Don Quijote*."
115. Fors, Luis Ricardo. *Espíritu del Quijote*.
116. Foulché-Delbose, Raymond. "Carta crítica sobre la obra de Cervantes."
117. Frank, Waldo. "The Will of Don Quixote."
118. Frye, Northrop. "The Four Forms of Fiction."
119. Ganivet, Ángel. *Idearium español*.
120. Gaos, Vicente. "El *Quijote:* Aproximaciones."
121. García Pavón, Francisco. "La Mancha que vio Cervantes."
122. Garciasol, Ramón de. *Claves de España: Cervantes y el Quijote*.
123. Garciasol, Ramón de. "Cinco aspectos de la vida en el *Quijote*."
124. Garrone, Marco A. "L'Orlando furioso considerato come fonte del *Quijote*."
125. Gerhardt, Mia I. *Don Quijote, la vie et les livres*.
126. Gillet, Joseph E. "The Autonomous Character in Spanish and European Literature."
127. Gilman, Stephan. "Los inquisidores literarios de Cervantes."
128. Gilman, Stephan. *Cervantes y Avellaneda*.
129. Goggio, Emilio. "The Dual Role of Dulcinea in Cervantes' *Don Quijote de la Mancha*."
130. Gonthier, Denys Armand. *El drama psicológico del Quijote*.
131. Goyanes, José. *La tipología de el Quijote: Ensayo sobre la estructura psicosomática de los personajes de la novela*.
132. Green, Otis H. "El *ingenioso* Hidalgo."
133. Green, Otis H. "Realidad, voluntad y gracia en Cervantes."
134. Grierson, Herbert. "*Don Quixote:* Some War-time Reflections on Its Character and Influence."
135. Guillén, Claudio. "Luis Sánchez, Ginés de Pasamonte y los inventores del género picaresco."
136. Guillén, Jorge. "Vida y muerte de Alonso Quijano."
137. Gutiérrez-Noriega, Carlos. "La contribución de Miguel de Cervantes a la psiquiatría."
138. Gutiérrez Noriega, Carlos. "La personalidad y el carácter en la obra de Cervantes."
139. Haley, G. "The Narrator in *Don Quijote*."
140. Hatzfeld, Helmut. "Boccacciostil im *Don Quijote*."
141. Hatzfeld, Helmut. *El Quijote como obra de arte del lenguaje*.
142. Hatzfeld, Helmut. "Das Stilproblem bei Cervantes."
143. Hatzfeld, Helmut. "Thirty Years of Cervantes Criticism."
144. Hatzfeld, Helmut. "Results from *Quijote* Criticism since 1947."
145. Hatzfeld, Helmut. "¿Don Quijote asceta?"
146. Hatzfeld, Helmut. "Artistic Parallels in Cervantes and Velásquez."
147. Hatzfeld, Helmut. "The baroque of Cervantes and the baroque of Góngora Exemplified by the motif 'las bodas'."
148. Hatzfeld, Helmut, ed. *Don Quijote: Forschung und Kritik*.
149. Hazard, Paul. *Don Quichotte de Cervantes. Étude et analyse*.

150. Hendrix, W. S. "Sancho Panza and the Comic Types of the Sixteenth Century."
151. Herrero-García, Miguel. "Cervantes," in *Estimaciones literarias del siglo XVII.*
152. Hilton, Donald. "Four Centuries of Cervantes: The Historical Anatomy of a Best-Selling Masterpiece."
153. *Hispania*, XXX, No. 3 (August, 1947). Cervantes Quadricentennial Number.
154. Howells, William Dean. "Cervantes," in *My Literary Passions.*
155. Hume, Martin. "The National Significance of *Don Quixote.*"
156. Ibáñez, Jaime. "Cervantes y la novela moderna."
157. Icaza, Francisco A. de. *El Quijote durante tres siglos.*
158. Immerwahr, Raymond. "Structural Symetry in the Episodic Narratives of *Don Quijote,* Part One."
159. Kayser, Wolfgang. "Origen y crisis de la novela moderna."
160. Ker, W. P. *"Don Quijote."*
161. King, Willard F. "Unamuno, Cervantes y *Niebla.*"
162. Kommerell, Max. "Humoristische Personifikation in *Don Quijote.*
163. Krappe, Alexander Haggerty. "La vrai philosophie du *Don Quijote.*"
164. Krauss, Werner. *Miguel de Cervantes. Leben und Welk.*
165. Krauss, Werner. "Cervantes und die moderne Welt."
166. Kruse, Margot. "Ariost und Cervantes."
167. Krutch, Joseph Wood. "Miguel de Cervantes," in *Five Masters.*
168. Krynen, Jean. "Don Quijote, ejemplar poeta."
169. Lascaris Commeno, Constantino. "El nombre de Don Quijote."
170. León Máinez, Ramón. *Cervantes y su época.*
171. Levin, Harry. "The Example of Cervantes."
172. Lewis, D. B. Wyndham. *The Lion and the Fox: The Role of the Hero in the Plays of Shakespeare.*
173. Lewis, D. B. Wyndham. *The Shadow of Cervantes.*
174. Lida de Malkiel, María Rosa. "De cuyo nombre no quiero acordarme..."
175. *Das literarische Werk von Miguel de Cervantes. Beiträge zur Romanischen Philologie* (Sonderheft, c 1967, 1968).
176. Lledó Iñigo, Emilio. "Interpretación y teoría de *Don Quijote.*"
177. Lloréns, Vicente. "Historia y ficción en el *Quijote.*"
178. Lloréns, Vicente. *"La intención del Quijote."*
179. Lollis, Cesare de. *Cervantes reazionario.*
180. López Navío, José. "Génesis y desarrollo del *Quijote.*"
181. Madariaga, Salvador de. "Our Don Quixote."
182. Madariaga, Salvador de. *Guía del lector del Quijote.*
183. Madariaga, Salvador de. "Cervantes and His Time."
184. Maeztu, Ramiro de. *Don Quijote, Don Juan y la Celestina: ensayos de simpatía.*
185. Maldonado de Guevara, Francisco. "El niño y el viejo: desmitologización en el *Lazarillo* y en el *Quijote.*"
186. Maldonado de Guevara, Francisco. "Del Ingenium de Cervantes al de Gracián."
187. Maldonado de Guevara, Francisco. "Dos estudios cervantinos."
188. Mañach, Jorge. *Examen del quijotismo.*
189. Mandel, Oscar. "The Function of the Norm in *Don Quixote.*"

190. Mann, Thomas. "Voyage with Don Quijote."
191. Marasso Rocca, Arturo. *Cervantes: La invención del Quijote.*
192. Maravall, José Antonio. *El humanismo de las armas en Don Quijote.*
193. Marqués Villanueva, Francisco. "Sobre la génesis literaria de Sancho Panza."
194. Medvedev, P. N. *Formalny metod y literaturovedenii.*
195. Meier, Harri. "Zur Entwicklung der europäischen Quijote-Deutung."
196. Menéndez Pidal, Ramón. "Un aspecto en la elaboración del *Quijote*."
197. Menéndez Pidal, Ramón. *Cervantes y el ideal caballeresco.*
198. Menéndez y Pelayo, Marcelino. "Cultura literaria de Miguel de Cervantes y elaboración del *Quijote*."
199. Menéndez y Pelayo, Marcelino. "Interpretaciones del *Quijote*."
200. Menéndez y Pelayo, Marcelino. *Orígenes de la novela, I.*
201. Merejkowski, Dmitri de. "Cervantes."
202. *Miguel de Cervantes Saavedra; homenaje de Ínsula en el cuarto centenario de su nacimiento, 1547-1947.*
203. Millé y Giménez, Juan. *Sobre la génesis del Quijote.*
204. Monroy, Juan Antonio. *La biblia en el Quijote.*
205. Montero, Lázaro, "Dulcinea."
206. Montero Díaz, Santiago. *Cervantes, compañero eterno.*
207. Montesinos, José F. "Cervantes Anti-novelista."
208. Montoliu y de Togores, Manuel de. *El alma de España y sus reflejos en la literatura del siglo de oro.*
209. Montoliu y de Togores, Manuel de. *Tríptico del "Quijote".*
210. Morel-Fatio, A. "Le *Don Quichotte* envisagé comme peinture et critique de la société espagnole du XVIe et du XVIIe siècle."
211. Morel-Fatio, A. "Le troisième centenaire de Cervantes."
212. Moreno Baez, Enrique. "Arquitectura del *Quijote*."
213. Moreno Baez, Enrique. *Reflexiones sobre el Quijote.*
214. Murillo, Luis Andrés. "Cervantic Irony in *Don Quijote:* The Problem for Literary Criticism."
215. Navarro González, Alberto. "La locura quijotesca."
216. Navarro González, Alberto. "El ingenioso Don Quijote en la España del siglo XVII."
217. Navarro González, Alberto. "El ingenioso Don Quijote, caballero andante cristiano y santo."
218. Navarro y Ledesma, Francisco. *El ingenioso hidalgo Miguel de Cervantes Saavedra.*
219. Nelson, Jr., Lowry, ed. *Cervantes: A Collection of Critical Essays.*
220. Neuschäfer, Hans-Jörg. *Der Sinn der Parodie im Don Quijote.*
221. Novitsky, Pavel. *Cervantes and Don Quixote: A Socio-Historical Interpretation.*
222. Olmedo, Félix G. *El Amadís y el Quijote; Soneto Famoso de Cervantes al túmulo de Felipe II; El Persiles.*
223. Ortega y Gasset, José. *Meditaciones del Quijote.*
224. Osterc, Ludovik. *El pensamiento social y político del Quijote.*
225. Palacín Iglesias, Gregorio B. *En torno al Quijote (Ensayo de interpretación y crítica).*
226. Palacín Iglesias, Gregorio B. *El Quijote en la literatura universal.*
227. Palacios, Leopoldo Eulogio. "La significación doctrinal del *Quijote*."
228. Parker, A. A. "*Don Quijote* and the Relativity of Truth."
229. Parker, A. A. "A Revaluation of *Don Quijote*."

230. Parker, A. A. "El concepto de la verdad en el *Quijote*."
231. Parker, A. A. "Fielding and the Structure of *Don Quijote*."
232. Peers, E. Allison. "Aportación de los hispanistas extranjeros al estudio de Cervantes."
233. Pemán, José María. "La 'armazón de cauallería' de Don Quijote."
234. Petriconi, H. "Kritik und Interpretation des *Quijote*."
235. Pfandl, Ludwig. "Der Ritter als Narr."
236. Predmore, Richard L. "La apoteosis de Don Quijote."
237. Predmore, Richard L. "El problema de la realidad en el *Quijote*."
238. Predmore, Richard L. *The World of Don Quixote*.
239. Prjevalinsky Ferrer, Olga. "Del *asno de oro* a *Rocinante*."
240. Puyol y Alonso, Julio. *Estado social que refleja "El Quijote."*
241. Quilter, Daniel Edward. "The Image of the *Quijote* in the Seventeenth Century."
242. Ramón y Cajal, Santiago. *Psicología de Don Quijote y el quijotismo*.
243. Real de la Riva, César. "Historia de la crítica e interpretación de la obra de Cervantes."
244. *Realidad, Revista de Ideas*, II, núm. 5 (Sept.-Oct., 1947).
245. Riegner, Helene I. "Humanitas cervantina."
246. Riley, E. C. "Who's Who in *Don Quixote?* Or an Approach to the Problem of Identity."
247. Riley, E. C. "Episodio, novela y aventura en *Don Quijote*."
248. Riley, E. C. *Cervantes' Theory of the Novel*.
249. Río, Ángel del. "El equívoco del *Quijote*."
250. Río, Ángel del. "Quijotismo y cervantismo."
251. Ríos de Lampérez, Blanca de los. "Algunas consideraciones sobre el *Quijote* de Avellaneda."
252. Riquer, Martín de. *Aproximación al Quijote*.
253. Riquer, Martín de. "Estilo del *Quijote*."
254. Riquer, Martín de. "El *Quijote* y los libros."
255. Rivers, Elias L. "On the Prefatory Pages on *Don Quijote*, Part II."
256. Rivers, Elias L. "El grave defecto del *Quijote*."
257. Rodó, José Enrique. "El Cristo a la jineta."
258. Rodríguez Marín, Francisco. *Estudios cervantinos*.
259. Romero, Francisco. "Don Quijote y Fichte."
260. Romero Flores, Hipólito R. *Biografía de Sancho Panza filósofo de la sensatez*.
261. Rosales, Luis. *Cervantes y la libertad*.
262. Rubin, Louis D. *The Teller of the Tale*.
263. Rubio, David. *¿Hay una filosofía en el Quijote?*
264. Rüegg, August. *Miguel de Cervantes und sein Don Quijote*.
265. Rüegg, August. "Le réalisme de Cervantes."
266. Rüegg, August. "Lo erásmico en el *Don Quijote* de Cervantes."
267. Russell, P. E. "*Don Quixote* as a Funny Book."
268. Salcedo, Emilio. "Cervantismo y quijotismo."
269. Salillas, Rafael. *Un gran inspirador de Cervantes: El doctor Juan Huarte y su "Examen de Ingenios."*
270. Sánchez, Alberto. "Historia y poesía en el *Quijote*."
271. Sánchez-Mariño, Rafael. "Un Alonso Quijano de carne y hueso."
272. Sánchez Rivero, Ángel. "Las ventas del *Quijote*."
273. Sánchez Rivero, Ángel. "Contestación" (to Américo Castro's "¿Cervantes, inconsciente?").

274. Sánchez y Escribano, Federico. "De la técnica realista en algunos cuentos pastoriles del *Quijote*."
275. Sánchez y Escribano, Federico. "Dos notas cervantinas."
276. Santayana, George. "Cervantes."
277. Sarmiento, Edward. "On the Interpretation of *Don Quixote*."
278. Savi-Lopez, Paolo. *Cervantes*.
279. Schevill, Rudolph. "Three Centuries of *Don Quixote*."
280. Schevill, Rudolph. *Cervantes*.
281. Schürr, Friedrich. *Cervantes: Leben und Werk des grossen Humoristen*.
282. Schürr, Friedrich. "Romanticismo, realismo y humorismo de Cervantes."
283. Serrano-Plaja, Arturo. *Realismo "mágico" en Cervantes; Don Quijote visto desde Tom Sawyer y el idiota.*
284. Shklovskii, Victor. "Kak sdelan Don-Kikhot."
285. Shroder, Maurice Z. "The Novel as a genre."
286. Sletsjöe, Leif. *Sancho Panza hombre de bien*.
287. Snetkova, Nina. "Quelques particularités du style du roman *Don Quichotte* de Cervantes."
288. Spitzer, Leo. "Die Frage der Heuchelei des Cervantes."
289. Spitzer, Leo. "Linguistic Perspectivism in the *Don Quijote*."
290. Spitzer, Leo. "On the Significance of *Don Quijote*."
291. Stagg, Geoffrey L. "Cervantes revisa su novela (*Don Quijote*, I.ª Parte)."
292. Stagg, Geoffrey L. "Sobre el plan primitivo del *Quijote*."
293. Stagg, Geoffrey L. "La primera salida de Don Quijote: imitación de sí mismo."
294. Stagg, Geoffrey L. "Castro del Río, ¿cuna del *Quijote*?"
295. Suarès, André. *Cervantes*.
296. Tarr, F. Courtney. "Recent Trends in Cervantes Studies: An Attempt at Survey and Prognosis."
297. Terrero, José. "Las rutas de las tres salidas de Don Quijote de la Mancha."
298. Terrero, José. "Itinerario del *Quijote* de Avellaneda y su influencia en el cervantino."
299. Terterian, Ioana. "Sobre algunas interpretaciones del *Quijote* en la España del siglo XX."
300. Toffanin, Guiseppe. "Il Cervantes."
301. Togeby, Knud. *La composition du roman "Don Quijote".*
302. Trachman, Sadie Edith. *Cervantes' Women of Literary Tradition*.
303. Trotter, G. D. *Cervantes and the Art of Fiction*.
304. Trueblood, Alan S. "Sobre la selección artística en el *Quijote*: '...lo que ha dejado de escribir' (II, 44)."
305. Trueblood, Alan S. "El silencio en el *Quijote*."
306. Ullman, Pierre Lioni. "The Burlesque Poems Which Frame the *Quijote*."
307. Unamuno, Miguel de. "Don Quijote en la tragicomedia europea contemporánea."
308. Unamuno, Miguel de. "Sobre la lectura e interpretación del *Quijote*."
309. Unamuno, Miguel de. *Vida de Don Quijote y Sancho*.

INDEX OF WORKS SUMMARIZED

310. Valera y Alcalá Galiano, Juan. *Discurso escrito por encargo de la Real Academia Española para conmemorar el tercer centenario de la publicación de "El ingenioso hidalgo Don Quijote de la Mancha."*
311. Van Doren, Mark. *Don Quixote's Profession.*
312. Varo, Carlos. *Génesis y evolución del Quijote.*
313. Vilanova, Antonio. *Erasmo y Cervantes.*
314. Villegas del Hoyo, Baldomero. *La revolución española: Estudio en que se descubre cuál y cómo fue el verdadero ingenio de D. Quijote y el pensamiento del simpar Cervantes.*
315. Wagner, Charles Philip. "The Sources of *El Caballero Cifar.*"
316. Wardropper, Bruce W. "*Don Quijote:* Story or History?"
317. Weinrich, Harald. *Das Ingenium Don Quijotes. Ein Beitrag zur literarischen Charakterkunde.*
318. Willis, Raymond S. "Sancho Panza: Prototype for the Modern Novel."
319. Willis, Raymond S. *The Phantom Chapters of the Quijote.*
320. Woodberry, George Edward. *Great Writers,* pp. 1-36.

1. Allen, John Jay. *Don Quijote: Hero or Fool? A Study in Narrative Technique.* Gainesville, Florida: University of Florida Press, 1969. Pp. 92.

   Cervantes, as a rule, is extremely careful to prepare the reader to accept the defeats which the Don is about to suffer. For example, the author pictures the Knight as quite content with himself after the Andrés episode, thus preparing the reader for the hero's defeat by the merchants from Toledo. Similarly, in the drubbing at the hands of the galley slaves we are prepared to laugh at the Knight because Cervantes allowed his protagonist to enjoy a victory in the prior episode (Mambrino's helmet). However, there is a definite lack of preparation for the hero's last two defeats in Part I (by the penitents and by Eugenio, the shepherd), and perhaps for this reason we feel a slight note of ambivalence toward both the curate and the canon at the end of Part I. Here Don Quijote does not seem to deserve the beatings he receives. It is increasingly true as the novel progresses that the reader will not laugh at the Knight in defeat unless specifically directed to do so by the author's rhetorical signals. Nevertheless, Don Quijote remains, at the close of Part I, a vain and meddling man with whom one does not identify strongly, at best occasionally pathetic, never tragic, almost always the object of the reader's and the other characters' laughter.

   There is a radical difference in the reader's attitude toward Don Quijote in Part II, but Madariaga's (182) theory of Sanchification of the hero is not adequate to explain this difference. Don Quijote becomes more and more aware that he cannot control events. He becomes more discreet, more self-doubting. He shifts from a reliance on his strength of arm to his strength of spirit. This shift begins early in Part II, and Cervantes prepares the reader to sympathize with a protagonist who increasingly reveals himself to be an intelligent, well-intentioned, self-doubting man, the victim of his fellow man as well as of his own presumption. Everything by way of pro-Don Quijote preparation comes to bear, and we are prepared to suffer with him, since he is shown to be generous, eloquent, noble, and patient. By the time Don Quijote is defeated by Sansón, the stage has already been set for his finest moment on the beach of Barcelona.

What is the object of Cervantes' satire? Outside the book it is bad novels of chivalry, criticized primarily for defective style and lack of verisimilitude. Within the novel, it is Don Quijote's undisciplined egocentricity, and Part II is the story of his recovery. If a man's life is a work of art, Don Quijote must correct in his life the same defects which disturb Cervantes in the novels of chivalry: a presumptuous and altisonant style, and lack of concordance with reality.

2. Alonso, Amado. "Don Quijote no asceta, pero ejemplar caballero y cristiano." *Nueva Revista de Filología Hispánica*, II (1948), 333-359.

Hatzfeld (145) is correct that Cervantes' Knight is not ascetic, but that critic is not correct in concluding that the hero was anthropocentric and a collection of weaknesses and vices. Hatzfeld is further mistaken to view the hero's insanity as immoral and to consider his defeats as punishment for his not being ascetic.

3. Alonso, Dámaso. "El hidalgo Camilote y el hidalgo Don Quijote." *Revista de Filología Española*, XX (1933), 391-397.

The episode of the outlandish hidalgo Camilote and his ugly sweetheart Maimonda in the *Primaleón* had a great influence on the *Quijote*. This Camilote episode has several parallels in Cervantes' novel: (1) both Camilote and Don Quijote are hidalgos; (2) both want adventures and first need to be knighted; (3) both men are ridiculously in love with women whom they falsely consider to be beautiful; (4) both seek to force others to recognize the beauty of their beloved; (5) both men act strangely in matters such as dress; (6) the reaction of the world to both is the same —ridicule; (7) there is a strange similarity between the names Camilote and Quijote. In view of these factors one must conclude that the Camilote episode in the *Primaleón* is one of the major germ cells of Cervantes' novel.

Gil Vicente adapted the Camilote episode to the stage in his *Don Duardos*, but Cervantes appears to have been influenced more by the novel than by the play.

4. Alonso, Dámaso. "La novela cervantina." *Revista de la Universidad de Cauca*, (Popeyán, Colombia), núm. 13 (1950), pp. 143-158.

Cervantes gathers in his works all the currents of the Spanish renaissance novel: pastoral, chivalry, Byzantine, Moorish, Italianate, and picaresque. In the *Quijote* he combines the realistic technique of *Lazarillo* with other types of renaissance novels, thus moderating the stark realism of the picaresque genre.

Cervantes is the creator of the true, fine humor of complicated characters, and England is the first country to appreciate this humor, this mixing of the sublime and the ridiculous. Why is the *Quijote* universal? Because it shows man's basic duality—spirit and matter, flesh and soul. Why was the *Quijote* produced when it was? Because God took away the hero from humanity at the same time that He took away the poem. In exchange, God gave man the novel. Thus when the poem dies, the novel arises, and *Don Quijote* is the exact moment of this change. The poem could no longer live after men lost a sense of common destiny, and felt that God had abandoned them.

5. Alonso, Dámaso. "Sancho-Quijote, Sancho-Sancho," in *Homenaje a Cervantes*, II. Edited by F. Sánchez-Castañer. Valencia: Editorial Mediterráneo, 1950, pp. 53-63.

Perhaps Sancho is Cervantes' greatest creation. He leaves home out of greed, lets himself be taken in by fantasies, and for a time even enters the Don's world of adventures. After the episode of Fierabrás' balsam, however, a counter-movement begins. Sancho withdraws from the world of imagination and soon ceases to believe in his master's world of enchantment. Sancho at times will make use of the Knight's fantastic imagination to deceive him, but the Squire does not become a permanent *pícaro*. Instead he hovers between rascality and idealism throughout the novel.

6. Arbó, Sebastián Juan. *Cervantes*. 3rd ed. revised. Barcelona: Noguer, S. A., 1956. Pp. 447.

[Arbó's remarks about the *Quijote* are of a very general nature. He finds Cervantes' masterpiece a work of consolation, not of doubt and pessimism. It is, to Arbó, a work that banishes the taste for the false by imitating the false. A particularly valuable feature of this biography is its graphic descriptions of the political activities in Spain during the various stages of Cervantes' life.]

7. Arco y Garay, Ricardo del. *La sociedad española en las obras de Cervantes*. Madrid: Patronato del IV centenario del nacimiento de Cervantes, 1951. Pp. 783.

[This work consists of twenty-three chapters and discusses many aspects of Spanish society in Cervantes' times. In Chapter I attention is devoted to Don Quijote's itinerary. Cervantes' references to various places are noted, as is his use of slang expressions for the inhabitants of various cities. Chapter II deals with the political, economic and social evils of Spain, such as the abandonment of agriculture, the growing disdain for work, and the increase in taxes. Chapter III studies Cervantes as a social person who projects himself in his work. Here Arco y Garay notes the highly autobiographical nature of the story of *El cautivo* and points out the legend that Cervantes actually brought back a Moorish girl with him when he returned from captivity and that Isabel de Cervantes was his daughter by that Moorish girl. Chapter IV discusses Cervantes' realism. To Arco y Garay the *Quijote* is a social novel that reflects the feelings, customs, and prejudices of the era. Chapter V deals with the question whether Cervantes was a freethinker. Arco y Garay concludes that the author did not actually criticize venerated customs; he merely condemned evils which moralists had maligned for years. Chapter VI discusses religion and Cervantes' attitude toward it. Arco concludes that the author was not truly sarcastic toward the Church. In Chapter VII is found a discussion of popular superstitions. Cervantes was not superstitious, Arco concludes. The royalty is dealt with in Chapter VIII, and women, love and jealously are discussed in Chapter IX, where it is observed that almost all of Cervantes' women live for love. Chapter X studies marriage and honor;

Chapter XI deals with the government; and Chapter XII discusses the nobility. Chapter XIII is concerned with such matters as the siesta, clothing, games, forms of address and food and drink. The following chapter discusses, *inter alia,* Cervantes' anti-*dueña* sentiments. Chapter XV deals with the *académicos* or *letrados.* In the next chapter Arco y Garay discusses the Spanish police in Cervantes' times, namely the two orders of the Santa Hermandad. Strolling players *(la farándula)* are described in Chapter XVII, and artists in the following chapter. Some attention is devoted here to Cervantes' theories of esthetics. Chapter XIX notes the problem of the returning soldier, and Chapter XX deals with the occupations of the lower classes. Adventure and getting rich quick are touched upon in Chapter XXI, and wanderers and vagabonds in the following chapter. Here Arco y Garay explains certain expressions used by the lower classes and by gypsies. The final chapter deals with village life and speech.]

8. Armas y Cárdenas, José de. *El Quijote y·su época.* Madrid-Buenos Aires: Renacimiento, 1916. Pp. 267.

The *Quijote* should not be viewed as merely an attack on chivalry novels. Furthermore, that novel is not a satire on the Spanish nobility in general, nor on the Duke of Medina Sidonia, in particular, as Daniel Defoe concluded. Nor does Don Quijote represent Charles V (as La Barrera believed), the Duke of Lerma (as Rapin asserted in 1674), or Cervantes' wife's uncle (as Manuel V. García claimed in 1867). There are, however, a number of subtle attacks in Cervantes' novel against Lope de Vega. Cervantes wrote his masterpiece during the worst part of his life, and for that reason there is a certain amount of bitterness in his novel. Yet it is not the bitterness of Rabelais or Swift. Cervantes has pity for all.

9. Asensio y Toledo, José. *Interpretaciones del "Quijote,"* in *Discursos leídos ante la Real Academia Española en la recepción del excmo. Sr. D. José María Asensio y Toledo el día 29 de mayo de 1904.* Madrid: Imprenta Alemana, 1904, pp. 3-20.

Even in Cervantes' day some readers saw veiled political references in the *Quijote.* There were, however, no profound philosophical interpretations of Cervantes' novel during the author's life. The *Quijote* was not considered an attack on public institutions, nor was it regarded as a book of social or political reform. Some seventeenth-century critics did believe, however, that the novel satirized Charles V (the lion adventure, the epitath on the Knight's tomb, and portions of the *escrutinio*), or the Duke of Lerma (*Décimas* of *Urganda la desconocida* at the front of Part I). Numerous later writers have made similar conjectures.

Nicolás Díaz de Benjumea in his *Comentarios filosóficos del Quijote* (in *La América*, 1859) concluded that the *Quijote* satirized all human weaknesses. Later that critic, in *La Estafeta de Urganda* (London, 1861), found a great deal of the autobiographical in the *Quijote* and concluded that several portions of the novel dealt with incidents in Cervantes' relationship with his enemy in Algiers, Juan Blanco de Paz. In 1878, Benjumea, in his *La verdad sobre el Quijote*, stated that Cervantes was the real protagonist of his masterpiece, and that he was always guided by his noble thoughts in the midst of his struggles against his powerful enemies. At the end of the nineteenth century several view Cervantes as a political radical, and Benigno Pallol ("Polinous") in his *Interpretación del Quijote*, 1893, goes so far as to assert that the *Quijote* is a veiled attack on the Holy Scriptures.

In reality Cervantes is neither a political philosopher nor a reformer. Instead, the *Quijote* is a most perfect picture of humanity. We are amazed at Cervantes' imagination, his style, his original way of describing people, feelings, actions and places. At the same time we become familiar with the author; we fall in love with the nobility of his heart. The political fortunes of Spain cannot help but be mirrored in the *Quijote*. Perhaps Cervantes reflected on Spain's decline at the height of its glory. In any event, a certain melancholy pervades all of his works.

10. Astrana Marín, Luis. *Cervantinas y otros ensayos.* Madrid: Afrodisio Aguado, S. A., 1944. Pp. 460.

[In Chapter I of this work Astrana discusses the celebrated letter from Lope de Vega to the Duke of Sesa, in which Lope attacks the *Quijote* as follows: "pero ninguno hay tan malo como Cervantes ni tan necio que alabe a Don Quijote." This letter was supposedly written in August of 1604, but Astrana concludes that the date assigned to it is incorrect. From internal evidence he seeks to prove that it was written late in 1605.

In Chapter VI the critic discusses the Don's route, finding it to be imaginary, not based on geography. Astrana concludes that Cervantes deliberately obscured the fact the Knight's village was Esquivias by stating that the hero left from the Campo de Montiel.

Chapter XI deals with Italian translations of the *Quijote*, especially the Giannini version. Chapter XII is concerned with translations of the *Quijote* in general. Astrana here notes that as of the date of publication of his work there were more than 1500 translations, not including reprints.]

11. Astrana Marín, Luis. *Vida ejemplar y heroica de Miguel de Cervantes Saavedra, con mil documentos hasta ahora inéditos y numerosas ilustraciones y grabados de la época.* Madrid: Reus, 1948-1957. 7 vols.

[In Chapter LXII of Volume V Astrana insists that the *Quijote* was begun at the noisy *Cárcel Real de Sevilla* and not at a jail in Argamasilla, as one legend would have it. In Chapter LXIII of this same volume the critic repeats his earlier (10) assertion that Esquivias was Don Quijote's home. In this same chapter there is discussed the theory that Cervantes' masterpiece was originally intended to be a short story. Attention is also devoted here to the question of the intention of the *Quijote*. In Chapter LXXXI of Volume VI the *Entremés de los romances* is dealt with. Astrana is of the school of thought that this playlet was written *after* the *Quijote*, not before it. Chapters LXXVIII, LXXXII in Volume VI, and Chapter LXXXV of Volume VII discuss the influence of the *Quijote* abroad.

Chapter XC lists the various editions of the *Quijote* in all languages. Here Astrana also discusses the possible real-life models for various characters in Cervantes' novel. The *Duque* and Diego de Mirando are dealt with in some detail.]

12. Aubier, Dominique. *Don Quichotte Prophète d'Israël*. Paris: Robert Laffont, 1966. Pp. 291.

[This treatise of fifteen chapters seeks to show the influence of the *Zohar* and other Hebrew writings on Cervantes. Anagrams are frequently used. Chapter IV gives a short history of the Jews in Spain and the sanctions imposed upon them from time to time. The struggle between the Old Christians and the New Christians is dealt with in some detail. The word *quixote* is examined by Aubier, who concludes that it is related to the Hebrew word *quechot* (certitude). Dulcinea is said to be a representation of the Hebrew female figure Shekhina, the Glory of God; and the reference to Dulcinea's modern lineage is considered a possible hint at her status as a New Christian. Chapter X is devoted to the windmills, which, the critic concludes, symbolize evil. In Chapter XII Aubier asks if the four parts of the 1605 *Quijote* are not an imitation of the four stages of emanation found in the *Masekhet Atsiluth*. Marcela is also studied here and is said to represent the *law*. In this same chapter Aubier examines the meaning of the fulling mills, concluding that they represent *rabbis*, the interpreters of the laws. Don Quijote, the critic observes, does not attack these mills, whereas he attacked the windmills (evil).]

13. Auden, W. H. "The Ironic Hero: Some Reflections on Don Quixote." *Horizon*, XX (1949), 86-94. [Reprinted in *Cervantes: A Collection of Critical Essays* (219), pp. 73-81.]

There are three basic types of heroes: (1) epic; (2) tragic; and (3) comic. However, Don Quijote fits into *none* of these categories. The epic hero is strong, brave, handsome, and performs supernatural deeds. He does not suffer unduly. The Don is old and weak, and performs no great feats. He suffers a great deal. The classical tragic hero knows the nature of the world, but his *hubris* leads him from one success to another, until all ends in misery. The tragic hero suffers to a considerable degree, and his suffering is caused by his collision with the universal law of justice, which is the same for all. Don Quijote does not know the nature of the world; his ideas are fantastic. He is not calculating like the tragic hero. The comic hero is an average man in a situation less dignified than average, such as the jealous old husband. He is thwarted not by the universal law but by other rogues equally outside the law. The comic protagonist suffers most unwillingly, and this suffering is temporary and educational. Don Quijote suffers willingly, but never despairs. The Christian saint has no special gift, only an obedient will. He is victorious through faith in God and in his fellow man. The saint is most difficult to portray; his suffering is ironic, for the saint-hero views it as a blessing. It is almost impossible to show that the Christian saint's faith is not pride. In any event the saint must be depicted as a failure in a worldly sense. While Don Quijote's madness appears to be *hubris,* it is not. It is a religious conversion. The Knight is a Christian saint who suffers intentionally.

14. Auerbach, Erich. "The Enchanted Dulcinea," in *Memesis: The Representation of Reality in Western Literature.* Translated from the German by Willard Trask. Princeton, N. J.: Princeton University Press, 1953, pp. 334-358. [As reprinted in *Cervantes: A Collection of Critical Essays* (219), pp. 98-122. Based on "Die verzauberte Dulcinea." *Deutsche Vierteljahresschrift für Litteraturwissenschaft und Geistesgeschichte,* XXXV (1951), 294-316.]

In the enchantment of Dulcinea, Chapter X, Part II, the Knight sees only reality — three ugly peasant girls on donkeys. Here we find the climax of Don Quijote's illusion and disillusion; the hero explains away reality by resorting to the idea that Dulcinea has been enchanted, and concentrates all his efforts on disenchanting her. The shock to the hero could have cured him or made him worse; but neither occurs. He persists in the role of the hero persecuted by envious enchanters, therefore, both cure and tragedy are avoided. The Knight's lofty speech to the peasant girl serves to make the stylistic anticlimax fully effective. But even this is not enough for Cervantes, who causes her to fall off her donkey and leap back on it with grotesque dexterity, while the Knight attempts to maintain the chivalresque style. His being so firmly fixed in his illusion that neither "Dulcinea's" earthy reply nor her springing on her donkey can shake him is the acme of farce. It is difficult to say whether the enchantment scene, and the *Quijote* as a whole, is comic or tragic. As presented, the scene is comic.

However, though the hero is foolish, we admire him in his foolish illusion, and Cervantes intended for us to admire him.

The *Quijote* is a comedy in which well-founded reality holds madness up to ridicule. Yet Don Quijote is more than just a ridiculous figure. He is lovable. He has natural dignity and is not vulgar like most comic types. In fact he is not actually a "type." He even develops and grows kinder and wiser while his madness persists. However, his madness is not "wise" in the Romantic sense that wisdom arises out of madness. Nor is he a Shakespearean fool who speaks wisdom through his madness. Instead he behaves like a robot when his idée fixe is upon him. He is wise and kind independent of his madness.

What orders the whole of the *Quijote?* Not the philosophy nor any didactic purpose. Neither human uncertainty nor the power of destiny. It is an attitude toward the world, and hence also toward the subject matter of his art, in which bravery and equanimity play a major part. Cervantes delights in multifariousness and has a certain Southern reticence and pride. This prevents his taking the play seriously. He remains neutral, except regarding poorly written books.

Cervantes saw that reality was complicated. He saw how a knight like his hero would collide with reality. Though Don Quijote's madness may be heroic and idealized (since it leaves room for wisdom and humanity), still the hero is not a tragic symbol. One may read the *Quijote* in this manner, but such an idea is not there of itself. So universal and multilayered, so noncritical and nonproblematic a gaiety in the portrayal of everyday reality has not been attempted again in European letters.

15. Avalle-Arce, Juan Bautista. *Deslindes Cervantinos*. Madrid: Edhigar, 1961. Pp. 242.

1. "Conocimiento y vida en Cervantes": Don Quijote has faith, but it is a literary faith, not a religious one. His faith goes so far that he denies his sensory experiences, as in the Maritornes bedside episode. Don Quijote expects others to have his faith (Toledan merchants episode) without examination. In the *Quijote* not only literary faith is satirized, but also empirical faith, for the

tale of *El curioso impertinente* shows the futility of injecting experience into vital matters.

2. ["Tres vidas del *Persiles*" is a discussion of the characters Antonio, Rutilio and Manuel in that novel.]

3. "Grisóstomo y Marcela (La verdad problemática)": Américo Castro in his 1941 "Prólogos al *Quijote*" (68) was the first to interpret Grisóstomo's death as a suicide. But suicide was a mortal sin after the Council of Trent. Also, bloody events had always been considered out of place in a pastoral setting. Cervantes is more influenced by the religious prohibition than by the esthetic injunction in obscuring the manner of Grisóstomo's death, for he did not hesitate to include a murder in the *Galatea*. Many factors indicate that Cervantes meant to convey the idea that Grisóstomo met his death at his own hands. But the ambivalence of his death ties in with the overall tone of *Don Quijote* as a series of ambivalences, of opposing components — Age of Gold versus Age of Iron, pretended shepherds versus real shepherds, suicide versus natural death.

4. "El curioso y el capitán (La verdad artística)": We must start with the assumption that the stories of the Curious Impertinent and the Captive Captain are pertinent to Part I of the *Quijote* — for there they are. It is not a question of whether they should be there but why and how they are there. The priest says that the tale of *The Curious Impertinent* will be read out of pure curiosity, disinterestedly and not for practical value. At the end the priest forgets that the tale was fiction and judges it as if it were history. *The Tale of the Captive* is set up as history, but at the end it is judged by fictional criteria, for Fernando says that in this history "todo es peregrino, y raro, y lleno de accidentes que maravillan y suspenden a quien los oye." Note that though the tale of the *Cautivo* is supposedly historical, its opening lines resemble the opening of the fiction of *Don Quijote:* "En un lugar..." This is part of Cervantes' irony. Both these inserted tales are compatible as correlates of an intricate system of fictitious lives and vital fictions. From the resulting amalgam surges for the first time in literary history a type of narration where all the opposites are in compatibility.

5. "El cuento de los dos amigos (Cervantes y la tradición literaria)": The motif of the two loyal friends in Spanish literature can be traced from the *Disciplina Clericalis,* at the beginning of the 12th century, through the late medieval and the renaissance epochs, and into the nineteenth century. At first the tale of the two friends loyal to death is moralistic. Later Boccaccio removes the didactic element in his version. Cervantes uses the motif twice. In the *Galatea* the version used is the traditional one; in *El curioso impertinente* the story becomes ironic, since the two friends are no longer friends. Considered in this manner, *El curioso impertinente* is the last stage in the development of the story of the two friends, and at the same time its destruction.

16. Avalle-Arce, Juan Bautista. "Don Quijote, o la vida como obra de arte." *Trabajo publicado en la revista "Cuadernos Hispanoamericanos."* (Febrero, 1970), núm. 242. Pp. 34.

Don Quijote's imitation of Amadís in the penance episode is an act of pure will, utterly without motivation. It is the first gratuitous act in literature. Here a man's will becomes his conscience. This leads later to Dostoyevski's Raskolnikov, who explores the gratuitous act, and to Gide's Wluki and Camus' Meursault, who commit senseless murders. Thus in modern literature the ethical sense of the gratuitous act has disappeared completely.

Montesinos' cave, like the Sierra Morena penance, shows life as a work of art. Here we are in the subconscious where there is a free association of ideas. All the figures in Montesinos' cave treat one another as if they were works of art, as figures without substance. The implication of this episode is that the hero, too, is without inner substance. After this adventure he is constantly in doubt and appears to be undergoing a complete moral disintegration.

Though many characters in the *Quijote* attempt to live life as a work of art, the possibilities of doing so are quickly revealed to be a chimera. The reason is that such attempts seek to make something absolute out of something relative. Furthermore, art is the work of man, but man is the work of God. Therefore, to try to live life as a work of art implies an irremediable confusion of objectives.

On his deathbed the Don abdicates his artistic personality by a supreme act of will. He makes the supreme sacrifice — his identity.

17. Avalle-Arce, Juan Bautista. "Tres comienzos de novela." *Papeles de Son Armadans*, Año X, Tomo XXXVII, núm. CX (Mayo, 1965), 181-214.

The *Amadís* presents a closed world of absolute virtues, and preaches the determinism of the nobility of blood. Using the literary device of calling his tale a history, the author views his material, from outside, as finished. The hero progresses from good to best. In *Lazarillo* there is also determinism, but not that of heroic blood. It is the determinism of a biblical curse, in which the sins of the corrupt forefathers are passed down to the following generations. Both these works, though written *a posteriori*, have an ordered *a priori* conception of life. Both heroes had to be the way they are.

Cervantes' novel is more subtle. The Knight is a hero without a known lineage. He is an average person put in a human, anti-heroic setting. The *Quijote*, unlike *Amadís* and *Lazarillo*, is not a deterministic work.

18. Avery, William. "Elementos dantescos del *Quijote*." *Anales Cervantinos*, IX (1961-1962), 1-28.

Arturo Marasso (191) concluded that the windmill episode was based on lines 6290-6294 of Virgil's *Aeneid*. However, the idea for this episode in fact came from Dante's *Inferno*, XXXI, 20: "Sappi che non son torri, ma gigante." Also, in the *Inferno*, XXXIV, 47, Dante believes that Lucifer is a windmill. Marasso also concluded that the *Aeneid* was the source of the adventure of the fulling mills. However, this episode is actually based on the *Inferno*, XIV, 76-77; XVI, 1-3, 92-93, 100-105. The *galeotes* episode is related to the condemned souls in hell whom Dante interviews, much as Don Quijote interviews the galley slaves.

Cervantes is so preoccupied with Dante's paganism that he seems to desire to discredit, by satire, certain elements in the *Divine Comedy* which contradict orthodox Spanish Catholicism.

Cervantes' statement that his novel would not be a mixture of the human and the divine appears to be a slur on Dante's work.

19. Ayala, Francisco. "La invención del *Quijote* como problema técnico-literario." *Realidad, Revista de Ideas*, II, núm. 5 (Sept.-Oct., 1947), 183-200.

The present-day reader has heard of Don Quijote and Sancho before he reads their story. The reader of 1605 was faced with an unheard of hero, and had no precedent on which to base his judgment of the Knight, other than the author's hints. Thus the reader of today is diametrically opposed to the reader of Cervantes' day. The modern reader, it should be noted, has difficulty with the minor, novelesque characters who are from a vanished world. To the reader of 1605 these minor characters and their historical world were more understandable than the two main protagonists. This historical-literary world of Spain, though difficult for us today, was essential, for it brings out the realness of the leading characters. The *Quijote* gains universality not from the plane of the *humano-general* but departing from a determined and most singular politico-social structure in time and space.

Cervantes' disappointment in life corresponded exactly with a decisive historical mutation in Spain. This gave the author the power to add such enormous projections to his personal experience. In Part I Cervantes erects an artistic complex capable of expressing the deformation suffered by the polished, heroic world of his youth, the disillusion, the complex game of reality and appearance. In Part II this drama moves toward the realm of the farce, artistically refined but of less poetic power. In Part II the grotesque becomes *quintaesenciado* and touches frequently on the magic. There is a predominance of the theatrical artifice: a cart of players, Camacho's wedding, Montesinos' cave, Maese Pedro's puppet show, complicated practical jokes.

20. Ayala, Francisco. "Nota sobre la creación del *Quijote*." *Cuadernos Americanos* (México), XXXV (1947), 194-206.

The modern reader, who sees madness as clinical, as something to be pitied, views the joking about the hero's insanity as repugnant. Thus today's reader does not see the sacred element in madness that was noted in earlier times. From the hero's madness Cervantes draws rich artistic results, from the pathetic to the grotesque, and paints them in rich baroque contrasts. Though he causes his hero to be a laughingstock, the author, by making the Knight insane, lifts him out of everyday reality and projects him toward the superhuman.

There are three levels in the *Quijote:* (1) the lower level of practical everyday life; (2) the level of spiritual interests, of eroticism, of idealism; (3) the level of the quixotic myth, of the transcendental. Today we do not understand the second level, but to ignore it is to misunderstand the novel, for here is where the hero's figure acquires its concrete profile, its transcendental, historical determination. There are delicate transitions in this middle level. From a study of the fatality of the Eros in a rarified, non-temporal atmosphere (Marcela-Grisóstomo) we move to a study of the Eros in society (Cardenio-Luscinda, Fernando-Dorotea). All the impassioned souls of this second level form an harmonious unit (which powerfully and richly modulates the theme of the Eros) and presents a wonderful entirety in which the individual voices become related to one another to form diverse groupings, arranged in turn in complex balance and in interminable interlacings, all around the deep tone with which the Knight sustains the axis of the whole composition. This baroque arrangement is undoubtedly what permits autonomy to individual elements within the packed *retablo* of the novel and adds variety and charm to the main plot. Cervantes, in this second level, is audacious in his linkings, moving from the use of a separate *novela*, the *Curioso impertinente*, to the introduction of the *cautivo* who brings his own *novela*, the story of his life. Here there are daring foreshortenings used by the author, as in the use of Princess Micomicona (Dorotea) whose story is also that of the real Dorotea. Cervantes multiplies the focuses on the reality he presents thereby giving that reality great substance.

21. Ayala, Francisco. *La invención del Quijote. Discurso leído en la Fiesta de la Lengua Española celebrada en la Universidad de Puerto Rico el día 24 de abril de 1950.* San Juan, P. R.: Editorial Universitario, Universidad de Puerto Rico, 1950. Pp. 38.

Cervantes conferred spiritual and mythic meaning on his hero, and this was intended to express in code the drama of Spain in the Counter Reformation, that desperate conflict between the vital and the spiritual. On the one hand, the insane hero is reviled; on the other, he is lifted up to a superhuman sphere. Between this upper spiritual level and the lower strata of everyday life there is another layer, one of intense cultural elaboration, of sentimental ideas and of the superior thoughts of the epoch. This level is that of the interpolated tales and episodes. The interpolated material has a greater function than merely complicating the main plot and adding charm to it. This material presents, in a stylized manner, Cervantes' historical actuality as a problematical life penetrated with ideals. These episodes add a rich perspective to the *Quijote* and bring out the hero with an unprecedented novelty of style.

The tale of the *Captive Captain* clearly shows Cervantes' world and contains the key to the quixotic myth. The vital experience of the author, as reflected in the *cautivo's* tale, trembles with baroque anguish. The returning captive is perhaps a young and sane Don Quijote, acting in a world worthy of his spirit. But in 1605, we are not in the age of Lepanto but in the era of the defeated Armada. The *cautivo* is like a spirit from the past; he reintroduces the youth of Cervantes into the environment of his old age. Cervantes' disillusionment corresponds to Spain's decisive change after Lepanto. Cervantes (as the captive captain) faces his own creation (Don Quijote) deformed by the baroque environment. The hero of Lepanto has artistically been turned into a poor, addled hidalgo who is struggling against the new social order.

22. Ayala, Francisco. "Nota sobre la novelística cervantina." *Revista Hispánica Moderna*, XXXI (1965), 36-45.

The different approaches to reality in the *Quijote* are the result of the use of different types of previous genre, all of which looked at the outer world differently. Thus the reverberant baroque structure of the *Quijote* is due to the inexhaustible combination of traditional styles and to the constant game of vital references to past and present literatures. The tendency in the *Quijote* is to connect, spiritually, spheres that appear to exclude each other. The result is the creation of a new dimension in space.

Cervantes does not turn his back on previous literature. Instead he uses the exhausted prior forms as construction material for his new creation, fashioning with it spiritual spaces whose possibility no one suspected. Don Quijote first appears to belong to the realistic level, since he is a village hidalgo. Soon he becomes part of the chivalric and pastoral worlds. There is, to be sure, an ambiguity at the beginning of the story as to the hero's identity and name. And this famous Cervantine tendency toward ambiguity, starting with names, gets us lost in a labyrinth of mirrors, through which labyrinth we search for an elusive reality.

23. Ayala, Francisco. "Experiencia viva y creación literaria (un problema del *Quijote*)." *La Torre*, núm. 6 (Abril-Junio, 1954), pp. 87-110.

In Luis Zapata's *Miscelánea*, written prior to Part II of the *Quijote*, there is an anecdote about a beard-washing prank played on the Portuguese ambassador. This episode appears to have been an historical event, and Cervantes probably heard of it rather than reading it in the *Miscelánea*. But even if he did read Zapata's work, this would not prevent Cervantes' beard-soaping scene at the palace of the *Duques* from being true literature. Literary creation concretizes not only the personal experience of the author but the myths of the day as well. The distinction between real-life experience and literary models is, in the last analysis, not at all clear. Cervantes makes his beard-soaping episode more artistic than that of Zapata in several details. More importantly, he causes it to become not something that happened to X and Y but an integral part of his hero's experience and his suffering.

The true transcendence of the *Quijote* is that it is a new genre. Cervantes manipulates the previous literary molds (from the most lyric to the most crude) in order to multiply perspectives. His new novel, not a loose string of events as in the romance, is an attempt to achieve a total feeling of human existence.

24. Azaña, Manuel. *Cervantes y la intención del "Quijote."* Mexico: Ateneo Español de México, 1955. Pp. 79. (Based on a lecture before "Lyceum," May 3, 1930.)

There are two currents in the *Quijote*, the realistic and the poetic, and the latter is deeper. The clash of these two currents determines the creation of the figure of the Don. The marvelous aspect of the composition of this novel — this is the sacramental act achieved by the author — lies in his having merged the realistic current and the mythological current into one emotion, a disturbing, bitter-sweet emotion. Myths become humanized, they become a part of concrete reality and of the experience of each person. On the other hand, the humanity of the *Quijote*, even when its realism seems the heaviest, moves as if stirred by a breeze that blows from some unknown place.

The *Quijote* is in part autobiographical. As a young man Cervantes thought himself a knight-errant. As an older man he dissects his heart with ironic pleasure. The profound resonance of the novel is due not to its being the story of a failure but due to the fact that it is the tale of every man's realization that life is inexplicable.

25. Azorín [Martínez Ruiz, José]. *La ruta de Don Quijote*. Buenos Aires: Losada, 1964. Pp. 140. (First published in 1905: Madrid, Biblioteca Nacional y Extranjera.

[Azorín colorfully tells of his preparations to travel through La Mancha. He visits Argamasilla de Alba, and there asks why Don Quijote had to be born at this particular place. Azorín concludes that Argamasilla was a town errant *(pueblo andante)* that moved several times in the sixteenth century because of epidemics. The nervous inquietude of the town became an inherited trait, a characteristic that Cervantes' hero possessed. Azorín visits with local pedants, "los académicos de Argamasilla," who insist that Cervantes was imprisoned in their town, and that Don Quijote was really Rodrigo de Pacheco, a local figure of some importance.

In Chapter VII Azorín describes his trip in a cart along the route of Don Quijote's first sally, and during the journey attempts to place himself in the hero's position. In Chapter VIII he visits the alleged site of the inn where Don Quijote was knighted. In Chapter X Azorín enters the cave of Montesinos, and in Chapter XI he discusses the windmills near Criptana. Chapters XIII and XIV are devoted to El Toboso, and here Azorín wonders about the truth of the legend that Dulcinea was really Ana Zarco de Morales. In Chapter XV the author visits Alcázar de San Juan where some believe Cervantes was born.

It is Azorín's conclusion that Cervantes condemned Don Quijote's mad outbursts but that he neither condemned love for an ideal nor self-confidence.]

26. Azorín [Martínez Ruiz, José]. *Con Cervantes*. Madrid: Espasa-Calpe, 1944. Pp. 213.

[In "Al margen del *Quijote*" Azorín imagines the Don on the porch of an inn and thinks of Álvaro Tarfe (from the false *Quijote*) poor and dying in Granada, yet cherishing his copy of the true *Quijote*. In his chapter "Sancho, encantado" Azorín pictures the Squire and Tomé Cecial in a dialogue at an inn. In "Su mejor amigo" the critic discusses Cervantes' imprisonment in Algiers and concludes that without it the *Quijote* would not have been what it is. An imaginary dialogue between Cervantes and Juan de Austria is also presented here. In "Claro como la luz" Azorín gives a lengthy list of those who have been suggested as the possible author of the false *Quijote*.

In "Cervantes irreductible" and "Depreciación de Miguel" Azorín comments on those, apparently meaning Maeztu (184), who find the *Quijote* to be a decadent novel, concluding, instead, that Cervantes' masterpiece is not *un libro enervador* but an inspiring work. In "La noche del 23" the critic imagines a visit from the Don. In the following chapter, "Don Quijote," Azorín envisions the Knight returning home in triumph. It is not really the Don, but an imposter sent by the Duke. In "El testamento" the critic declares the Don's last will and testament to be null and void because he was insane with fever when he renounced generosity and nobility of spirit. In "El retrato" Azorín imagines the circumstances surrounding the painting of Cervantes' portrait by Jáuregui. In the chapter entitled "Viaje a Sevilla" the deep influence of Sevilla on Cervantes' works is discussed.

In "Su retrato" Azorín discusses the concept of time in Cervantes' works. The critic observes: "el tiempo es un factor primordial en la obra cervantina... si Lope es el espacio, Cervantes es el tiempo. Hay un cansancio de inefable dulzura en la segunda parte del Quijote."

In "Alto en El Pedernoso" the influence of Cervantes on Diderot is briefly examined, it being concluded that there was no direct imitation by the Frenchman, but "una lejana, ideal y bella resonancia de nuestro gran libro."

Francisco Márquez Torres (who wrote the *aprobación* to the 1615 *Quijote* and told of the visit to Spain of certain French diplomats) is the topic of discussion in "El primer Cervantista." Here Azorín comments briefly on Cervantes' style which the critic finds to be repetitious and careless at times, yet generally uncomplicated. In his final chapter, or "Epílogo, si se quiere," Azorín discusses several works about Cervantes, including Cotarelo's *Efemérides Cervantinas* (82) and Mayáns' biography of the master. Mayáns, states Azorín, noted long ago Cervantes' "involucraciones" or "retrocedimientos" in time. To Azorín, the total impression of *Don Quijote* on the reader is of "tiempo desvanecido," a fundamental factor in the author's spirit.]

27. Azorín [Martínez Ruiz, José]. *Con permiso de los Cervantistas*. Madrid: Biblioteca Nueva, 1948. Pp. 241.

Cervantes lived on the road, on the edge of society. He grew up among the common people, not the aristocracy. He hated the *moriscos* but not on religious grounds nor because he was captured by them; he hated them because they were rich and he was poor.

Cervantes is drawn to the feminine. All his women have curiosity; all follow their instincts. The feminine dominates the masculine in the *Quijote,* and ten to twelve women make up the spiritual atmosphere of that novel. While the author may disagree with the impulsive attitude of his female characters, he cannot deny their sincerity.

There is a certain "désarroi" in Part II of the *Quijote* after the appearance of the false *Quijote*. But there are many beautiful things in the last fifteen chapters of Part II. Would they have been there had there been no false *Quijote?*

Some believe that the *Quijote* is decadent. It is not; there is instead a great affirmation of independence in the novel, as in the Marcela episode. However, there is in Cervantes' works an open inclination toward dissidence revealed by the many cases of mental unbalance which he pictures — Don Quijote, the Glass Licentiate, Basilio, Cardenio. Also, his characters, like himself, are at times on the edge of society.

28. Basave Fernández del Valle, Agustín. *Filosofía del Quijote.* Mexico: Espasa Calpe Mexicana, S. A., 1959. Pp. 279.

The Knight of La Mancha lives in two worlds, the real and the ideal, without being able to live well in either. He attempts to go against time; he strives for irreducible essences. But while the Don knows how to discover eternal values, he lacks a sense of the historical.

Don Quijote tries to make his life an expression of the highest ideals. He builds his own world, leaving out what does not suit him. The essential feature of Don Quijote is that he feels himself to be the bearer of a personal value, the chivalresque.

We admire Don Quijote. He speaks to our imagination, to our sensibility and to our intelligence. The Knight shows us the harmony of the noble life. We love him because he produces pleasure in us. He inspires us, and when we are with him we feel as if we were in an unlimited world. His ideals are not fantastic, but his visions of the world of the senses are indeed unreal.

29. Bataillon, Marcel. *Érasme et l'Espagne: Recherches sur l'histoire spirituelle du XVIe siècle.* Paris: E. Droz, 1937, pp. 819-849.

[This work, as the title indicates, deals with the general influence of Erasmus on Spain. Only those portions dealing with the *Quijote* are discussed here.] Menéndez y Pelayo, in his study of heterodoxies in Spain, saw a latent influence of Erasmus on Cervantes, though he did not consider the author of the *Quijote* a modern freethinker. Américo Castro in his *El pensamiento de Cervantes* (63) finds a great deal of the Erasmian in Cervantes' works but tends to confuse *erasmismo* with Rationalism. Is Cervantes a hypocrite as Castro claims? No! He does, however, share Erasmus' smiling irreverence at outward religious practices. Both are also skeptical about miracles. The Knight of the Green Cloak is Cervantes' moral ideal — pious, simple, modest. This conforms to Erasmus' ideal. Cervantes states that half-hearted works of charity are of no value, an Erasmian and Valdesian concept. But Cervantes is a devout Catholic who is living in an age when one can no longer jest about the difference between true religion and outer religious practices. Also, let no one see in Cervantes' remark about freedom of conscience in Germany a condemnation of the exile of the *moriscos*.

30. Bataillon, Marcel. "Publications cervantines récentes." *Bulletin Hispanique*, LIII (1951), 157-175.

[Bataillon does not pretend to present an exhaustive list of the works written in honor of the fourth centennial of Cervantes' birth, nor does he seek to be selective. The critic briefly discusses collective volumes of Cervantine material published in 1947 and 1948; bibliographical studies such as Helmut Hatzfeld's (143) and E. Allison Peer's (232) summaries of Cervantes criticism; biographies of Cervantes, such as those of A. F. G. Bell (31) and Astrana Marín (11); and works dealing with the cultural and literary influences on Cervantes, such as Arturo Marasso's (191) and Antonio Vilanova's (313) studies. Under "Pensée et thèmes" Bataillon discusses Menéndez Pidal's *Cervantes y el ideal caballeresco* (197), J. A. Maravall's *El humanismo de las armas en Don Quijote* (192), A. A. Parker's "El concepto de la verdad en el *Quijote*" (230), and Helmut Hatzfeld's "¿Don Quijote asceta?" (145). Under "Création littéraire et structure" he devotes his attention to Américo Castro's "Incarnation in *Don Quixote*" (69), Joaquín Casalduero's *Sentido y forma del Quijote* (58), E. Moreno Báez' "Arquitectura del *Quijote*" (212), J. Camón Aznar's *Don Quijote y la teoría de los estilos* (53), and other works. Under "Langue et style" several works are discussed, including Helmut Hatzfeld's *El Quijote como obra de arte del lenguaje* (141). Also noted by Bataillon are Dámaso Alonso's "Sancho-Quijote, Sancho-Sancho" (5), Francisco Romero's "Don Quijote y Fichte" (259), Francisco Ayala's "La invención del *Quijote* como problema técnico-literario" (19), and numerous works on the influence of Cervantes on later literature.]

31. Bell, Aubrey F. G. *Cervantes*. Norman, Okla.: University of Oklahoma Press, 1947. Pp. xxi + 256.

Cervantes' criticism of the Spain of his times is typically Spanish. The Inquisition did not bring gloom and repression to Spain. However, Cervantes saw the hollowness of his age. The divorce between theory and practice, promise and fulfillment, external show and inner reality, furnished the main subject for his philosophy and for his art. He combined the spirit of the Renaissance (a sense of "new immediacy") with the medieval sense of the preciousness of the human soul. He believed in absolute values and in divine justice. Yet he is delicately perceptive and, therefore, modern.

The *Quijote* is an epic in prose though not what Pinciano had in mind as a prose epic. Cervantes extends this concept to include humor and humanity. Though low reality is found in the *Quijote*, Cervantes' genius is essentially romantic. He was impelled toward the fantastic. He says he avoids the impossible but comes very close to it on several occasions, as in the cave of Montesinos episode. The fact is that Cervantes was continually tempted to see how much of actual life and of fantastic imagination he could fit into his literary sack.

The *Quijote* is an audacious novel in its attempt to contain a multiplicity of heterogenous thoughts, events, episodes, scenes and characters and to weld them together into an harmonious whole. Some believe that Cervantes' novel has no unity. Perhaps not, but it is a consumate work of art. Besides there is one great unifying force — its humor. The *Quijote* is a divine patchwork. Though Cervantes favored a broad canvas, he was really best at the brief sketch, the *entremés* and the short story. Don Quijote himself is a unifying force in the novel as is his village, which as always in the background. Cervantes' chief originality is that his marvelous imagination is brought to bear on the common things and ordinary events of everyday, illumining them with extraordinary power.

32. Bell, Aubrey F. G. "The Wisdom of Don Quijote." *Books Abroad, An International Literary Quarterly* (Okla.), XXI (1947), 259-263.

Cervantes' fantasies are based on reality and reflect Henry James' twin demons of observation and imagination. Like most classics, *Don Quijote* is more praised than read. This is a pity since Cervantes' masterpiece has great humor and deals with the problems of existence. The *Quijote* was written in a time like ours, an epoch of crisis, of inflation. The author had a tragic conception of life but was courageous, full of humor and stoic. Cervantes' wisdom was that of a man who had traveled much and suffered much, physically and spiritually.

33. Bell, Michael. "The Structure of *Don Quixote*." *Essays in Criticism*, XVIII (1968), 241-257.

The effect of the second-hand narrator is to throw doubt on the ontological status of Don Quijote. With the intrusion of the historical idea Cervantes disturbs our comfortable assumption that the story is all purely fictional. The ambiguity on this point is held intact by the gap between the two narrators, Cide Hamete and Cervantes.

Don Quijote's own awareness of himself as a character in a fictional setting tends, however, to remove him from the fictional frame, for a purely fictional character is not entitled to such a self-awareness. It is a logical absurdity for the Knight to be able to think of himself as a character in a book, but his being allowed to do so gives him a sort of autonomy. The episodic structure of the *Quijote*, the feeling of randomness in that novel, also makes the hero more real, as does the fact that the hero is archetypal, even in Part I.

The people who organize the Don's adventures in Part II are readers of Part I. In this earlier part people tended to yield to the hero, whereas in Part II they only appear to yield to him. In reality they deprive him of initiative; they undermine his confidence in himself and his ideals. This is the "real" world's response to the hero's recklessly having abandoned his fictional frame where he would have been largely safe from his final humiliations.

In Part II Don Quijote not only enters a more "real" world but also a social world, and the people in Part II oppose the Knight *qua* fictional character. Though people from the "real" world enjoy reading about the Don, they resent his intruding into their world. From the point of view of the reader of Part II, the Knight is doubly fictional: (1) he is someone they have read about and come to know in a book; (2) he is a real historical figure pretending to be a character from the world of fiction.

34. Benardete, M. J. "Los galeotes (Capítulos XXII, XXIII, XXV, XXIX de la primera parte del *Quijote*)." *Revista Hispánica Moderna*, XXXI (1965), 57-70.

The episode of the galley slaves investigates the problem of justice. But what sort of justice? We agree that a lawbreaker should be punished but at times we are perplexed. The laws in Spain were harsh. Agreements with minorities were broken, and the Indians were cruelly exploited under the law. Some, such as Bartolomé de las Casas, spoke out against the mistreatment of the Indians, but no one spoke out directly against the persecution of the Jews and *moriscos*. However, Cervantes suggests the possibility that historical decisions against the minorities in Spain were not sacred decisions. In the *Quijote* he examines all the institutional beliefs of his age and obliquely attacks their grotesqueness and absurdity. In the adventure of the galley slaves Cervantes suggests deep and mysterious lessons of morality and metaphysics. Though the outcome of this adventure is melancholy and depressing, it deserves to be in the Bible because of the lessons implicit in it. All in all, Don Quijote did well in freeing the slaves, in spite of their ingratitude.

35. Benardete, Maír José, and Flores, Ángel, ed. *The Anatomy of Don Quixote: a symposium*. Ithaca, N. Y. The Dragon Press, 1932. Pp. xiv + 120.

[This collection contains the following four works translated into English: (1) Ramón Menéndez Pidal's "Un aspecto en la elaboración del *Quijote*" (196); (2) A. Morel-Fatio's "Le Don Quichotte envisagé comme peinture et critique de la société espagnole du XVIᵉ et du XVIIᵉ siècle" (210); (3) portions of Helmut Hatzfeld's (141) work on Cervantes' style in the *Quijote;* (4) Ivan Turgenev's "Hamlet y Don Quijote," 1879.]

36. Bergson, Henri [Louis]. *Laughter: An Essay on the Meaning of the Comic*. Translated from the French by Cloudesley Brereton and Fred Rothwell. New York: The MacMillan

Company, 1921. Pp. 200. (First published in 1900 as a series of three articles in *Revue de Paris*.)

To produce its whole effect, the comic demands momentary anesthesia of the heart, for its appeal is to the intelligence, pure and simple. The basis of the comic is inelasticity, something mechanical grafted upon the living. Absentmindedness is a form of inelasticity, and Don Quijote is an absentminded figure. His strange, reasonable madness excites us to laughter by playing on the same chords within us as does the victim of a practical joke or the passer-by who slips and falls down in the street. The Knight's absentmindedness is systematic and organized around one central idea, and his mishaps, thanks to the inexorable logic which reality applies to the correction of dreams, are such that they kindle in those around them, by a series of cumulative effects, a hilarity capable of unlimited expansion. Systematic absentmindedness, like that of Don Quijote, is the most comical thing imaginable: it is the comic itself, drawn as nearly as possible from its very source.

Common sense represents the endeavor of a mind continually readapting itself. It is the mobility of the intelligence conforming exactly to the mobility of things. It is the moving continuity of our attention to life. Common sense is often the ability to forget, as well as to remember. Don Quijote cannot forget the stories of chivalry with their accounts of giants. Therefore, he needs to encounter giants. The idea of giants, imbedded in his mind, is bent on entering the material world. Thus the Knight sees giants where we see windmills. This is comical; it is also absurd. But is it a mere absurdity, an absurdity of an indefinite kind? No! It is a very special inversion of common sense. It consists in seeking to mold things on an idea of one's own, instead of molding one's ideas on things, — in seeing before us what we are thinking of, instead of what we see. Good sense would have us leave all our memories in their proper rank and file; then the appropriate memory will every time answer the summons of the situation of the moment and serve only to interpret it. But in Don Quijote, on the contrary, there is one group of memories in command of all the rest and dominating the character himself: thus it is reality that now has to bow to the imagination, its only function being to supply fancy with a body. Once the illusion has been created, Don Quijote develops it logically enough in all its consequences; he proceeds with the certainty and precision of a somnambulist who is acting his dream. Now, is this logic peculiar to the Knight? No. All comic characters err through obstinacy, through absent-mindedness. In short, through automatism. At the root of all comic characters there is a sort of rigidity which compels its victims to keep strictly to one path, to shut their eyes and refuse to listen, to refuse to adjust their thoughts to things. Society suspects such inelasticity because it is a possible sign of slumbering activity as well as separatist tendencies, for such tendencies swerve from the common center around which society gravitates.

37. Bertrand, J.-J. A. "La naissance du chef-d'œuvre." *Anales Cervantinos*, VI (1957), 193-226.

Very little is known of the genesis of *Don Quijote*. Cervantes was about fifty when he conceived his famous knight and fifty-seven when Part I was published. There are a number of theories as to when the *Quijote* was begun. Cervantes refers to L. Barahona de Soto (died 1595) as *was*. Therefore, it appears that the *Quijote* was started after 1595. It was probably begun in Seville in 1597.

Cervantes pictured the *Quijote* as a confrontation between two worlds, the romantic and the brutally realistic. Book I of the 1605 edition (the *Urquijote*) is a picaresque novel, and the impression that the *Quijote* is a pure satire springs from these early chapters. The second sally of the hero is a new conception; Cervantes raises his sights. In Book II Don Quijote begins to become transfigured. In Book III he becomes a "loco-cuerdo," only partially mad. Don Quijote now appears to be the one with reason, not the world. His error is his use of force to carry out his ideas. The end of the 1605 *Quijote* is enigmatic, though it seems to portray the painful triumph of a superior man.

Part II has a totally different spirit from Part I. Some, like Goethe, do not care particularly for Part II and condemn it. They are wrong to do so. Others, like Le Sage, wrongly conclude that Cervantes plagiarized Avellaneda's *Quijote*. Part II is better constructed than Part I, and there are many differences: the character of Don Quijote's love is altered; his desire for fame grows dim, and the need to disenchant Dulcinea becomes the dominant theme. Cervantes seems to hesitate about Dulcinea. He had stated that she and Don Quijote would marry, but later the author realized that this ideal could not be achieved. In Part II Don Quijote is no longer a knight errant; he is merely a victim of human nonsense who is passed from hand to hand. At the end of the 1615 *Quijote* the protagonist dies because Cervantes feels himself dying. Cervantes' satire, in his last years, loses its bite. Inner peace reigns, and we enter the realm of the divine.

38. Bickermann, Joseph. *Don Quijote y Fausto, los héroes y las obras*. Prólogo del P. Félix García. Barcelona: Araluce, 1932. Pp. 422. (First published in 1920 as *Don Quijote und Faust. Die Helden und die Werke:* Berlin, A. Collignon.)

How could Cervantes make his comic protagonist a hero? How could he elevate the comic? The hero is pictured as eloquent and tenacious, therefore a sympathetic figure. But what is the need of these good qualities if the purpose of the story is to make him a laughingstock? How does Cervantes achieve the concordance of the uplifting and the humiliating? He accomplishes this by making the story the myth of a redeemer, faithful even in defeat.

Don Quijote is not a romantic. His fantasy is sterile. He is a fussy and exaggerated ritualist, though a great dialectician. To be a prisoner of a concrete scheme of things is not to be a dreamer; it is the opposite. He is mad, and his madness is not based on a vital belief but on a dead letter. Yet he is a representative figure, for all of us are Don Quijotes, though inferior ones. Don Quijote has no desire for truth. Not only does he not see; he does not want to see. His hardheadedness does not arise from a profound faith but merely from the fear of being disillusioned.

Don Quijote believes in *universalismo*, since he wishes to liberate mankind for all times (an idea not found in chivalry novels). The Don is a *monista* in that he regards reality as an organic whole. In addition he is an *institucionalista* in that he realizes that he must have an institution (knight-errantry) behind him. In the figure Don Quijote, Cervantes created the prototype of all future reformers, and giving him all the gifts of God, the author showed us the destructiveness of that type of madness, even in a privileged type.

Don Quijote and Faust have much in common, though they are different in many ways. Both are inactive until late in life. Both recognize their excess at the end. Both want to achieve everything yet accomplish nothing. Both Don Quijote and Faust yearn to return to the human fold at the end. They are both heroes, not because of their deeds, but because they find themselves. Their renunciation is the cause of their greatness.

39. Blanco Aguinaga, Carlos. "Cervantes y la picaresca: Notas sobre dos tipos de realismo." *Nueva Revista de Filología Hispánica*, XI (1957), 313-342. [Translated into English and abridged by Lowry Nelson, Jr. in *Cervantes: A Collection of Critical Essays* (219), pp. 137-151.]

Picaresque naturalism and chivalresque idealism are both deterministic; they are different from the *Quijote*, which does not allow fixity either in theme or in form. Cervantes, both in the *Coloquio de los perros* and in the *Quijote*, immediately undertakes to divest of any importance what happened prior to the beginning of the novel. What is about to happen is the crucial idea. Cervantes shows a complete openness in his works. The reader and the novelist retire from the scene feeling that more life is always possible.

Cervantes' realism is gorged with idealism. In his works the levels of reality always intersect, so that no one of them seems to represent absolute truth. Opposites coalesce to underscore the ambiguity of reality and to show us that "realism" does not necessarily mean complete disillusion.

For Cervantes, composing a story meant creating a world in the image of the one we perceive, one which, from its very creation, is independent of its creator, a world always fragmentary, though complete in every fragment: a world which, like our own, is in the process of becoming outside of us, while we are becoming in it and in the interplay between each of us and the rest. Writing a novel, for Cervantes, is, in a sense, letting do and letting live in the created world of half-truths and half-lies which no one has yet known how to demarcate satisfactorily. Cervantes is first a creator, then a spectator who observes ironically and benevolently the progression of what he has created, unable to censure any of its parts or creatures.

40. Blasco Ibáñez, Vicente. "The Greatest Novel." [As summarized in *Bulletin of the Pan American Union*, L (1920), 529-531.]

The chivalry novel became so fantastic that a reaction set in, and this reaction produced *Don Quijote*, the first and greatest of the modern novels. All literatures of the world are shot through with the spirit of the *Quijote*. But the novel goes beyond literature; it is life made eternal in words, just as *Las meninas* is life in colored lines. Moreover, I do not know any other book which better symbolizes the superiority of the idealist and the dreamer over the jeering and materialistic common herd, despite the fact that Cervantes seems at times to laugh at the misfortunes and disappointments of his hero.

The ending of the story is profoundly human. Those who had jeered at the hero beg him to go on living, and Sancho inherits his master's madness. Don Quijote represents the greatest human virtues: the protection of the weak, self-sacrifice, and the suppression of selfishness. The vulgar, such as Sancho, are unwittingly the servants of the dreamers and madmen.

41. Bodensieck, Annemarie. "The Comic of Expression." Unpublished Ph. D. dissertation, University of Wisconsin, 1928. Pp. 152.

[Chapter I consists of a short summary of seven theories of humor: the degradation theory, the surprise theory, the incongruity theory, the release theory, the defensive theory, the self-including element theory, and the oscillation — conflict theory. Chapter II deals in part with the question whether Cervantes is humorously attacking ideals or not. Here Miss Bodensieck observes that the mainsprings of Cervantes' humor consist in the ever-recurring paradox: he is an enigma; he seems to criticize and yet he does not. In Chapter III the critic discusses Cervantes the linguistic comic. Under the heading "Intentional Linguistic Comic" Miss Bodensieck includes wit, parody proper, and irony. She concludes that in the *Quijote* parody prevails and that the humor arises out of the characters themselves. Chapter IV deals with parody in some detail. Its usual purpose, she observes, is to degrade a respected subject without revealing any profound truth. However, the critic hastens to add, Cervantes' parody does not take on the aspect of derision; it enobles the dying parent-novel of chivalry. Cervantes, Miss Bodensieck here notes, uses neologisms, strange words formed by new endings; he also makes verbs out of nouns, adverbs out of nouns, juxtaposes real and ideal concepts, and uses the masculine as well as the feminine form for a parodic type of exaggeration: "No había barca ni barco"; "no había ínsula ni ínsulo." Other linguistic devices used by Cervantes are pointed out: the use of lofty-sounding but nonsensical prefixes *(proto-encantador)*; coined words with adjectival endings *(dueñasco)*; the accumulation of superlatives; puns; and overexactness. Chapter VI discusses wit. Here Miss Bodensieck concludes that the most generous source of linguistic wit in Cervantes' work is motivated genuinely in the character's make-up. The critic further states that the reader laughs more at the incongruity between the means of expression and the unexpected results than at the stupidity displayed.]

42. *Boletín de la Real Academia Española. Número especial para conmemorar el cuarto centenario del nacimiento de Cervantes,* XXVII (Oct., 1947-Abr. 1948).

[This collection contains the following articles: (1) José María Pemán's "La 'armazón de cauallería' de Don Quijote (Apuntes sobre el capítulo III de la primera parte)" (233); (2) Duque de Maura's "Miguel de Cervantes Saavedra, fracasado genial"; (3) "Las tres edades del *Quijote*" (59) by Julio Casares; (4) Armando Cotarelo Valledor's "Obras perdidas de Cervantes que no se han perdido"; (5) Lorenzo Riber's "Al margen de un capítulo de *Don Quijote* (El LX de la segunda parte)"; (6) Eugenio d'Ors' "Fenomenología de los Libros de Caballería"; (7) Ángel González Palencia's "Cervantes y los moriscos"; (8) Luis Martínez Kleiser's "La universalidad externa e interna del *Quijote*"; (9) Narciso Alonso Cortés' "Tres amigos de Cervantes"; (10) Santiago Montoto's "Juan de Mestanza, poeta celebrado por Cervantes"; (11) José Manuel Blecua's "Un nuevo soneto atribuido a Cervantes y un romance del Conde de Lemos"; (12) Eduardo Juliá Martínez' "La serena muerte en Cervantes"; (13) Jaime Oliver Asín's "La hija de Agi Morato en la obra de Cervantes."]

43. Bonilla y San Martín, Adolfo. *Don Quijote y el pensamiento español.* Madrid: Imprenta de Bernardo Rodríguez, 1905. Pp. 26. (Conferencia pronunciada el sábado 6 de Mayo de 1905, en el Ateneo de Madrid.)

Patricio de Azcárate, in 1861, concluded that Cervantes was the initiator of the rational method of thought later followed by Descartes, in that the author of the *Quijote* considered evidence to be the first criterion of truth. Campoamor, in 1862, generally followed Azcárate, affirming that Cervantes and Gómez Pereira were the founders of modern psychology in that they were the first to seek to confirm their own existence.

By Cervantes' time the integral early Renaissance had faded away, leaving only its erudite, bookish side behind. The early Renaissance had been more Humanistic and literary than philosophical, but by Cervantes' age three schools of philosophy had established themselves in the universities: (1) traditional Scholasticism, more or less purified of errors; (2) Aristotelian Scholasticism; (3) independent philosophy, based on Aristotle, Plato and Vives. Cervantes is more or less Aristotelian, though his knowledge of philosophy is neither deep nor methodical. However, he did clearly distinguish the vital early Renaissance from the later decadent state into which it had fallen.

Spanish philosophy is neither the Knight's intellectual philosophy nor the Squire's practical philosophy. It is both philosophies, united and combined; and though appearing to be divergent they are *formas de idéntica materia.* At various times in its history Spain has produced moral and psychological philosophers such as Seneca; in other eras it has given forth metaphysical thinkers such as Lulio, Averroes, and Maimónides. It is foolish to say that one of these approaches to philosophy is *the* Spanish philosophy.

Don Quijote, when all is said and done, is the center of the story. He seeks to revive something no longer in use. He wishes to transform ideas. The Knight is heavily influenced by Humanism, and literarily he is a product of the Carolingian cycle of chivalry legends. He represents individual justice, and is opposed to all authority, even Church authority. He is a contradiction, especially in the highly controlled period in which he is living. We are fascinated by his desire to bring back primitive justice. We are not impressed by the Knight of the Green Cloak, who is a circumspect, meticulous, self-satisfied Philistine.

The quest for individual justice is what Cervantes sought to describe in his hero. At the end, however, both author and hero summon the priest. Don Quijote is not like Ibsen's Brandt who died as he lived. The Knight strove to achieve a goal, and, like many of the heroes who searched for the Holy Grail, failed. Yet he died satisfied because he had aspired.

There are works that are superior to the *Quijote* in style, entertainment value, and philosophy. The secret of Cervantes' novel is the deep sympathy which the quixotic ideal inspires in us all, although not all seek to carry it out and many laugh at it. Because it is both a universal and human conviction that if we followed the Knight's ideal, the Golden Age would return and the world would be happy.

44. Bonilla y San Martín, Adolfo. *Cervantes y su obra*. Madrid: Beltrán, [1916]. Pp. 262.

Though it is difficult to find a concrete body of esthetic theory in Cervantes' works, it is definite that he did not write unconsciously. The theories which he appears to adhere to are drawn largely from his reading of Pinciano and Leon Hebreo. Cervantes' thought is clear and his technique is descriptive. Lope's thought is artificious and his technique is dramatic. Quevedo's thought is natural but his style is artificious. Cervantes narrates, Lope converses, Quevedo chides. Cervantes and Quevedo have more truth than Lope, and Cervantes is more natural than Quevedo.

Cervantes' *discreción, decoro, invención,* and *ingenio* were often praised by his contemporaries, and the *Quijote* was enjoyed by many in the early seventeenth century. However, this masterpiece was praised by few. Did the people understand Cervantes? Better put, did he understand himself? Later generations do not necessarily understand the *Quijote* better than Cervantes' contemporaries, merely differently.

[Many of the ideas expressed in this work are also found in his earlier essay of 1905 (43) and are not repeated here. In addition, Chapter II of *Cervantes y su obra* is devoted to the expression "los bancos de Flandes," and Chapter VI deals with *La tía fingida*.]

45. Bonilla y San Martín, Adolfo. *De crítica cervantina*. Madrid: Ruiz Hnos., 1917, Pp. 105.

[The first portion of this work deals with the 1614 *Quijote* of Avellaneda and the various theories as to the true identity of that author. Part II of Bonilla's treatise is concerned with interpretations of Cervantes' masterpiece. Here are discussed various philosophical and political interpretations of the *Quijote* by such critics as B. Pallol [*Interpretación del Quijote*, 1893]. Bonilla concludes that the first writer to call attention to a possible occult meaning in *Don Quijote* was José Cadalso, 1741-1782, who, in his *Cartas marruecas*, observed that beneath the nonsense in that novel there lay a "conjunto de materias profundas e importantes."]

46. Booth, Wayne C. "The Self-Conscious Narrator in Comic Fiction Before *Tristram Shandy*." *PMLA*, LXVII (1952), 163-185.

Cervantes' *Quijote* is the first important work to use a self-conscious narrator, and in that novel this technique is developed to an extent not equalled until well into the eighteenth century. Perhaps only Cervantes can claim a position of greater importance than Marivaux in the history of the European novel before Fielding. The Spaniard is quite important to Sterne and to other novelists because of his experiments with sentiment and with the combination of sentiment and ridicule. He is also important for his pre-Richardsonian exploration of psychological detail.

47. Borges, Jorge Luis. "Nota sobre el Quijote." *Realidad, Revista de Ideas* (Buenos Aires), II, núm. 5 (Sept.-Oct., 1947), 234-236.

It is perhaps true that the Don Quijote and Sancho Panza of legend are symbols, abstractions, or myths, but not the Knight and the Squire of the book, who are individuals, and very complex ones too. Prior to the *Quijote* the characters created by art were either to be pitied or to be admired. The Knight is the first who deserves and wins man's friendship, after he wins Cervantes as a friend.

48. Borges, Jorge Luis. "Magies partielles du *Quichotte*." *Les Temps Modernes*, X (1955), 2127-2130.

Cervantes enjoys confusing the objective and the subjective, the world of the reader and the world of the book. In the *escrutinio* in Chapter VI, Part I, he even brings himself and his novel *La Galatea* into the *Quijote* and describes the barber as a friend of Cervantes. In Chapter IX, Part I, we are surprised to hear that the whole novel was translated from the Arabic by a *morisco*. This game of strange ambiguities reaches its peak in Part II where the protagonists become readers of the *Quijote* as well as fictional characters. This is like the Sanskrit poem of Valmiki, the *Ramayana*, where the lost children of Rama become pupils of the author himself. It is also similar to the structure of *The 1001 Nights* where the writer never attempts to demarcate the different levels of reality and presents all levels as being on the surface, as in a Persian tapestry. In fact, in Tale 602 of this collection of fantastic stories the narrator tells of her own life, a story which includes all the other tales and itself as well. Why are we disturbed that the Knight himself should be a reader of the *Quijote* or the 1001 nights be within *The 1001 Nights?* Because such inversions suggest that if characters of fiction can be readers, then we, as their readers, can also be fictional characters.

49. Borges, Jorge Luis. "Análisis del último capítulo del *Quijote*." *Revista de la Universidad de Buenos Aires*, I (1956), 28-36.

Cervantes avoids using surprise in the last chapter, telling us in the chapter heading that the hero will die. Cervantes is sly in this chapter for he states that all flesh and blood must perish, whereas Don Quijote is not flesh and blood but a purely fictional character.

The *Quijote* was not conceived of as a short story, but as a long tale which would end in disillusionment. In effect, the whole novel was written for the death scene. Cervantes was puzzled as to how to bring about the disenchantment of his hero. He uses the improbable device of a mysterious sleep to serve this purpose. Cervantes does not tell us what happened in this feverish sleep, but this omission, oddly enough, adds more credibility to what is stated.

50. Brenan, Gerald. "Cervantes," in *The Literature of the Spanish People From Roman Times to the Present.* Cleveland and New York: The World Publishing Company, 1963, pp. 175-198. (First published in 1951: Cambridge, Cambridge University Press.) [Reprinted in *Cervantes: A Collection of Critical Essays* (219), pp. 13-33.]

The interest of the reader of *Don Quijote* is maintained by the tension of a series of fixed contrasts. For example, there is the contrast between the actual situation and what it appears to be to Don Quijote; there is that between his noble and exalted way of feeling and Sancho's peasant shrewdness and self-interest; and, if one likes, that between the Knight's wise and sane ratiocinations and his violent fantasies whenever the subject of chivalry enters his head. Every situation that turns up brings at least two of these into play, and the reader is kept in suspense until he knows precisely how it will be decided. By these means the weakness inherent in the picaresque form — a chain of events loosely strung together — is overcome and the greatest concentration brought to bear on each incident.

The relationship between the Knight and the Squire is like a marriage, and their familiar dialogues are like those of a married couple. This type of dialogue has the effect of lacing together the various incidents. Don Quijote is the unmitigated male, while Sancho is the semi-dependent female. Hence the long story of Sancho's fidelities and infidelities, which is one of the most revealing things in the book.

As the Montesinos' cave episode reveals, Don Quijote is fundamentally a dry and prosaic person. Through the dream we receive an oblique yet penetrating glimpse into the deeper layer of Don Quijote's mind. We see that knight-errantry, even in a dream, has not conquered every portion of his mind.

One must examine the *Quijote* on a metaphysical plane, although in doing this we are going far beyond the author's intentions. The material for metaphysical interpretations is in the novel, and there is pleasure to be got from the queries it raises about human certainties. If we cannot pin down this most elusive of writers to any definite attitude, we may at least say that he contrasts the biological need which man has for faith with the difficulty his intellect has in finding grounds for it. We may sum up Cervantes' contribution to philosophy by saying that, like Montaigne and Descartes, he set in motion a chain reaction of doubt.

51. Brenes, Dalai. "The Sanity of Don Quixote: A Study in Cervantine Deception." Unpublished Ph. D. dissertation, Graduate School of Cornell University, 1957. Pp. iv + 244. [Appreciation is expressed to Connie Maxfield and Susan Little for their assistance in preparing this summary.]

[Brenes, in his introduction, concludes that Cervantes was neither an Erasmian nor a party-line Catholic, and that *Don Quijote* was the product of an intelligent and cultured Catholic whose questioning mind critically examined the problems raised at the Council of Trent and the solutions there given to those problems. Chapter I deals with Cervantes' life. Chapter II discusses the question of the influence of Erasmus on Cervantes' thought. Chapter III is devoted to a sharp, detailed attack on Casalduero's (58) belief that the *Quijote* is baroque in structure. Chapter IV challenges Spitzer's theory (289) that the variations in names for persons and places in Cervantes' novel calls for a perspectivistic outlook on life. Chapter V discusses the genesis of the *Quijote*. The possible influence of Huarte's theory of insanity is dealt with. Brenes concludes that Ignatius Loyola was the principal model for Cervantes' hero. Later in this chapter the critic discusses Castro's (63) theory that the *Quijote* is a Platonistic study of the truth and falsity of appearances. Brenes disagrees with Castro, concluding that certain episodes, such as that of the basin-helmet dispute, may well be Cervantes' reaction to a non-Platonic idea such as the doctrine of transsubstantiation. The dispute over wine and blood in the episode of the wineskins is, to Brenes, another possible reference to this doctrine. Chapter VI discusses the repressive conditions in Spain in Cervantes' times. In this chapter Brenes reaches the conclusion that the attack on chivalry novels is a disguised attack on the historicity of the Holy Scriptures.]

52. Buchanan, Milton A. "Extraneous Matter in the First Part of Cervantes's *Don Quijote*," in *Estudios eruditos in memoriam de Adolfo Bonilla y San Martín (1875-1926) con un prólogo de Jacinto Benavente*, I. Madrid: Universidad Central, Facultad de Filosofía y Letras (Imprenta Viuda e Hijos de J. Ratés), 1927, pp. 143-149.

Cervantes, in seeking to explain the inclusion of interpolated episodes in the *Quijote*, withholds from the reader the fact that these intercalations were old material not originally intended for the *Quijote*, and that there were other interpolations besides the short stories: namely the poems. In interpolating episodes and other material Cervantes was not using a new technique, nor was he necessarily violating any canon of esthetics. In the *Persiles* he defends the practice of intruding episodes, provided the intrusions are not lengthy. One basic reason for Cervantes' interpolations was that the main plot of the Knight's deeds lacked love episodes and poems, which Cervantes' readers demanded and which the pastoral and the chivalry novel provided.

Early in the Cardenio episode Cervantes includes a sonnet that is also found in his *La casa de los celos*. The sonnet in *El curioso impertinente* is also found in that *Comedia*. Why did Cervantes do this? Because the play, though written already, had neither been performed nor published. In addition, Cervantes, never fully convinced that he was an unsatisfactory poet, seeks opportunities to force his poems on his readers and to indulge in a little propaganda in behalf of his efforts. The ballad of *Olalla* [Chapter IX, Pt. I] was also an earlier poem though it is not found in any work that has come down to us. The same is true for other poems in both parts of the *Quijote*.

There are several prose interpolations in Cervantes' novel: the *Tale of the Curious Impertinent*, the *cautivo's* story, the Marcela and the Eugenio episodes. The *Curioso* has no connection with the main plot. It was a much earlier work by Cervantes, his earliest *novela*, perhaps. If he had not used it in the *Quijote*, he would have placed it among his *Novelas ejemplares* in 1613. The story of the *Captive Captain* was not written for the *Quijote* either. It is a soldier's autobiography, a fairly common genre in Cervantes' time. It appears to have been written in 1589 or 1590. Structurally it is similar to Cervantes' memorial to Felipe II, 1590, and may have been the author's first attempt at realistic prose. The interpolated episodes of Fernando-Dorotea, Cardenio-Luscinda, Marcela-Grisóstomo, were, in all probability, earlier material which Cervantes, with little success, wove into the main plot. The scrutiny of the library and the critique of contemporary drama are also earlier works that are essentially irrelevant to the main plot.

The style of the main plot is simple, flexible and at times ungrammatical. Cervantes uses a poetic prose style in grandiloquent passages, and here are found many flowery epithets written in a baroque, pseudoclassical manner. The style of the interpolated episodes is different from the above two styles. It is more the Boccaccioesque style of the *Novelas ejemplares*, a style of forensic pleading and debate.

53. Camón Aznar, José. *Don Quijote en la teoría de los estilos.* Zaragoza: C. S. I. C., 1949. Pp. 51.

Is the *Quijote* a renaissance or a baroque work? There are some renaissance elements (Platonism), as well as baroque elements (crude naturalism and subtleties). Actually, Cervantes' masterpiece is written in *estilo trentino*, a style found at the end of the sixteenth, and beginning of the seventeenth, century. *Estilo trentino* is at the crossroads of platonic abstraction and baroque naturalism. In effect, Cervantes' narrative storytelling is based on the handling of a renaissance creation with a Counter-Reformation mentality. Man and his environment were dislocated around 1600, for the Renaissance and the Baroque were not compatible trends. Don Quijote, however, seeks to be the impossible ring that joins them.

Part I and Part II of Cervantes' masterpiece have several essential differences: in vocabulary, in tone, and in the presentation of the leading figures (who become more human in Part II). In Part I Cervantes plants the adventures of his hero as the product of an insuperable duality between Don Quijote and his environment.

In Part II the hero is not incompatible with his environment; he moves through society. The author becomes quixotic and blurs the contrast between his hero and his hero's surroundings. Part II, however, contains more baroque pessimism and naturalism.

The hero of the *Quijote* is rightly identified with the Jesuits. His mental system is Jesuit. The Knight always has sufficient capacity to be cured. Don Quijote's insanity is intellectual, and the idea of an intellectual conversion is a typically tridentine concept.

54. Cannavagio, Jean François. "Alonso López Pinciano y la estética literaria de Cervantes en el *Quijote*." *Anales Cervantinos*, VII (1958), 13-107.

Pinciano's *Philosophia Antigua Poetica* appeared in 1596 at a decisive moment in Cervantes' literary development. In general, Pinciano follows Aristotle and renaissance Italian estheticians. Both Cervantes and Pinciano appear to believe that delighting the reader is more important than teaching him; both recommend a clear style; both feel inferior to classical writers. Cervantes and Pinciano arrive at the same result through different methods. Pinciano's work is a three-way dialogue, a dialectic. Cervantes is definitely more interested in writing a story than in composing a literary treatise. Nevertheless, all of Pinciano's essential doctrines are in the *Quijote*, though scattered about. Both writers contend that poetry is the supreme science; both consider Aristotle's three principles to be essential (imitation, verisimilitude and teaching while delighting); both justify fiction; both define poetry as the interaction of nature and art; both writers assert that meter is unnecessary in fiction. Cervantes and Pinciano also have a similar outlook on the theatre. Both object to anachronisms; both are concerned about the unities of action and time (and Cervantes adds the unity of place). El Pinciano and Cervantes both deal with the question of verisimilitude and with the concept of catharsis. Pinciano interprets the latter concept physically (the spectator should fortify himself against life), whereas Cervantes interprets it morally (the spectator should be made happy by the jokes, taught by the truths, amazed by the events, made wise by the examples, angered by vice, and enamored of virtue). Thus for

Cervantes the moral lesson of a work is not a purifying of passions but an inculcating of virtues. Both Cervantes and Pinciano are concerned about the effect of episodes on the overall unity; both condemn the lack of verisimilitude and bad style in chivalry novels; both believe that comic and tragic elements could be mixed in the prose epic.

55. Carbonell y Basset, Delfín. "Don Quijote desde un punto de vista existencio-fenomenológico." *Duquesne Hispanic Review,* II (1963), 21-32.

Don Quijote's life prior to the beginning of the story is unimportant. It was a quiet, peaceful life of pure vegetating. The hero was ignorant of the world, thinking that it was peaceful like La Mancha. The Don, however, is capable of change. He reads chivalry novels, and the world seems different. These books give the hero light, the opportunity to change his condition, his being. They take away his peace but give him glory in return. They make him the most existencial of all men in literature.

The Knight feels a lack inside him. But he is superior to other characters because he feels the anguish of this lack. He does not become resigned to his fate. Instead he elects what he wants to be, having faith in his complete liberty. Don Quijote is the most important figure in the novel because he is the only one who chooses, the only one who does not let himself be carried along by circumstances.

The Don decides to be a hero but finds that the world has no enchanters and giants such as those found in books of chivalry. He needs to create a world that is consistent with his new condition. But he does not create a new world; he interprets the existing world subjectively. What is one thing to him is something entirely different to another. This demonstrates Heidegger's observation that all is relative where one is interpreting phenomena. As far as Don Quijote is concerned, he himself is the center of the universe; he is superior to phenomena and need not defer to them.

56. Casalduero, Joaquín. "Explicando la primera frase del *Quijote*." *Bulletin Hispanique*, XXXVI (1934), 137-148.

The first words of the *Quijote* ("En un lugar de la Mancha...") should be carefully interpreted. They do not refer to any particular town such as Argamasilla. Nor should one conclude that Cervantes, by using vagueness, was seeking to create a poetic atmosphere, as some contend. Finally, one should not accept the idea that Cervantes was attempting to conceal the real-life model of the hero [Rodríguez Marín, ed. *Don Quijote*, 1927-1928, Vol. VII, pp. 80-81].

Cervantes actually was endeavoring to make the *Quijote* the very antithesis of a chivalry novel. Since the chivalresque hero was never hungry or tired, Cervantes pictures his protagonist as constantly famished and worn out. Since chivalry-novel heroes were never faced with paying bills, Cervantes sees to it that his Knight is constantly reminded of the need for money. In view of the fact that maidens in books of chivalry did not have to concern themselves about their chastity, even in the company of men and in remote places, the author of the *Quijote* makes a point of the fact that Dorotea does have such a problem.

In the opening lines of Part I of the *Quijote* Cervantes does not tell us what the authors of chivalry novels clearly reveal to us: the name, ancestry and place of birth of the hero. By not naming the hero clearly and not specifying his origin and birthplace, Cervantes is deliberately following a procedure opposite from that found in novels of chivalry. Also, if a chivalresque hero is young, Don Quijote must be old; if the knights in books of chivalry came from the remote past, the Knight of La Mancha must be from a recent era.

57. Casalduero, Joaquín. "El desarrollo de la obra de Cervantes." *La Torre* (Sept.-Dic., 1966), núm. 54, pp. 65-74.

Cervantes believed that he had to change the static form of such works as Montemayor's *La Diana* and replace its simplicity of lines with the interpolation of levels. He did not wish to enclose the world in an abstract arabesque, but instead sought to leave it open to the dynamic state of life, for to Cervantes life was a continual conflict, not a static condition.

Cervantes, a product of the Baroque era, makes marriage the goal of love. He finds the themes of being-seeming and love-marriage both united in a new manner, that of conceiving of time as a historical reality: the present imposing and demanding its form in face of the past. The modernness of the *Quijote,* however, is not only in its new manner of seeing and feeling certain eternal themes, but in taking possession of them in a consciously literary and novelesque manner. The whole *Quijote* is a confrontation between the forms which it has to destroy (chivalresque, pastoral) and what is being created.

In 1605 Cervantes gave a separate form for each aspect of his work: for chivalry, adventure; for love, the short story; for literature, the discourse. In 1615, the author changes his technique, seeking the root of life, the unity of being. In Part II the sallies are reduced to one. The author no longer presents a historical-metaphysical-sentimental experience; instead he examines the relationship between idea, society and art.

The trajectory of Cervantes' work is as follows: starting with the inquietude of a dramatic love conflict in *Galatea,* he studies man in the present, in a society, and sees to it that love is not only a tragic and individual adventure but that it has a social and transcendent end (marriage). Later, in the *Persiles,* man fulfills himself and finds peace in the bosom of the Church.

58. Casalduero, Joaquín. *Sentido y forma del Quijote (1605-1615).* Madrid: Ínsula, 1966. Pp. 405. (First published in 1949: Madrid, Ínsula.) [Appreciation is expressed to Robbie Tatum and Janina Montero for their assistance in this sumary.]

Baroque art gives the impression of great disorder, but is (as Cervantes states in Chapter 50, Part I) an *ordered* disorder. The original 1605 edition of the *Quijote* contained four parts. Part One had eight chapters; Part Two had six; Part Three had thirteen; and Part Four had twenty-five chapters. Thus Part Three is equal in size to Parts One and Two, and Part Four has almost as many chapters as Parts One, Two and Three together. This creates a baroque cascade effect. Chapters XXVI and XXVII form the mechanical axis of the story, the central point, where the priest and barber reappear to bring Don Quijote home. In renaissance composition the mechanical axis always coincides with the spiritual or organic axis, the highest point of tension. This is not true in baroque composition, for there the function of the mechanical axis is to mark the displacement of the spiritual axis. The spiritual axis of the *Quijote* was reached in Chapters XVIII through XXII, the five central adventures.

The composition of the *Quijote* is circular. A man leaves home, seeks adventures and returns home. The process is repeated in the second sally. This circular idea represents destiny. The first sally was conceived of to give the basic idea of the second sally, where complications are brought in. This technique is common in the Baroque. The determinant of the novel is the contrast between: (1) the condition and occupation of an hidalgo; and (2) his strange idea of becoming a knight-errant and reviving the Middle Ages. The *Quijote* is loaded with antithetic suggestions: society versus spirit, *ser* versus *parecer*, idealism versus realism, poetry versus prose. However, there is no Gothic confrontation between opposites here, but an interlacing.

Love is a secondary theme and is found in the second part (Marcela episode) of the 1605 *Quijote*. In the third part this secondary theme becomes united with the main theme of chivalry; and this chivalry theme is linked to the third theme, that of literature. In all three themes there is the overall conflict of the past in confrontation with the present.

Sancho is introduced after seven chapters, and through him we are able to see the dialectics of the Knight's transformation of reality. Don Quijote and his Squire do not oppose each other. They are the same thing in a different key. The Knight is grotesque; Sancho is comic. Don Quijote is grotesque because his ideal and absolute world clashes with the relative world (reality). Sancho is comical because he treats his master's ideal world as if it were relative and real; he actually believes that he will receive the island which his master has promised him.

The 1615 *Quijote* consists of seventy-four chapters, not grouped in parts. It is slow-starting, for it takes seven chapters to cause the hero to depart from his village. The chapters tend to fall into groups of two and three, and the central adventure of Trifaldi takes up six chapters. In 1615 there is rambling, pausing, retracing of footsteps, going in and coming out, and one explores with pleasure, one goes about with joy, one likes to visit places, one satisfies his curiosity. If in 1605 tales and stories were told and discourses were held, in 1615 one talks unceasingly. The 1615 *Quijote* is full of deception, and one deception leads to another so that several characters in turn are deceived. In 1605 the mystery of life was presented; in 1615 life is a maze, and the author has to explain it. In 1605 Cervantes expressed his own personal conflict, the past versus the present. In later works, including the 1615 *Quijote*, he dedicates himself to explaining his era.

In 1605, Sancho and Don Quijote neither opposed each other nor complemented each other; they were one and the same. In 1615 their mutual dependence is underlined, which emphasizes the different quality of each.

59. Casares, Julio. "Las tres edades del *Quijote*." *Boletín de la Real Academia Española*, XXVII (1947-1948), 43-60.

The first age of *Quijote* criticism is the healthy laughter of the seventeenth century. Here we are at a stage in European letters that corresponds to an ingenuous and frivolous mentality. The second stage is romantic adolescence where people begin to take the Knight seriously, possibly too seriously. In this era the Don and the Squire become purified of national traits and are made into symbols. The third stage of *Quijote* interpretation, the mature attitude, was reached in eighteenth-century England, where the novel was regarded as an example of universal humor, a harmonious synthesis of the comic and the tragic, an overcoming of the opposition between medieval laughter and the tears of Romanticism.

60. Casella, Mario. *Cervantes. Il Chisciotte*. Florence: F. le Monnier, 1938. 2 vols. [The Introduction to this work is translated from the Italian into English as "Critical Realism" by Joseph DeSimone in *Cervantes Across the Centuries* (112).]

Don Quijote, in its remotest and occasional conception, is derived from the first skirmishes which occurred in Spain in the latter part of the sixteenth century between the followers of Platonic, Augustinian and scholastic aesthetics and the fervent and intransigent followers of Aristotle's *Poetics*. In his *Quijote* Cervantes makes concrete this struggle which presented itself as being pregnant with possibilities. Aristotle's poetic universal is an abstract universal, an absolute which owes nothing to anyone else and everything to itself. Furthermore, Aristotle's distinction between history and art had, in Cervantes' time, overshadowed the beautiful Augustinian idea of the irreversible becoming of history. Cervantes, in his novel, sets up a contrast between ideal poetic beauty and documentary truth, the universal of art and the particular of history. The Canon of Toledo is an Aristotelian idealist; the village priest represents the historical particular.

Don Quijote's adventures, like all romances of chivalry, rest on the poetic irrational. Sancho's comic adventures rest, like those in a picaresque novel, on the instinctive irrational. The New Aristotelian commentators, with their theory of art idealizing reality according to fixed rules and conventional preconceptions, would have claimed the right to eliminate these two irrationals of nature from history. Cervantes, however, saw that one could not possibly judge a work of beauty except by means of the poetic reason which is immanent in it.

Don Quijote and Sancho are individualities and must be interpreted in their subjective and ineffable truth, for what they long to become, in relation to the idea which each of them aspires to realize. Don Quijote declares for the beauty of virtue and honesty. Sancho declares for utilitarianism. They are thus two universal tendencies.

Seventeenth-century France dismembered the *Quijote* to enjoy the isolated stories in it. Rationalism saw no unity in the work and interpreted it as a farce. England identified Don Quijote with Loyola and ridiculed both. Voltaire saw Cervantes' story as reason's critique of ideal values. The naturalistic followers of Rousseau wept over the hero who, to them, personified the good man that is derided by a society that cannot understand him. German Romanticism, from the Schlegels to Heine, romanticized the *Quijote's* content and derived logical symbols from it. Documentary historicism, from Herder on, broke it up anew in order to derive from it the biographical details of the author's life and the representation of the society that was contemporary to him. Erudite positivism considered Cervantes as a man without thought who gathered together only empty fantastic molds. Pure aestheticism, which puts its trust in the false transparency of images, asserted its own hedonistic subjectivism and made a theory out of it in the name of the unconscious poet who creates without knowing what he is creating. Learned commentators boast of their understanding but are mostly impertinent.

61. Cassou, Jean. *Cervantes*. Paris: Éditions Sociales Internationales, 1936. Pp. 244. [A portion of this work is translated into English as "An Introduction to Cervantes" in *Cervantes Across the Centuries* (112).]

[Cassou's work consists of sixteen short chapters, followed by selected texts. The first eight chapters deal with background material. Chapter IX discusses Cervantes' life. Chapter X deals with the culture of the author of the *Quijote*, and Chapter XI is devoted to the renaissance elements in his works. Chapter XII discusses the chivalry novel, and Chapter XIII is concerned with destiny. The following chapter is devoted to the picaresque novel. Chapter XV pictures Cervantes' genius. The final chapter, "Cervantes et nous," describes the author's tragic intensity, his power of transcription.

In general, Cassou is a follower of Américo Castro's *Pensamiento* (63), in that he emphasizes the strong influence of renaissance themes on the master's works — liberty, reality versus illusion, good sense, instinct. Cassou also emphasizes (p. 73) the ambiguity of the *Quijote*. With Cervantes, he exclaims: "on est perpétuellement dans l'équivoque."]

Cervantes' *Quijote* is the first work in the history of modern literature that seems to have felt a breath of universal sympathy for man's inescapable attachment to his fate. Cervantes is not, however, fatalistic in the manner of the picaresque novel. He turns the picaresque world into a paradise. He is not vile like Quevedo, for Cervantes covers his world with a veil of exquisite delicacy. The author's goodness is his most striking feature. It illuminates all his characters. He shows that beneath the self-interest and passion in life there is always the possibility for charity. Cervantes does not look to the future; he is content with the present, which he endows with amazing life and integrity. At every turn he balances reality with a dream.

62. Castro, Américo. "Cervantes y Pirandello," in *Hacia Cervantes*. Madrid: Taurus, 1967, pp. 477-485. [Based on a summary submitted by Robbie Tatum.]

[This essay was originally published in *La Nación* (Buenos Aires) on November 16, 1924. Here Américo Castro examines Pirandello's *Six Characters in Search of an Author*, Unamuno's *Niebla* and Calderón's *El gran teatro del mundo*, along with *Don Quijote*. In all cases, it is noted by Castro, the characters have become conscious of their existence within a work of art: in Pirandello the absurd characters' anguish stems from their not having been completely formed by their author, whereas in Cervantes the characters have a consciousness of possessing a full life. Castro concludes that Cervantes is the initiator of the character who rebels against his literary creator.]

63. Castro, Américo. *El pensamiento de Cervantes*. Madrid: Hernando, 1925. Pp. viii + 406.

Previous literary criticism of Cervantes' works has ignored the author's critical capacity and viewed his mind as a mere receptacle. This is incorrect. One should examine his perspective to see how he transforms things into a *mundo cervantino*. His feelings and ideas are more important than what he saw and read.

In the sixteenth century, literature was becoming more mundane, less religious and ideal. But the Council of Trent changed this. After 1550 there is an anti-Platonic reaction toward Aristotle. The Aristotelian preceptists told Cervantes that universal truth (art, poetry) was opposed to historical truth (particularity). But once he has accepted this distinction Cervantes enjoys opening breaches in it and showing the impossibility of distinguishing between the two.

There is a unity of thought in all of Cervantes' works, and thus the *Quijote* is not separate from his other literary productions. The main distinction is that only in the *Quijote* is there a synthesis of poetic truth (the universal) and historical truth (the particular).

The Baroque wants literature to teach; the Renaissance is interested in art for art's sake. Cervantes must be placed within the Baroque epoch. He likes to regulate, and often looks for rules; but at times he reacts against excess regulation in favor of vitalism and spontaneity. Hence he is dualistic, and his dualism leads along new and strange paths.

The *Quijote* was written by Cervantes' applying his critical faculty to his imaginative faculty — something we find in the *Coloquio*, the *Licenciado Vidriera* and even in the *Persiles*. Cervantes' main concern is: What is reality? Like the Humanist Erasmus, Cervantes thought that one should mistrust outer appearances. *Don Quijote* is also the great depository of the theme of la *realidad oscilante*. Truth depends on each person's perspective.

In Cervantes' works error and harmony are important themes. If a character misinterprets a physical reality (venta-castillo), the result is comic; if he misinterprets a moral reality (Anselmo believing in absolute virtue), the result is tragic, often leading to death *post errorem*.

It is difficult to say what Cervantes' religious ideas were. Heinrich Heine thought he was a true Catholic. Others see him as a liberal progressive. Cervantes did not consciously embrace a set of ideas either favorable or unfavorable to the Church. There are occasional contradictions in his thinking. He is a great *disimulador* who covers up his thoughts with irony and skill. He is *un hábil hipócrita,* and we must interpret him with reserve. Cervantes, though devout, is an intellectual Catholic and at times heterodox (e.g., his idea that Nature was a divine power that creates man), and his Christianity at times is more like that of Erasmus (who sought to bring the Church in line with Humanism) than that of the Council of Trent. To him religion was liberty, country, civilization in the face of the Turk. At times the author is devout, at times ironic, especially about alleged miracles. Was Cervantes tolerant? What does the Ricote episode reveal? [Castro here indicates that Cervantes was anti-Semitic.] Cervantes' Christianity is essentially Erasmian. He wanted simplicity and a return to the Scriptures. Without Erasmus Cervantes would not have been as he was.

The eighteenth-century Englishman Bowle concluded that Cervantes believed in free will, but this is doubtful. In reality, Cervantes thought that each person's character had its own trajectory set by nature; *libre albedrío* to Cervantes meant the right of each person to follow unobstructed his own destiny.

64. Castro, Américo. "¿Cervantes, inconsciente?" *Revista de Occidente*, XXVII (1927), 285-290.

It is true that Cervantes was dragged along by the theme of his story to regions he had not imagined when he wrote the first lines of the *Quijote*. However, Sánchez Rivero in "Las ventas del *Quijote*" (272) is wrong to follow prior critics who believe that the author reached his goal by chance, or unconsciously. Though Cervantes did not know the whole trajectory of his story before he wrote it, he was fully aware that he was going to confront the world of illusion with the real world, the poetic universal with the historical particular.

Why does Cervantes first say that the hero's real name is unimportant, but then state that his story does not depart one bit from the *truth?* The reason is that Cervantes has a double concept of the truth and is saying that for the purpose of poetic truth the historically true name of the living model of the story is of little or no consequence. For the purpose of poetic truth it is only necessary that the story follow the law of verisimilitude. Poetic truth and historical truth go hand in hand throughout the *Quijote*, and the author *consciously* causes these two concepts to confront each other.

Madness is essential in Cervantes' novel, for it turns the prosaic historical into poetic reality. Sánchez Rivero (272) is wrong to imply that insanity is not basic to the story.

65. Castro, Américo. "Cervantes y la Inquisición." *Modern Philology*, XXVII (1930), 427-433.

Cardinal Zapata ordered, in 1632, that in Chapter 36, Part II of the *Quijote*, there should be expunged the statement that half-hearted works of charity were of no value. Cervantes had no complicated motive when he referred to such works. In general he is very cautious in dealing with religious matters. Both Saint Paul and Erasmus emphasized the inner man, not the outer man, and Cervantes may well have been influenced by them. What Cervantes wrote about half-hearted works of charity was a popular idea in the early sixteenth century, but an idea which later became dangerous.

66. Castro, Américo. *Cervantes.* Paris: Rieder, 1931. Pp. 80.

Prior to Cervantes, literature dealt with fantasy. The author of the *Quijote* joins the world of fantasy with the everyday world and thus creates the modern novel. But the *Quijote* is not merely the result of the opposition of reality and fantasy; it shows the solidarity of these two forms of "reality," each one a function of the other.

Tamayo de Vargas, the seventeenth-century critic, was incorrect in implying that Cervantes was uncultured ("ingenio festivo, aunque lego"). But let us not demand of him profound ideas about life nor points of view not in accord with his times. Cervantes is a man of the Renaissance living during the Baroque Counter Reformation. He is for liberty, for the right of each individual to affirm the spontaneity of his own personality.

67. Castro, Américo. "Erasmo en tiempos de Cervantes." *Revista de Filología Española,* XVIII (1931), 329-389, 441.

The works of Erasmus were prohibited by the Inquisition in 1559 and in 1583. However, they continued to be read by a few, since inquisitorial decrees were not enforced with equal rigor in all cases. Cervantes even quotes works on the Index, and his teacher, López de Hoyos, cited Erasmus ten years after the latter's works had been placed on the Index. Where Cervantes acquired a knowledge of Erasmus' doctrines is not perfectly clear — perhaps from Hoyos — but the influence of the theologian from Rotterdam is strong on the author of the *Quijote*. Cervantes cites one work heavily influenced by the Dutchman, *Luz del alma.*

One had to be extremely careful about religion in Spain, and Cervantes' statements are at times so piously cautious as to amount to hypocrisy; but his hypocrisy was justified as a measure of self-protection and by the fact that through such caution he was able to continue to say things of the highest value.

68. Castro, Américo. "Los prólogos al Quijote," *Revista de Filología Hispánica,* III (1941), 314-338. (English version "The Prefaces to *Don Quixote,*" *Philological Quarterly,* XXI (1942), 65-96.) [Appreciation is expressed to Robbie Tatum for her assistance in this summary.]

Much is written about the jail in which the *Quijote* was presumably written. It seems evident, however, that the work was more likely conceived in the deepest recesses of Cervantes' soul, "donde toda incomodidad tiene su asiento."

Lope de Vega took a serious view of the chivalry myth. To Cervantes, Lope was a man going along with the tastes of the crowd and with tradition. At the other extreme from the traditionalist Lope stood Quevedo, who took a disillusioned and scathing view of the chivalric myth. Cervantes sought a middle ground between these two approaches. He becomes vague and elusive in his attitude toward the myth, even in regard to the birthplace of the Knight.

The essential pecularity of the *Quijote* lies in the fact that the characters seem real, they pursue their own goals, take cognizance of themselves, in short, do whatever they please. From this firm basis of individuality the personalities in the *Quijote* project themselves in all directions, manifesting such qualities as imagination, illusion, irony, prudence and violence. They are unlike picaresque characters who cannot change. Cervantes, in presenting figures with their own core of personality, drew upon the pastoral novel, which, despite its conventional nature, provides a projection of the innermost consciousness of the characters. The pastoral figure is the opposite of a *pícaro*, for the shepherd's vital impulses spring from his soul, with complete disregard of all external circumstnaces. In such an atmosphere the Knight nourishes his own vital self-sufficiency, his disdain for outward circumstances. Cervantes' novel is the result of a process the reverse of that of the mystics, who aspire to a mysterious union with the divine transcendence, within which they feel themselves fully existing. *Don Quijote*, instead, becomes possible only when the individual cuts all ties and ventures to row his boat with no equipment other than the mere fact of his existence.

Cervantes was driven to use insanity as a vehicle, since he could not leave this new type of expression entirely unmotivated. But insanity is a minor factor; the important thing is Don Quijote's will, peculiarly his own and unhampered by external forces. After the *Quijote* the genre "novel" will be determined by lives of characters conceived of as "novels," that is, as lives in the making. The essential, in Cervantes' creation, is the fact that he came to feel an equal appreciation of the innermost being of the individual and the outward appearances which masked it, a miracle which was fully realized in his representation of the lives of Don Quijote and Sancho. But Cervantes would never have arrived at this unique comprehension without the use of irony, which separates what is valuable and estimable from what is adventitious and unauthentic. By means of irony one discovers the misplacement of external human appearances, and attempts to put them in their proper position. Irony is functional in the art of Cervantes. If the pastoral furnished him his weapons, it was irony which made their use possible. Cervantes has a passion for testing the actual solidity of what presents itself to his observation with claims of lasting value. At times the author's tendency toward irony will take him beyond the limits which reason has established (e.g., the Don's using a shirttail to fashion a rosary). The resulting process of retraction is not adventitious to, nor superimposed upon, the work of Cervantes, but is rather a functional element in it. After he has gone too far, the author will often become morally and religiously unctuous.

Cervantes is circumspect about certain matters, such as suicide. Grisóstomo's death is self-inflicted, but the author, in the prose portions of the novel, makes the manner of death vague. Only in the poems does it become clear that Grisóstomo died by his own hand; and Cervantes knew that many readers would skip over the poems.

69. Castro, Américo. "Incarnation in *Don Quixote*," in *Cervantes Across the Centuries*. Ed. Ángel Flores and M. J. Benardete. New York: The Dryden Press, 1947, pp. 136-178.

The novelty and success of *Don Quijote* are not due exclusively to its wealth of episodes, its exemplariness, its imaginative richness, its arrangement, its variety in literary genre, nor to its vivid presentation of Spanish life. In reality the greatness of Cervantes' novel is its characters. At first, it is true, his figures appear to be stock characters but they become transformed unexpectedly from a static state to a dynamic life. These transformations are not gradual and psychological; they are "vital." We might say that the process of life, as conceived by the author, is a dialogue between a life-giving, formative *logos* and an inert passivity ready to receive it. This new approach leads to the liberation of fiction centuries later. Prior to the *Quijote* it had not been possible organically to harmonize the expression of the imaginary or fictitious and the concrete, contemporary experience of the character or the author without falling into moralizations or grotesque farce. The unreal time of the narration and the contemporary time of the author were irreconcilable.

The *Quijote* shows us that the reality of existence consists in receiving the impact of all the influences that can affect man from without, and in transforming these influences into outwardly manifest life processes. Thus the major theme of Cervantes' masterpiece is the interdependence or interrelationship of what lies beyond man's experience and the process of incorporating that into his existence. Cervantes' art consists in blending the conception of life as a purely phenomenalistic succession of "withins" and "withouts" with the Stoic, Judaic, Christian idea of man's rising upon the rock of his will and upon the consciousness of his personal liberty.

In *El pensamiento de Cervantes* (63) we indicated that Cervantes was primarily interested in searching for the reality behind fluctuating appearances. This was an excessively Occidental approach to the *Quijote*. The problem of logical truth or error does not preoccupy the author. The true innovation of his novel consists in establishing as true what is authentically interlaced with vital experience, and not what is determined by the cognitive process. The reality of the style of the *Quijote* lies in a vital articulation of its values; beliefs, be they what they may, are made acceptable to us to the degree that they are held and lived by those who interweave them into their existence. We are convinced because the characters are convinced, not because what they believe is logically true. Only through this criterion of personalized vitalizations can we analyze whether the *Quijote* was written as an attack on chivalry novels. The author's statements that his book *is* such an attack are inside the novel and depend upon the rest of the book. Thus even if we knew that the author's purpose sometimes has validity as a logic-moral judgment, the truth is that the moment it penetrates into the avalanche-like movement of the work, it submits itself to the existential system of the rest.

70. Castro, Américo. "La estructura del *Quijote.*" *Realidad* (Buenos Aires), II (1947), 147-170.

Prior to the *Quijote* literature, with the exception of the *Cid*, dealt with the distant past or was comical. Pre-*Quijote* writings were often moralizing. Such works were a mixture of incompatible elements; and fiction, in general, had become a hybrid form incapable of procreation.

The *Quijote* is unique. It has an *irreductible peculiaridad*. The principal theme of the novel is the interdependence, the interreality, of the extrapersonal world and of the process of its becoming incorporated into the life of a person. The outer world acts upon a man, and he, thus inspired, gives forth imaginings and beliefs. Cervantes loves people who will come out of themselves. He prefers the abnormal and is openly disdainful of the temperate Caballero del Verde Gabán. The hero of the *Quijote*, and certain other characters, are consumed with the idea of carrying out their objectives, without objectifying them in thoughts (as Goethe or Milton would have had them do) or in useful results (as in Defoe's *Robinson Crusoe*). Cervantes is able to achieve characters of multiple dimensions, and each character relates himself with the rest in extremely varied forms and combinations. By use of introspection an abstract type becomes alive and individualized. In addition, everything extrapersonal becomes incorporated into the lives of the literary figures. In general, no person and no thing plays a purely ornamental role in the *Quijote*.

Cervantes is a secular, not a religious, writer. The transition from the contemplative religious attitudes to the attitudes in the *Quijote* found an easy way through Erasmus' teachings, which were insistent on preferring inner Christianity to outer practices.

71. Castro, Américo. "El cómo y el por qué de Cide Hamete Benengeli," in *Hacia Cervantes*. Madrid: Taurus, 1967, pp. 409-450. [Based on "El sabio Cide Hamete Benengeli," *Bulletin of Hispanic Studies*, XXXIII (1956), 218-225.]

The *function* of Cide Hamete Benengeli, the fictitious author of the *Quijote*, is more important than his literary origin. One of the main purposes of Cide Hamete is to make it possible for Cervantes to enjoy himself in his own contemplation and to escape direct responsibility. In the *Quijote* Cervantes is submitting creative activity itself to the same artistic treatment as that which he gives to what is created by such activity.

72. Castro, Américo. "Cervantes y el *Quijote* a nueva luz," in *Cervantes y los casticismos españoles*. Madrid - Barcelona: Alfaguara, 1966, pp. 1-183, and Appendix. [Appreciation is expressed to Robbie Tatum for her assistance in this summary.]

The desire of New Christians to become adjusted pervades Spanish literature and explains the vast difference between Spanish literature and the literature of the rest of Europe. The Jewish *conversos* cultivated a literature that was neither Judaic nor Old Christian, but oriented toward new horizons.

Sancho represents the Old Christian and Don Quijote the *intercastizo*. Cervantes is less a man of the Renaissance and Baroque and more a New Christian who wrote in the Spain of Felipe III. He incorporates in *Don Quijote* his attitude toward the circumstances of his times, literary as well as social. Cervantes does not directly attack the Old Christian obsession on race, yet he does not adopt the Old Christian point of view.

One novelty of Cervantes' style lies in his pointing out the contrast between the visible aspect of an object and its latent functional purpose. Another aspect of his new style is his presentation of a human being *not* as being, doing, suffering this or that, but as a point of departure for unfolding latent possibilities and surprising us with them. His figures overflow their frames, revealing their inner motivations. His personages are strange flowerings of stock figures such as the priest.

Cervantes is an outsider in his times. At the end of the sixteenth century there was a crisis of blood in Spain, and we should focus on this circumstance rather than on some vague concept of the Baroque, which is an international phenomenon. In 1599 the maximum of bitterness of the converts is expressed in *Guzmán de Alfarache*, the work of the *converso* Mateo Alemán. Cervantes was influenced by Alemán in a number of respects (e.g., the interpolation of stories). However, though *Guzmán* and the *Quijote* are related works, they are very different. Alemán's characters are guided by circumstances in a world without order;

Cervantes' figures have their own horizon. Alemán faces *un mundo malcreado*, whereas Cervantes prefers to create his own world.

Cervantes was not anti-Semitic [as indicated in *El pensamiento* (63), 1925]; instead he expressed the point of view of the New Christians and of the Jews. Cervantes forgets Alemán's hatred and presents Spaniards humanly united without distinction as to lineage.

73. Castro, Américo. "La palabra escrita y el *Quijote*," in *Hacia Cervantes*. Madrid: Taurus, 1967, pp. 359-419. [First published in 1947, *Asomante*, San Juan, P. R.; also found in *Cuadernos de Insula* (202), pp. 9-44. Based on a summary submitted by Robbie Tatum.]

The entire *Quijote* is forged from the active material of other books. Part I is deduced from the books that the Don has read; Part II is based on Part I. The books in question are not included for decorative or illustrative purposes, but are articulated with the very existence of the people. Literature thus becomes personalized. Throughout European thought books had long been the objects of man's thoughts and emotions, but with Cervantes, a book becames a friend or an enemy to live with. An important innovation of Cervantes is the idea that life is not merely changed by literature, but that a character attempts to live within literature.

The author of the *Quijote* is not inferior to his work, as Unamuno (308) and others assert. It is merely that the reader becomes so involved in the story that he cannot get an overall perspective. Cervantes' center of attention is the flowing reality of realizing one's own existence, including in this realization the very act of writing.

74. Castro, Américo. "El Quijote, taller de la existencialidad." *Revista de Occidente*, XVIII (1967), 1-33. [Based on a summary submitted by Eileen McFadden.]

One of the new and most important elements of style in the *Quijote* is that the imaginary characters succeed in constructing their existence as their own, i.e., their lives are not determined by fixed or transcendental circumstances. In the theater of Lope de Vega everything in the social system is predetermined; and conflict, such as that between inner religiosity and that practiced by society, is non-existent. This is not so in the *Quijote*, where that which is created by the different beliefs, preferences and interests of the various characters makes it a multidimensional work; order and disorder depend always on the individual.

In the *Quijote* each individual is able to see the world in his own way: Don Quijote defends his *libros de caballerías* while the Canon of Toledo is also an individual, for he leaves the generic outline of his profession and confesses to know more about *libros de caballerías* than about a work more connected with religion. This all comes from an interior dynamism or inclination of the characters and is dependent upon individual action: nothing is fixed or preordained in their world. The *Quijote* is filled with agents who are capable of forming their own lives. By far the most significant element of the *stylistic revolution* of Cervantes is found in his going from narrative description to *autobiografismo*, in which not only human beings and animals but also the author will let their presence be known as individuals who are unfolding before us in a state of being and becoming. But we must be careful not to call this existentialism; what is brought into being in the novel is a tension and pressure in which individual existences are made and dissolved.

Cervantes never praises the Spanish nobility in his works as it never rewarded him adequately for his efforts in its favor. It did not offer him employment nor did it permit him to travel to the Americas. *Conversos* were prohibited from doing this, and Cervantes appears to have been of Hispano-Judaic descent. In the *Coloquio de los perros*, Cervantes spoke against the statute of *limpieza de sangre*, and because the Jesuits never paid great attention to this law, Cervantes always regarded them highly.

The *Quijote* is a modern work because in it the author felt the need to express his aversion to the society in which he lived; in doing this he created characters able to fulfill themselves without being forced by society to conform to its preconceived molds and ideas.

75. Castro, Carmen. "Personajes femeninos de Cervantes: las mujeres del *Quijote*." *Anales Cervantinos*, III (1953), 43-85.

No female character in the *Quijote* is complete in her own figure. What is said about one applies to others. This is a peculiarity of Cervantes. His women form a thick and firm bond among themselves which is the network of the story. Each female character is an open possibility.

Part I and Part II of the *Quijote* are different in regard to women. In the first part there are stories of women, while in the second part possible true stories are turned into a mockery, until in the midst of the mockery — an ingenious technique — there erupt true stories. The women of Part II are no longer lifted, like Marcela or Dorotea, from a certain *apariencia* to a reality which they themselves reveal; instead they are lifted from a story-like aspect, performed by them, to a less mythic state, burdened by human weaknesses which they themselves, or their environment, reveal to us.

76. Castro Silva, José Vicente. *Epílogo de Don Quijote*. Bogotá: Editorial Centro, S. A., 1939. Pp. 117.

The hero's life as Don Quijote covers a very brief period of time (only about five and one-half months), and takes place at the end of an ordinary life. Though thirty days of book time elapse between the second and third sallies, actually ten years of chronological time pass by; and the author's suffering and thought during this period are reflected in Part II. The Knight is very different in Part II. In the 1605 *Quijote* his madness contrasts markedly with his environment because the hero cannot imagine the real world to be different from the world of chivalry novels. In the 1615 *Quijote* the Knight surrenders to reality, and his imagination becomes attuned, in part, to the real world. In Part I the hero stoically suffers hardships at the hands of the lower classes; in Part II he converses and lives with the powerful. This new life in Part II leads to the Knight's mental recovery. This means that the politeness and courtesy which make social intercourse pleasant were able to accomplish more than the beatings and stonings of Part I in the correcting, at least in part, of certain lunacies of the hero. The force and reasoning used in Part I in order to cause the Knight to give up his fabulous undertaking and to help him regain his sanity were not successful since this force and reasoning was not dressed in the trappings, and did not speak the language, of the madness that was afflicting the Knight.

In Part II there is a subtle mutual influence and communication between Don Quijote and the people who surround him, though they do not accept each other completely. Though people deceive the hero, they give him a role to play in society, the role of a burlesque figure. In Part I cultivated people generally ignore the Don. In Part II they receive him as a buffoon. Yet the Don's madness makes him a transcendental buffoon, an unfettered critic of society, not a deliberate, calculating fool of the stage.

77. Cernuda, Luis. "Cervantes." *Bulletin of Hispanic Studies*, XX (1943), 175-195.

The reader of the seventeenth century was aware of the Knight's noble features as well as his comical attributes. These two aspects of his nature exist side by side, and neither should be ignored at the expense of the other.

In the *Quijote* Cervantes presents two types of stories, the embellished and the unembellished, and blends them together. This technique leads the way to the modern novel. In effect Cervantes believed that fiction should contain all of life and that it should be much more than a series of adventures. Another modern feature of the *Quijote* is its presentation of a hero acting in a real world of real evils. It is thus the first modern epic.

78. Chambers, Leland H. "Structure and the Search for Truth in the *Quijote:* Notes Toward a Comprehensive View." *Hispanic Review*, XXXV (1967), 309-326.

Don Quijote stresses the relativity of man's worldly experience, the fluidity of all that seems most before him. In that novel all decisions are problematical. However, free will is constantly emphasized by the author. But if Don Quijote is insane, is he responsible for his acts? If he is insane, why all the discussion about free will? It is typical of Cervantes' technique that unequivocal ideas are cast into doubt by their contexts and must, consequently, be examined in connection with other related passages.

In Part I of the novel events are primarily woven around the display of faulty judgment in regard to human affairs and physical realities. In Part II the misuse of judgment in human affairs comes to be seen as having to do with the health of the soul. Knighthood becomes sainthood to the hero.

Cervantes pictures his characters poised on the shifting borderline between cognitive self-assurance and doubt, and the result is that the *Quijote* gives the impression of being principally concerned with reality.

79. Chasca, Edmund de. "Algunos aspectos del ritmo y del movimiento narrativo del *Quijote*." *Revista de Filología Española*, XLVII (1964), 287-307.

If there is no structural connection between the episodes of the *Quijote*, how does it achieve an organically structured form? By a system of conscious actions and reactions of the dynamic hero, which produces the fundamental rhythm of the novel. There are active and reflective stages in the story, but the hero is always aware of his mission. The periods of reflection relieve the monotony of a string of adventures. Cervantes also varies the adventures, inserting comic or false victories; and the defeats are quite different one from the other. Nevertheless, twin adventures stand out (the Andrés episode and the adventure of the galley slaves deal with justice; the windmills and the army of sheep are concerned with *engaño a los ojos*).

In the contexture of main and secondary actions, the matter which is repeated most often is the love affairs of a series of couples. They contrast directly with Don Quijote's love for Dulcinea, for the affairs of the couples often work out happily, while the hero's love is only possible in the heart.

80. Chesterton, G. K. "The Divine Parody of *Don Quixote*," in *A Handfull of Authors*. Edited by Dorothy Collins. New York and London: Sheed and Ward, 1969, pp. 24-27. (First published in the *Daily News* in 1901.)

The great truth in *Don Quijote* is that the world is a conflict between goods. The eternal glory of Cervantes' novel in the literary world is that it holds perfectly even the mysticism of the Knight and the rationalism of the Squire. Deep beneath the superficial wit and palpable gaiety of the story there runs a deep irony — an irony that is older than the world. It is the irony that tells us that we are living in a maddening world in which we are all in the right. *Don Quijote* is not a saddening work; it assumes, instead, that human nature is good. The story, however, preaches that we mind our own business.

The greatness of Cervantes' novel is not due to its style or diction. It stems from the author's impartiality, for Cervantes is a writer who condemns no one.

81. Corley, Ames Haven. "Word-Play in the *Quijote*." *Revue Hispanique* XL (1917), 543-591.

Word-play is quite common in satirical works and is one of the cardinal features of Cervantes' style in the *Quijote*. In this novel all social classes make plays on words, and the author, even when speaking for himself, makes puns. Cervantes not only plays *on* words, he plays *with* words, as in *Rocin-ante, Dulci-nea*. All in all, the author has an overfondness for word-play. One of the most common types of his verbal games is the play on compounds of words, as in *canta-encanta, coger-escogèr*. [Corley divides Cervantes' word-plays into two main categories, sense play and sound play, and presents an elaborate scheme of subcategories under each of the two main divisions. An appendix lists further word-plays not mentioned in the body of the article.]

82. Cotarelo y Mori, Emilio. *Efemérides cervantinas o sea resumen cronológico de la vida de Miguel de Cervantes*. Madrid: Tip. de la "Revista de Archivos," 1905. Pp. 315.

[At page 268 *et seq.* Cotarelo discusses four types of *Quijote* criticism: (1) philosophical; (2) historical; (3) philological; (4) scientific. Under (1) the critic notes that some consider the *Quijote* to contain, in veiled form, a series of truths of high intellectual and moral speculation, which makes the story a scientific handbook of the rules of good living. Others, states Cotarelo, believe the *Quijote* to be a political tract — for example, Villegas (314) — on the art of governing. There are, the critic observes, those who consider the *Quijote* a socialistic work.

Under (2), the historical group, Cotarelo notes that numerous critics believe the *Quijote* to be a work that contains numerous veiled references to people of the day. The third group, the critic states, is made up of two types of critics: (A) those who seek to explain the "giros y frases" of Cervantes and who praise or criticize his grammar; (B) those who seek to correct the *Quijote* in later editions. The final school, Cotarelo notes, studies the *Quijote* from the point of view of a particular science and notes down what Cervantes had to say about the subject.

A few words are devoted to those who search for living models for Don Quijote. Some, he notes, believe that the Knight represents Charles V; others say Lerma; still others conclude that the Don is the representation of an uncle or cousin of Cervantes' wife; another group considers the Knight to be Rodrigo Pacheco of Argamasilla, while still another school believes him to be Alonso Quijada of Esquivias.]

83. Cotarelo y Mori, Emilio. *Últimos estudios cervantinos.* Madrid: Tip. de la "Rev. de Arch., Bibl. y Museos," 1920. Pp. 66.

[Chapter I of this work presents the three leading currents of Cervantine studies in the first part of the twentieth century: bibliographical works, studies on the identity of Avellaneda, treatises on the origin, development and import of Cervantes' masterpiece. The second chapter discusses catalogues of the editions of Cervantes' works, such as that of Juan Suñé y Benages and Juan Suñé Fonbuena [*Bibliografía crítica de ediciones del Quijote impresas desde 1605 hasta 1917*]. The third chapter of Cotarelo's work deals with the Avellaneda question, and here the author discusses the various theories presented. The fourth and final chapter treats the origins of the *Quijote*. Here the critic discusses the Argamasilla legend as well as the tradition that Rodrigo Pacheco was the living model for the Knight of La Mancha. The Esquivias legend is also commented upon. Extensive study is given to the question of the influence of the *Entremés de los romances*. The critic strongly disagrees with Menéndez Pidal's view (196) that this one-act farce was the forerunner of the *Quijote*. Cotarelo concludes that if Cervantes had imitated that *entremés*, his enemies would definitely have pointed it out. To the critic the *Entremés de los romances* is clearly and adaptation of the early chapters of the 1605 *Quijote,* and was probably written about 1611 when it was first published.

In the latter part of his book the critic discusses the fragmentary structure of the 1605 *Quijote* and concludes that it was originally intended to be a short story. He largely bases this conclusion on a sentence toward the beginning of Chapter IX of Part I of the *Quijote* in which Cervantes states that the reader might get as much as two hours of enjoyment from the story. Cotarelo concludes that the author simply forgot to erase this sentence after he had turned the tale into a full-length novel.

The composition of the 1615 *Quijote* is briefly discussed. The critic concludes that the first two chapters were written around 1607. These chapters discuss the reception of Part I, and hence, states Cotarelo, it is more logical to assume that they were written shortly after the appearance of the earlier volume. The last chapters of the 1615 *Quijote* were, Cotarelo concludes, hastily composed, though ably written. Cervantes, the critic believes, was seeking to get into print quickly in order to neutralize the effect of Avellaneda's novel. In the last chapters of Part II, Cotarelo states, Cervantes' Knight acquires a sweet melancholy that is consistent with his approaching death.]

84. Criado de Val, M. "*Don Quijote,* como diálogo." *Anales Cervantinos,* V (1955-1956), 183-208.

The difficulty with the criticism of *Don Quijote* stems from the attempt to encase it within the framework of the novel, instead of considering it a dialogue — which it mostly is. The *Quijote* is related to Erasmus' dialogues and other Renaissance works of that type which were quite influential in Spain. But Cervantes also had the dialogues of *Lazarillo* and *Celestina* as guides. Furthermore, the third *tratado* of *Lazarillo* was Cervantes' immediate source for his main characters — the poor, idealistic hidalgo and the realistic squire.

The plot of the *Quijote* is disjointed, the grammar is bad and careless, the philosophy grows vulgar, and the interpolated stories are boring. Only the dialogue remains alive and effective. The chapters of the *Quijote* follow one another without cohesion. Only the dialectical process of the two central figures follows a clear and intentional line, modifying itself progressively. Some of the main features of Cervantes' dialogues are intimacy, cordiality, competition for predominance, and sincerity. Cervantes could not have written such beautiful dialogue if he had not observed the evolution through which his protagonists were going. The author, in effect, became converted along with his characters.

Most of Cervantes' derogatory remarks about his hero are found in Part I. In the 1615 *Quijote,* beneath the humor, the author is on the side of his hero. Unfortunately, Part II was hastily written because Cervantes was hurrying to get into print to offset the effect of Avellaneda's *Quijote.* The author's references to Avellaneda, in Part II, are most distracting. The last chapter, however, is capably done, quite dramatic and realistic.

85. Croce, Benedetto. "The 'Simpatia' of Don Quixote," in *Cervantes Across the Centuries.* Edited by Ángel Flores and M. J. Benardete. New York: Dryden Press, 1947, pp. 179-182. (Translation by Frederick F. Fales.) [Based on a passage from *Poesia antica e moderna, interpretazioni,* 2nd edit., 1943.]

We feel *simpatia* toward the Knight of La Mancha, a feeling of tender understanding, not a feeling of pity. There is a certain voluntary quality to his illusions, but there is a true reality in illusion, a reality that makes us live and work, suffer and die. Man must create illusions in order to live.

To be sure, not all of *Don Quijote* has a purity of portrayal and of poetry, for Cervantes was a man of letters who wanted to compose a work of entertainment value. He introduced, for ornamentation and variety, many extraneous elements and followed the first part with a second, which, no matter how many very fine passages it may have, has also, in some instances, the defect of forcing the narration to the point of farce.

86. Crocker, L. G. "*Hamlet, Don Quixote, La vida es sueño:* The Quest for Values." *PMLA,* LXIX (1954), 278-313.

Hamlet, Don Quijote, and Segismundo are all involved in situations where the problem of evil in man, concretized in deeds of injustice, becomes the key to their conduct. Their situation compels a decision on values and norms of action; this decision necessitates in turn a world view of the nature of reality, the meaning of life, the cosmic status of mankind. All three protagonists are searching for a way out of anarchy towards right, a search that raises them to heroic heights and enables them to epitomize some of the deepest perplexities of their times and ours. All three works are tragedies, though not in the same sense. *Don Quijote* is a work in which the comic is superficially predominant, although it serves ultimately to enhance the tragic.

The Knight starts with an appearance — reality dualism, in which appearance is the material, evil, limiting world, and the hero's ideal world, the true reality. The Don ends up with the disillusioning realization that what he considered appearance is reality and that his ideal world is merely appearance. Hamlet, beginning with a similar dualism, has been disenchanted before the play commences, and so he already bitterly applies the word "appearance" to the ideal world ("the painted face"). Segismundo, initially free of dualism and *a priori* concepts, comes to learn that reality and appearance, *engaño* and *desengaño,* are the conditions of our world; but he has recourse to an interpretation that accounts for the discrepancy: all here is dream, reality is elsewhere.

The similarities between *Don Quijote, Hamlet,* and *La vida es sueño* derive from common problems and from a common concept, typical in baroque literature, of man as unbalanced, as struggling between sensuality and spirituality, between lust and death.

In Part I of *Don Quijote* Cervantes reveals to us that the hero's ideal is impossible because of things as they are; in Part II the author shows us, further, that it is unrealizable because of the evil in men, because of the powers that be, the mediocre and the wicked. The attempt to surpass the human condition is self-defeating, since it involves the human weakness of self-delusion.

87. Croft-Cooke, Rupert. *Through Spain with Don Quixote.* New York: Knopf, 1960. Pp. 278. (First published in 1959 as *The Quest for Quixote,* London: Secker and Warburg.)

[Croft-Cooke discusses the Knight's route in some detail, noting that it is full of sheer fantasy. The secret of Cervantes' realism, the critic states, is that he writes in a cool, unhurried, detached way, in simple language, without elaboration or figure of speech, as curtly as a man dictating a report. Yet, Croft-Cooke continues, with a few hundred words of prosaic narrative Cervantes has made a parable for the entire world, has enriched the idiom of most peoples with a metaphor, and has held every reader breathless.]

88. *Cuadernos de Literatura,* III, núms. 8-9 (Marzo-Junio, 1948). *Homenaje a Cervantes.*

[This volume contains the following ten articles on Cervantes or his works: (1) "Los Cortinas de la villa de Barajas," by Narcisco Alonso Cortés; (2) "El uso de La Sagrada Escritura en Cervantes," by Teófilo Antolín; (3) "Historia y poesía en el *Quijote*" (270), by Alberto Sánchez; (4) "Historia cinematográfica de *Don Quijote de la Mancha,*" by Carlos Fernández Cuenca; (5) "Cervantes y la evolución de su época," by Rafael Benítez Claros; (6) "Cinco aspectos de la vida en el *Quijote*" (123), by Ramón de Garciasol; (7) "Del *asno de oro* a *Rocinante:* Contribución al estudio del *Quijote*" (239), by Olga Prjevalinsky Ferrer; (8) "El autor de la frase más célebre de Cervantes: Lepanto, Cervantes y el Dr. Don Pedro de Fuentidueña," by J. González Díez; (9) "Notas al margen: Realidad y ficción en las *Novelas ejemplares,*" by Enrique Sordo; (10) "Doce opiniones sobre el *Quijote,*" by Antonia Sanz Cuadrado.]

89. Darío, Rubén. "Un soneto a Cervantes" and "Letanía de Nuestro Señor Don Quijote," in *Obras completas,* V. Madrid: A. Aguado, 1953, pp. 917, 937-939. (Poems composed in 1905.)

[In "Un soneto a Cervantes" Darío praises the author as "la vida y la naturaleza." Cervantes, the poet continues, "parla como un arroyo cristalino." Darío concludes this sonnet as follows: "Así le admiro y quiero. Viendo cómo el destino hace que regocije al mundo entero la tristeza de ser divino!"

In "Letanía de Nuestro Señor Don Quijote" Darío speaks to the Knight, naming him "rey de los hidalgos, señor de los tristes," and "noble peregrino de los peregrinos que sanctificaste todos los caminos con el paso augusto de tu heroicidad." Darío begs the Knight to pray for those who have lost faith.]

90. Descouzis, Paul Marcel. "*Don Quijote* y la generación del 98." Unpublished Ph. D. dissertation, University of Maryland, 1959. Pp. 175. [Subsequent to the preparation of this summary Dr. Descouzis' work was published as: *Cervantes y la generación del 98; la cuarta salida de Don Quijote*. Madrid: Ediciones Iberoamericanas, 1970. Pp. 158. We have not examined the published version in detail.]

The conditions in Spain in 1588 and 1898 were similar, for in both epochs there was discontent and great discordance between the past and present. However, the reactions of the authors of 1588 and those of 1898 were quite different. In Cervantes' time one had to use veiled criticism, while the Generation of '98 was openly bitter in its denunciation of Spanish life. This generation sought inspiration not in historical deeds of the past but in spiritual values exemplified by great figures of bygone years — the mystics and Don Quijote. The writers of the Generation of '98 try to overcome Don Quijote's image of quixoticness. They dress him up and sublimate his virtues.

Unamuno sought out actions and virtues that would move the Spanish people to awaken. In his hands Don Quijote becomes a prototype of the Spanish people: (1) the ideal hero; (2) the creative spirit. Unamuno changed his position on several occasions, but in 1902, in *Amor y pedagogía*, he came to the conclusion that madness is, after all, desirable, a view repeated in his *Vida de Don Quijote y Sancho* (309) in 1905.

Maeztu discussed *Don Quijote* on several occasions. In 1903, in the columns of *Alma española*, he referred to that work as decadent. Later [see (184)] he sought to explain that the work was decadent because it was pessimistic. Valle-Inclán (in *La corte de los milagros*) questioned the value of *Don Quijote* as a force for regeneration, since it was to him anti-idealistic. Ganivet (119) attacked the injustice of Spanish laws, using the episode of the galley slaves to show the distinction between formal law and natural law. Azorín, like Unamuno, considered the Knight an actual being and felt that regeneration required the restoration of the elevated moral values of truth and justice. Looking at Azorín's work as a whole, Pedro Laín Entralgo has concluded [*La generación del 98*, 1945] that for Azorín three factors make up the *arquetipo quijotesco:* Castillian graveness, an affirmation of life, and a strong desire to know and understand.

91. Descouzis, Paul Marcel. *Cervantes, a nueva luz. I. El "Quijote" y el Concilio de Trento.* Frankfort a/M: V. Klostermann, 1966. Pp. 200. (*Analecta Romanica,* Heft XIX.)

[Descouzis points out that there is no express reference in the *Quijote* to the Council of Trent but gives examples of how the decrees of the Council affected Cervantes' characters. For example, the priest changes out of female garments lest he offend the Council's injunction against lack of decorum. Also, Cervantes, in the Tosilos episode, makes it clear that the Duke is violating the Council's prohibition against dueling. Descouzis also discusses Roque Guinart's state of imperfect contrition (attrition) and the Council's favorable attitude toward that state. The critic further asserts that Zoraida's pious reaction to Church images may be an illustration of the Council's belief that such images aided the believer to draw nearer to God.]

92. Deutsch, Helene. "Don Quijote und Donquijotismo." *Almanach der Psychoanalyse,* X (1935), 151-160.

Alonso Quijano, as an elderly man, falls in love with a peasant girl. He is not successful in his courtship for he is timid and even afraid to see her. His choice of a husky girl tells us a good bit about the Knight, namely that he is passive-feminine and that he has probably been impotent all his life. The hero's frustration causes his fantasy to become inflamed and he imagines himself to be superpotent. His ties with reality become broken. His oppressed ego surrenders to an ideal ego, and he loses all capacity for self-criticism. The Knight becomes so enmeshed in his fantasy world that he cannot get out. To bolster this new world of his he makes use of enchantment. Like a child he enchants the world and comes to believe in this enchantment.

Don Quijote, in his narcissistic overconfidence, believes himself to be immortal. Like a small boy he appears to know no danger. Later, when he senses death approaching, he becomes reconciled with reality and regains his sanity.

Sancho is a figure that Don Quijote *induces* out of a need to cope with reality. The Squire is thus a split-off part of the Knight. Sancho is motherly and practical, and represents the Knight's inherent desire to affirm reality.

Some view the *Quijote* as a mockery of a by-gone age. But the age involved is not an historical age but the hero's early life. The Knight is an anachronistic caricature of a father as seen in the unsexual period of childhood. He represents the castration wish of a child toward its father. Sancho also has some resemblance to the castrated father figure. But Sancho has a maternal side; he seems to be the author's humorous mockery of motherhood.

93. Díaz-Plaja, Guillermo. "La técnica narrativa de Cervantes." *Revista de Filología Española*, XXXII (1948), 237-268.

[Díaz-Plaja, in discussing the renaissance and baroque elements in Cervantes' works, concludes that the *Novelas ejemplares* are more linear (renaissance) than painterly (baroque). However, the *Quijote*, to the critic, is quite different from the short stories of the master: the latter have a clearly defined dynamic movement, whereas the masterpiece wanders along in a curve which can be extended into the infinite. The *Quijote*, the critic concludes, has a lack of goal, and therefore the reader is constantly ill-at-ease in a genuinely baroque manner. Díaz-Plaja is of the belief that the plot of the *Quijote* reaches an end only because Cervantes allows the foolishness, which maintains the plot psychologically, to disappear and permits his hero to die sane.]

94. Durán, Manuel. "Cervantes y el realismo fluido." *Ínsula*, XVIII, núms. 200-201 (1963), p. 3.

To say that Spain is realistic in her literature is only partially true. It is a notion supported by three columns: The *Cid*, Cervantes and Galdós. But what is Cervantes' realistic technique? His point-of-view toward the external world is a variant of the loss of medieval innocence in the refined environment of the Renaissance. The neo-Aristotelians stated that the verisimilar and the fabulous should be separated, and they felt that a certain order could be created in an epoch in transition. But these estheticians did not foresee the complications in the artistic viewpoint. Some writers imitated models, such as Virgil, but this was sterile. Others, to escape sterility, became ironic, and literature became introverted, full of illusions and optical tricks, such as plays within plays. These tendencies, along with the perspectivism, relativism and introspection which the Renaissance had introduced into the conscience of the writer, caused his optical instrument to vacillate, to become blurred, to turn into a gallery of mirrors.

For Cervantes and others two factors contributed to the increase in the confusion between fantasy and reality; (1) the Italian-neoplatonic idealization of love; (2) the fantastic events of the day as told by travelers. In the *Galatea* as well as in the *Persiles* there is an idealization of love. To Cervantes love was not a distortion, but the source of beauty, harmony and knowledge. In the *Quijote* Cervantes makes fun of this platonic myth which he accepted earlier without reserve in the *Galatea* and later in the *Persiles*. Thus Don Quijote is a step backward in the idealization process.

How do we explain Cervantes' boredom with the everyday, his continuation of the idealization process in the *Persiles?* In part, the attitude of the times made it hard to separate the real from the fantastic. Fables came in from newly explored lands and superimposed themselves on old myths without replacing them altogether. Thus if the epoch was full of fantastic events, the literature (epic, lyric, theatre) was not far behind.

Though the *Quijote* is, in a sense, realistic, it is pierced with idealism, open and fluid. It is a realism which includes the external world as well as the internal reactions of the characters, the presence of the author himself as well as the presence of the reading public, and the impact of the work on the characters. In the *Quijote* there is a whole gamut of delicate shades, a stairway of situations which permits us to pass from the realistic realism of the inns to the interior world of *idealismo "virtual,"* loaded with literature. Cervantes' realism is open, liquid, tolerant, and does not have as its object the destruction of idealism. Instead it seeks to enrich idealism through a new dimension.

95. Durán, Manuel. *La ambigüedad en el Quijote.* Xalapa, México: Universidad Veracruzana, 1960. Pp. 279.

From the late Middle Ages to the height of the Renaissance, there is an ascending line of subjectivism — Petrarch, Erasmus, Montaigne. During this same period there is a descending line of disbelief in the power of certain external myths, such as knight-errantry. These two lines cross at *Don Quijote;* and Cervantes demythicizes certain myths but retains the subjective attitude, so that the degradation of the myths is accompanied by an interiorizing of them. Thus, while the desire to degrade the chivalry myth was necessary for the writing of the *Quijote*, a desire for an internal vision was also needed. In this respect *Celestina* and *Orlando furioso* were more important to Cervantes than the *Entremés de los romances*, which only gave the point of departure for the *Quijote*.

The interrelation of artistic elements in the *Quijote* might be outlined as follows: There is an initial ambivalence by the author as regards the convenience of destroying or radically weakening certain myths; this leads to Cervantes' endowing his hero with some sympathetic and some ridiculous characteristics. The periods of adventures are followed by moments of rest. In both periods the Knight has an attitude different from those around him toward objective reality. Rationally the reader agrees with the secondary characters, but emotionally he is attracted to the hero, the only figure who has a life-plan and who escapes reality. There are two types of ambiguity in *Don Quijote:* (1) the interpretation of reality, ontological relativism, a renaissance idea of "engaño a los sentidos;" (2) the ambiguity of the author toward his characters.

The fact that the *Quijote* reminds us of modern [existential] thought is not pure anachronistic caprice, nor a curious coincidence. It is not a question of converting Cervantes into an existentialist, for that would be absurd. However, both the *Quijote* and existentialism derive from the Christian interpretation of life, — an insistence on individual responsibility, the relationship of man to God, salvation, the interior man with all his doubts and hopes.

96. Efron, Arthur. "Satire Denied: A Critical History of English and American *Don Quixote* Criticism." Unpublished Ph. D. dissertation, University of Washington. Pp. 557.

In general, the history of English and American criticism is that of a few basic assumptions, never supported by the text of the novel, and though criticism has become more complex, it has not progressed. There are three established readings of *Don Quijote:* (1) idealistic; (2) cautionary; and (3) perspectivistic. All three are deficient. *Don Quijote* begins as a satire on chivalry novels and naturally gravitates toward a satire in depth of idealism. Sancho's function is to expose the progressive irrationality of the attempt to live out a prearranged code of conduct which the Knight represents. Cervantes shows that Don Quijote's idealism is not only fundamentally unimaginative, but involves severe self-sacrifice for no discernible benefits. Cervantes is attacking the ideal, not just the ideal within the chivalry framework. He casts doubt on the value of the norms of Western civilization.

97. Eguía Ruiz, Constancio. *Cervantes, Calderón, Lope, Gracián: Nuevos temas crítico-biográficos.* Madrid: Instituto "Miguel de Cervantes" de Filología Hispánica, 1951, pp. 3-45. (Anejos de *Cuadernos de Literatura,* VIII.)

[Chapter I of this work discusses in some detail the suggested living models for Don Quijote and Dulcinea. Numerous earlier books and articles are cited, including Rodríguez Marín's 1918 article *El modelo más probable del Don Quijote* (258) and Manuel Víctor García's *El museo universal,* 1867.]

98. El Saffar, Ruth Snodgrass. "The Function of the Fictional Narrator in *Don Quijote.*" *Modern Language Notes,* LXXXIII (1968), 164-177.

Cide Hamete claims attention and shows his distance from the characters and his control of them by: (1) arbitrarily stopping events; (2) ending a chapter in the middle or referring to the preceding or following chapter; (3) appearing in his own voice to express the difficulties involved in describing an event or character; (4) breaking in and revealing the end; and (5) intruding extraneous material unrelated, or only slightly related, to the main characters.

Don Quijote is not the basis of the novel; the basis is the dialectic represented by the opposition of Don Quijote and Cide

Hamete. The comments by and about Cide Hamete must be handled by someone external and distant from him, and the translator and the second author fulfill this role. But ultimately they too must have an author through whom they can be presented in the third person. The only appearance of the ultimate author is at the end of Chapter VIII of Part I where he appears in order to tie the end of the first part of the manuscript to the Second Author who immediately takes upon himself the responsibility of finding and transmitting the remainder of the history. The ultimate author remains anonymous and uses the impersonal reflexive rather than the first person. The reason for the disappearance of the true author behind a series of fictional authors is control and distance, and distance is the prerequisite of control.

99. Ellis, Havelock. "Don Quixote," in *The Soul of Spain*. Boston: Houghton Mifflin Company, 1937, pp. 222-243. (First published in 1908: London, Archibald Constable & Company; Boston and New York, Houghton, Mifflin & Company.)

Cervantes, in his great story, combined for the first time the chivalry novel with the picaresque, creating something altogether original, an instrument that was capable of touching life at every point. The ideal and the real are equally welcomed in the *Quijote;* the serious and the gay are blended. As in *Lear* the madman and the fool are brought together in a concord of divine humor.

Don Quijote has a religious significance for the consolation of men. It is not only the type and pattern of our greatest novels; it is a vision of the human soul, woven into the texture of the world's spiritual traditions.

Even though the *Quijote* is national in flavor, it is the most cosmopolitan, the most universal of books. Neither Chaucer nor Tolstoy shows a wider humanity than Cervantes, for there is not a single villain among the 639 characters in the *Quijote*.

100. Entwistle, William J. *Cervantes*. Oxford: Clarendon Press, 1940. Pp. 192.

Don Quijote is no literary accident as some claim. Cervantes' style shows great care and planning, and his technique has the same impediments when he fails as when he succeeds. There is also a great consistency in his style and thought. Cervantes' genius is unequal in all his writings, and the *Quijote* is a mosaic of parts of unequal interest. Cervantes' true genius is that of a writer of exemplary short stories, and it was the skill and moral purpose of the exemplary novelist, vivified by a rich idea, which gave birth to *Don Quijote*.

Cervantes was overly influenced by medieval aesthetics, which emphasized variety (a web woven of various fair strands), and partly for that reason included extraneous episodes in his novel. But the broadening of the narrative stream in *Don Quijote* led to divided currents and episodic islands. These interpolations are not congruent with the main history. Some episodes are idealistic and jarring in a realistic setting; the motivation rings false. Other episodes are merely irrelevant.

In Part II the formula was to stick to the main plot. However, this was not adhered to in practice. Camacho's wedding is actually a pastoral episode in a semi-realistic setting; Claudia Jerónima and her woes are essentially irrelevant. In Part I the events merely follow one another; in Part II they rise to two climaxes, the two jousts with Sansón Carrasco.

To Cervantes the ability to keep his narration moving is tied in with the concept of verisimilitude. The point of departure is the Aristotelian distinction between history and fiction. Verisimilitude goes beyond literal truth; it is more universal, and even includes the impossible. According to El Pinciano the author must select material to create harmony; and skill in style will determine the verisimilitude. The fictitious must be married to the reader's mind. Cervantes sometimes fails to accomplish these objectives because he overdoes the style. We resent the intrusion of a romantic style in the interpolations more than we resent the lack of verisimilitude found in these episodes.

The worth of *Don Quijote* is not its plot or its narration, but in the revelation of the inner man. For the essential step from the medieval romance to the modern novel is that in the latter the plot becomes the mere outward semblance of character. Prior to Don Quijote characters were not rounded. At first, to be sure, the Knight is a *Johnsonian humour*, a *figurón*. The revelation of his character is slow and even largely unforeseen and unplanned by Cervantes. Both Don Quijote and Sancho grow in Part II; they are not static. Madariaga's (182) theory of Sanchification — Quixotization is, in general, correct, but both Sancho and Don Quijote follow their own orbit. Quixotization does not deepen Sancho; it is simply that we know more about him when we reach Part II. Nor is Sancho responsible for Don Quijote's change from lunacy to doubt and then to sanity.

101. Farinelli, Arturo. *Cervantes zur 300jährigen Feier des "Don Quijote."* Munich: Allgemeine Zeitung, 1905. Pp. 39.

The *Quijote* was originally intended to be a mere satire on chivalry novels but it grew into a deep, valid, eternal picture of man's life and struggles. Thus out of an attempted destruction there arose a noble construction.

Cervantes is not a forerunner of modern philosophical thought, as some falsely contend. In fact he avoids original observations. Cervantes was also more concerned with creating new and surprising situations than in the development of secondary characters. His minor figures are mere sketches. While there are many types of figures in the *Quijote,* Cervantes does not have the variety of characters that Shakespeare and Lope have.

Part I and Part II of the *Quijote* are quite different. The 1615 *Quijote* is deeper, and the parody is softened. However, the central episode at the palace of the *Duques* is long and boring. The fall of the hero at Barcelona is too sudden, and there is entirely too much novelistic material toward the end of Part II. The author appears to be in too great haste to finish his work.

Cervantes never loses his inner balance. Thus he is a classical writer, as Goethe contended. Cervantes' irony is goodhearted and thus quite unlike that of Rabelais, Swift, Quevedo and Voltaire. The irony of the *Quijote* has a childish naïveté about it.

Cervantes was not attempting to be philosophical in the *Quijote.* Nor did he intend to be mythological or abstract as Schelling thought. If the *Quijote* is a symbol at all, it is that of two souls in one breast, one soul aspiring heavenward, the other clinging to the earth. It was a stroke of genius for Cervantes to heal his hero at the end. Though the Don is cured of his illusions about chivalry novels, he maintains his high ideals.

102. Farinelli, Arturo. "Cervantes con ocasión del cuarto centenario de su nacimiento." *Boletín de la Academia Argentina de Letras*, XVI (1947), 541-587.

Cervantes was more a man of feeling than a man of thought. He was not concerned with dogma. Cervantes did not feel constrained by his times nor was he a person capable of concealing his feelings. Furthermore, he was not preoccupied with the edicts of the Council of Trent. Though there is some kinship between Cervantes and Erasmus, Américo Castro (63) is wrong to conclude that Cervantes would not have been as he was had there been no Erasmus.

103. Farinelli, Arturo. "Cervantes," in *Aufsätze, Reden und Charakteristiken zur Weltliteratur*. Bonn and Leipzig: Kurt Schroeder, 1925, pp. 1-37.

Cervantes let his story run on in an unrestrained flow of speech, in a natural style full of light and colors. His manner of writing is nature itself, a living organism in which all the gradations of thought are shown. Cervantes can be charming, elegant, serious and pathetic. He reaches into the innermost part of life. The author paints his two protagonists with loving care. To Cervantes they were not abstract symbols; they are real beings.

The plot of the *Quijote* is not single and unified. Cervantes believed that the reader might become bored with a single plot and therefore poured in additional material. In doing this he did not use the artistic selection of Ariosto.

Beginning with an insignificant item Cervantes was able to create something delightful. He was able also to mix gaiety and healthy humor with deep seriousness, and give charm to his irony, an irony full of naïveté and pity. Though he laughs at people he never goes so far as to degrade them.

104. Faure, Élie. "Cervantes," in *Montaigne et ses trois premiernés*. Paris: G. Grès et Cie, 1926, pp. 115-171.

Whether or not Cervantes ever read Montaigne he has offered the solution of an idealistic illusion to the intellectual drama which

Montaigne opened up: idealism, though it never achieves its goal, enlarges the interior man.

The genius of Spain, part plastic part psychological, reaches its peak with Cervantes. Like Homer, the author of the *Quijote* gives the impression, in his apparent simplicity, that he does not realize his own power. Cervantes, like all Spaniards, is an improviser. He starts without a fixed plan, stops on the way, doubles back and engages in digressions.

105. Fernández Suárez, Álvaro. *Los mitos del Quijote.* Madrid: Aguilar, 1953. Pp. 203.

The circumstances of the Knight's death are puzzling. Why must he die, and sane to boot? Why does Cervantes kill his hero twice, once when he makes the Knight sane, and then when he physically kills Alonso Quijano? This was done to spite future Avellanedas. But this violence brought in by an outside factor (Avellaneda) plus such anomolies as repentance, make us wonder whether the Alonso Quijano who died was really Don Quijote. Perhaps he was merely another person who thought he was Don Quijote. Perhaps the often confused historian was mistaken. Perhaps there was a Don Quijote, or his *prefigura carnal*, who died around 1570, having repented, and another, living in 1605 and later, who was the great Don Quijote. But even if we do not accept these hypotheses, Don Quijote's life is saved, because he becomes a myth and lives on. The Knight is not made of salt and will not melt in the first rain; nor is he made of unchanging bronze. He is a myth and can change with time and gain new meaning as he changes. What is he for us today? A hero, brave though weak. Even with his fear he refuses to submit. He pictures the struggle between renaissance Rationalism and the mythical Medieval, but this struggle is not resolved in the novel. Therefore, the problem remains standing. Furthermore, it is not a question of one age against another. The problem of the rational versus the mythic endures because these two qualities exist in every man in every age.

Don Quijote is not insane. If he were mad, he could not become a myth. He is an optimist who does not accept things as they are. He is an escape from analytical thought. He is sure of certain values and convinced that life has a meaning.

When Don Quijote was born his prefigure died. But Dulcinea was not strong enough at first to erase Aldonza Lorenzo. Nevertheless, Dulcinea grows by a process of progressive affirmation of the ideal entity. At first Don Quijote is not completely sure of his ideal Dulcinea. He doubts yet does not want to doubt, as when he failed to test his helmet the second time. He knows his myths are myths but cannot live without them. In Part II the Knight sufficiently believes in the Dulcinea myth to test it. Yet he both yearns for and flees from a meeting with her. When Cervantes states that Don Quijote has never seen Dulcinea is he teasing the reader and himself? No! The idea is that the Dulcinea myth has grown so strong that she has become a separate entity from Aldonza Lorenzo. Yet deep in his heart the Don is fearful that he will destroy the myth. Sancho affirms the Knight's description of Dulcinea when he enchants her. Thus the myth is saved. Even after the sentence of the lashes, the Squire does not reveal his trickery to his master.

Don Quijote spares Sancho from oblivion. Why did the Knight choose Sancho? Because there was a hidden communication between them. They were attracted to each other before the story began. Don Quijote chose Sancho because Sancho was honorable, goodhearted and simple. The Knight, like Christ, did not disdain simplicity in a disciple. Why did Sancho follow Don Quijote? Not because of ambition nor because of greed nor in order to have a guaranteed wage. Even though Sancho is materialistic, the real reason is that he loves the Don. Why is Sancho a myth? In spite of his excessive humanity Sancho becomes a myth because the Knight leads him by the hand. Don Quijote could not have lived on this earth without his Squire. For this reason alone Sancho deserves glorification. In essence, the myth of Sancho is the glorification of the flesh through love.

Rocinante becomes elevated to a myth. This is not unusual since other horses have become myths. But Rocinante, like his master, is weak. On occasion, however, the spirit of the Knight enters Rocinante, and they become like a centaur. Rocinante's greatest virtue is his love for the Knight. This is apparent throughout the story, although it is not insisted upon by he author. Rocinante, skinny, generous, valiant and wretched, is the Don Quijote of the horse world. Like Rocinante and the Knight, Dapple and Sancho are one. In his love for his donkey Sancho shows a childlike love for animals. For the Squire, his donkey is more than a beast of burden. It is a friend and companion.

106. Fichter, William L. "Estudios cervantinos recientes (1937-1947)." *Nueva Revista de Filología Hispánica*, II (1948), 88-100.

[This article continues the 1940 study of F. Courtney Tarr (296). Fichter first deals with recent bibliographical material such as Suñé Benages and Suñé Fonbuena's *A Critical Bibliography of Editions of Don Quijote*, 1939. Erudite articles which seek to interpret a given passage in Cervantes' works are noted briefly: for example, María Rosa Lida's (174) and Joaquín Casalduero's (56) notes on the opening line of the *Quijote*. Works which examine the influence of Cervantes in a given country are discussed, and Harri Meier's article (195) on European interpretations of the *Quijote* is particularly praised. Studies dealing with the literary sources of Cervantes' works are noted, a brief discussion being presented of Arturo Marasso's book (191) on Virgil's influence on Cervantes. At the end, leading works during the survey period are briefly examined: those of Entwistle (100), Bell (31), Croce (85), and Casella (60), as well as Américo Castro's *Prólogos al Quijote* (68).]

107. Fitzmaurice-Kelly, James. "Introduction" to *The History of Don Quixote of the Mancha*. Translated from the Spanish of Miguel de Cervantes by Thomas Shelton, annis 1612, 1620. Vol. I. New York: AMS Press, Ins., 1967, pp. ix-li. (First published in 1896, London, D. Nutt.)

Cervantes is to be judged solely as an extraordinary talent, as a consumate artist in humor, and as a prince of invention. He is no scholar; he dashes down quotations at random; he confuses the events of history; he has bad grammar. As a craftsman he has no claim to the first, nor to the second, place among Spanish writers.

108. Fitzmaurice-Kelly, James. *The Life of Miguel de Cervantes Saavedra: A Biographical, Literary and Historical Study with a Tentative Bibliography from 1585-1892 and an Annotated Appendix on the "Canto de Caliope."* London: Champion and Hall, Ld, 1892. Pp. xiv + 396.

In the late sixteenth century chivalry novels were dead, and thus the *Quijote* only tolled their knell. The modern psychological, introspective romance was not yet born. But there was perhaps a more excellent way, for there was still room for a declaration, an exposition, of the true and the false; of the painful, necessary contrast of the ideal with the actual; of the pathetic difference between aspiration and accomplishment; of the story ocean which divides the vision from the retrospect; of the immeasurable interval which separates the magnificent blue of poetry from the subdued drab of prose.

[Fitzmaurice-Kelly notes Rawdon Brown's theory, c. 1873, that Sancho is based on the historical figure Pedro Franqueza, once a servant of Lerma and later Secretary of State. Landor's theory of 1876 that the *Quijote* is a veiled attack on the Virgin Mary is also noted, as is Defoe's belief, in 1720, that Cervantes was lampooning the Duke of Medina Sidonia. In analyzing Cervantes' masterpiece Fitzmaurice-Kelly observes: In *Don Quijote* one sees the idiosyncracy of the man, interpenetrated as it were with lofty, sustained enthusiasm, that romance, that dash of oriental exaggeration, that dignity of sentiment, that inexhaustible good humor, that tenacious vigor in the prosecution of an object which Carlyle and Victor Cherbuliez are agreed in thinking characteristic of the Spanish race. So incomparable is the verve with which the portrait of the Knight is rendered that Don Quijote may be said to have supplanted the Cid Campeador as the popular hero and the national type.]

109. Fitzmaurice-Kelly, James. *A History of Spanish Literature.* New York: D. Appleton and Company, 1898, pp. 211-274.

Cervantes is a literary artist, stronger in practice than in theory. His learning is naught, his reasonings are futile, his speculation is banal. He can be a great stylist but lapses into Italian idioms, or into composing sentences packed with needless relatives. Cervantes is immortal not as a stylist nor as an intellectual. He is immortal by reason of his creative power, his imaginative resource, his wealth of invention, his penetrating vision, his inimitable humor, his boundless sympathy. Hence the universality of his appeal; hence the splendor of his secular renown.

Cervantes never saw the scope of the *Quijote*. He began it as a short story, but it grew into a whole human comedy. It was not intended to be an allegory of human life, for the author was inspired solely by the desire to create living characters.

110. Fitzmaurice-Kelly, James. *Cervantes and Shakespeare.* London: Humphrey Milford, Oxford University Press, 1916. Pp. 23.

Though Shakespeare may have heard of Cervantes (and could well have read Shelton's 1612 English translation of *Don Quijote*), Cervantes did not know of Shakespeare. Both Cervantes and Shakespeare are geniuses and have certain similarities. Sancho's and Falstaff's soliloquies are similar. Both authors discuss the theatre. But Cervantes lacks Shakespeare's endowment of divine utterance. The Spaniard's expression also lacks Shakespeare's ecstacy of beauty, although it is always adequate to its purpose and has the charm of natural simplicity and dramatic appropriateness. Cervantes, however, excels in realism and humor. Shakespeare is polished, self assured; Cervantes makes false starts, and hesitates. Both authors were intrigued by insanity, and both their masterpieces, *Hamlet* and *Don Quijote,* were written at almost the same time. Both Hamlet and Don Quijote evolve, yet both are consistent. Don Quijote lacks Hamlet's psychological intensity and his intellectual subtlety. Cervantes is weak in portraying female characters, Teresa Panza and the Duchess being exceptions to the rule.

Although Cervantes was neither a real poet nor a dramatist, his masterpiece is penetrated with poetic imagination and is pregnant with dramatic suggestion. Cervantes is the first novelist to make his characters talk as real people. Yet he is not above tricks and mannerisms. Nor is his taste impeccable. Absolute beauty of phrase is not his preoccupation. He aims at being natural and at conveying and exact impression of manifold life.

111. Flecniakoska, Jean-Louis. "Reflexions sur la parodie pastorale dans le *Quichotte*." *Anales Cervantinos*, VIII (1959-1960), 371-378.

Don Quixote is a satire both of chivalry books and pastoral novels. The author satirizes Alonso Quijano's intent to become a shepherd just as he makes fun of the Don's efforts to become a knight-errant. The episodes of Grisóstomo and of the New Arcadia are both cases of pretended shepherds, the only real difference being that Grisóstomo and his friends are much more serious about the game. In both cases, the false shepherds are overly intoxicated with literature. The pastoral novel was overly erotic, and Marcela, in her speech at Grisóstomo's grave, criticizes this characteristic of the pastoral.

It is not possible to separate the pastoral myth from the chivalry myth in Cervantes' novel, for the *Quijote* is a unity. Both genres are parodied in the story, and Dulcinea is the center of this parody.

112. Flores, Ángel, and Benardete, M. J., ed. *Cervantes Across the Centuries*. New York: Gordian Press, 1969. Pp. vii. + 386. (Originally published in 1947 and reprinted in 1969 with corrections.)

[The nineteen essays reprinted here in English are divided into four parts. In Part One are found Jean Cassou's "An Introduction to Cervantes" (61), Ramón Menéndez Pidal's "The Genesis of *Don Quixote*" (196), Joaquín Casalduero's "The Composition of *Don Quixote*," Helmut Hatzfeld's "The Style of *Don Quixote*," and A. Morel-Fatio's "Social and Historical Background" (210).

The second group of articles contains Miguel de Unamuno's "Of How Don Quixote Fell Sick and Died," Américo Castro's "Incarnation in *Don Quixote*" (69), Benedetto Croce's "The 'Simpatia' of Don Quixote" (85), Waldo Frank's "The Career of the Hero" (117), and Mario Casella's "Critical Realism" (60).

In the third group of studies are found Harry Levin's "*Don Quixote* and *Moby Dick*," Mack Singleton's "The *Persiles* Mystery," Pavel I. Novitsky's "Thematic Design" (221), Stephan Gilman's "The Apocryphal *Quixote*," and Charles Haywood's "Musical Settings to Cervantes' Texts."

Part Four contains Edwin B. Knowles "Cervantes in English Literature," Esther J. Crooks "Translations of Cervantes into French," Lienhard Bergel's "Cervantes in Germany," and Ludmilla B. Turkevich's "Cervantes in Russia."]

113. Forcione, Alban K. *Cervantes, Aristotle and the Persiles*. Princeton, N. J.: Princeton University Press, 1970, pp. 91-166.

The Canon of Toledo is *not* a rigid puritan on the subject of books of chivalry. Like Torquato Tasso he appreciates the pleasure to be derived from them, but wishes to purify them by eliminating their flaws. Also like Tasso, the canon cannot divorce pleasure from a literal belief in the truth of the events in a story.

Cervantes appears to follow Pinciano's belief that verisimilitude depends, in the last analysis, on the *individual* reader's outlook and not on that of the hypothetical reader conceived of by Tasso. The author of the Quijote seems to see no connection between literal truth and pleasure. He wishes to liberate art from the mimetic renaissance theories of verisimilitude and the imitation of nature. However, the author of the *Quijote* does not flee into pure fantasy; he moves toward everyday reality, creating what came to be the modern novel.

Tasso had suggested that adding *new customs* to a story would increase its verisimilitude. Cervantes disagrees, lampooning the idea on a number of occasions, as where the knight, when caged, insists that there are *new customs* in enchantment. The real point of that episode, however, is that Don Quijote believes that he is enchanted and that is enough to make his enchantment verisimilar to him.

The Montesinos' cave adventure ties in with the debate between the canon and Don Quijote in Part I. Cervantes brings a standard of objectivity into this episode and adds a series of incongruous observations which subject the phenomena in the cave to a process of analysis and explanation by then current standards of natural science (e.g., Durandarte's heart is salted to prevent its smelling and its decomposition). Don Quijote appears to submit to the scientific explanations of the fantastic, but the episode is in reality a satire on the humanistic-scientific perspective and its attempt to encroach on the realm of imaginative literature. Montesinos' cave, thus, is a parody on the neo-Aristotelian confusion between artistic and empirical truth. It is a satire on Tasso's bringing in empirical details to enhance the appearance of truth.

Maese Pedro's pupet show is likewise a satire on literary theories. Here Don Quijote reverses his role and objects to the lack of empirical reality in the presentation of the story of Gaiferos and Melisendra (the Moors did not use bells to sound the alarm, he notes). What Cervantes is really suggesting here is that the reader or spectator enjoys a scene more if he is *not* aware of their lack of empirical reality. Don Quijote soon becomes carried away by the *admiratio* of the presentation and intervenes in the story. This is dramatic proof of the power of fantasy and its independence of laws of empirical truth.

114. Ford, J. D. M. "Plot, Tale, and Episode in *Don Quijote*," in *Mélanges de Linguistique et de Littérature offerts à M. Alfred Jeanroy par ses élèves et ses amis*. Paris: E. Droz, 1928, pp. 311-323.

When Cervantes refers, in Chapter XXVIII of Part I, to the tales included in his story, it is not clear whether he considers them out of place. In Chapter III of Part II we find that Cervantes' readers considered the *Curioso* unessential and we also hear that Don Quijote considered this interpolation to be mere padding. In Chapter LIV of Part II Cervantes again raises the question of these intrusions, referring both to *The Captive's Tale* as well as the story of *The Curious Impertinent* as being interpolations. Here Cervantes' half-hearted defense of the inclusion of these *novelas* veils a roguish complacency, for he was proud of both these tales.

There are four important novelsque episodes in Part I: (1) Grisóstomo-Marcela; (2) Cardenio (interwoven with Dorotea); (3) *El curioso;* and (4) the tale of *El cautivo*. The *Curioso* is the only episode that is absolutely extraneous, though the Marcela interlude is barely connected to the main plot. The *Curioso*, however, *is* relevant in the sense that it is another example of monomania.

While the novel is a medieval genre historically, the idea for inserting short stories in the main narrative is ancient. It is found in the Greek Epic. Also, two Latin novels, Apuleius' *Asinus aureus* and Petronius' *Satyricon,* contain one interpolated story each. The

Satyricon includes the tale of the *Matron of Ephesus* and *The Golden Ass* contains the story of *Cupid and Psyche*. It is unlikely that Cervantes knew of the *Satyricon*, but it is probable that he was familiar with the *Asinus aureus*. In *Palmerín de Inglaterra* there is found an interpolated tale, that of the *Four French Ladies*, Chapters 137 to 147, or about one-twelfth of the whole novel, and *Orlando furioso* devotes more than seventy stanzas to the episode of Giocondo. Ariosto did not apologize for the inclusion of this unessential tale, and the Cervantes of Chapter XXVIII of Part I had no compunction about interpolations. It is only after criticism that the author of the *Quijote* felt it necessary to abandon the practice.

Since Cervantes' time other writers have used the device of interpolations. For example, Fielding includes the story of *The Man of the Hill* in his *Tom Jones*.

115. Fors, Luis Ricardo. *Espíritu del Quijote*. 2ª edición ilustrada y adicionada con las supercherías literarias sobre el escudo de la edición príncipe del Ingenioso Hidalgo, procedido todo de una carta-proemio del señor Julián J. Solveyra. Buenos Aires: Laso, Pardo y Cía, 1916. Pp. 117. (First published in 1901: La Plata, Imp. y Enc. 'La Popular.)

Cervantes lived in fanatical and oppressive times, and only a spirit like his could have confronted such an era calmly and with an ironic smile. *Don Quijote* is more than an attack on books of chivalry and on certain contemporaries of the author. It is a very human book, and yet a book that has something unknown and supernatural on each page, something fascinating that leads the reader to the point of recognizing the sublime greatness of the Mad Manchegan and of realizing the disconcerting reality that it is noble madness to defend justice and proclaim the truth while all the powers that be conspire against the law and liberty of nations and races.

There are numerous mysteries in Cervantes' novel: his choice of the word *ingenioso* in the title of the book, for example. Many translators have been puzzled by this word. The fact is that hardly any deed by the Knight could be described as *ingenioso*. The true meaning of this word is that the *book* is *ingenioso*, not the hero.

That Cervantes' novel has a hidden meaning can be seen in the poem of Urganda at the beginning of the story, where the fictitious enchantress predicts that no one will fathom the true meaning of the novel. Actually the *Quijote* attacks the oppression of the Church and the Inquisition. Cervantes never forgot the Dominican priest — inquisitor Blanco de Paz who betrayed him in Algiers. For that reason Cervantes' hero makes a purely gratuitous attack on the Church in Chapters VIII and XIX of Part I.

Dulcinea is a contraction of Nueva (Nea) and Dulcura (dulci), and represents the "dulzura y dicha" of future ages. She is liberty, independence and a yearning for justice in the midst of despotism.

The coat-of-arms of the *principe* edition has an arm emerging from a cloud or smoke. On this arm is a stole and on the wrist a tied and hooded falcon. Above is a human head pressed down by a screw, and below is a sleeping lion. The cloud or smoke represents ignorance. The arm with the stole symbolizes the Church. The tied and hooded falcon is the human intelligence and the sleeping lion, Spain.

[In the last portion of this work Fors elaborates on the symbolism of the above coat-of-arms. He insists that it was created by Cervantes, although admitting that this same *escudo* appeared in two works printed prior to Part I of the *Quijote*.]

116. Foulché-Delbosc, Raymond. "Carta crítica sobre la obra del *Quijote*." *Revue Hispanique*, XIII (1905), 229-255.

It is not correct to compare the *Quijote* to the works of Homer and Virgil. Cervantes' novel, as a book of witty sayings, is inimitable, but compared to the great epics it is weak, without invention, and not at all poetic. The *Quijote* was primarily intended to be entertaining, and the author did not set out to compose an epic.

Don Quijote is an excellent picture of customs and contains great dialogue. However, Cervantes' imagination is limited. The endings of the adventures are too uniform, and the author is too inclined to bring in extraneous matter to prolong the story.

117. Frank, Waldo. "The Will of Don Quixote," in *Virgin Spain: The Drama of a Great People*. New York: Duell, Sloan and Pearce, 1942, pp. 187-238. (First published in 1926: New York, Boni and Liveright. Revised and enlarged in the 1942 edition.)

Don Quijote's God is justice, and he creates a world that consists solely of opportunities for him to bring about justice. The Knight is Christ-like, though comical, and in laughing at him we are, in effect, crucifying him.

There are two actions in *Don Quijote*: the "surface of action" (picaresque Spain) and a "line of action" (the Knight's pilgrimage). There is, however, a subtle synthesis of these two actions, and this synthesis gives the novel its unity.

The prose in which the author of the *Quijote* writes is a heavy and pregnant prose, but it often lacks swiftness and sharpness. Cervantes' masterpiece has other technical shortcomings. For example, the minor scenes are often clumsily described.

118. Frye, Northrop. "The Four Forms of Fiction," in *The Theory of the Novel*. Edited by Philip Stevick. New York: The Free Press; London: The MacMillan Company, 1967, pp. 31-43. (From *Anatomy of Criticism*, Princeton, 1957.)

Three are four types of fiction: (1) the novel; (2) the romance; (3) the anatomy; and (4) the confession. The essential difference between the novel and the romance lies in the conception of characterization. The romancer does not attempt to create real people so much as stylized figures which expand into psychological archetypes. Romance reflects Jung's libido; it is thus subjective. The novelist deals with people wearing their social masks. It is not surprising that an important theme of the more bourgeois novel should be the parody of the romance and its ideals. The tradition established by *Don Quijote* continues in a type of novel which looks at a romantic situation from its own point of view, so that the conventions of the two forms make up an ironic compound instead of a sentimental mixture.

A confession (autobiography) is interested largely in ideas, and is alien to the novel, which is mainly concerned with man and society. Confessions, following the form of St. Augustine, later under Rousseau flow into the novel and produce the fictional autobiography, the *Künstlerroman* and kindred types. The *anatomy* derives from the Menippean, or Varronian, satire. It deals more with mental attitudes than with people as such. The Menippean satire thus resembles the confession in its ability to handle abstract ideas and theories, and differs from the novel in its characterization, which in the *anatomy* is stylized rather than naturalistic, and people become mere mouthpieces of the ideas they represent.

Genres, however, are not pure, but mixed, and there are six possible combinations of the four basic forms of fiction. The novel has combined with each of the other three, and exclusive concentration on one form is rare. *Don Quijote* is a combination of novel, romance, and anatomy.

119. Ganivet, Ángel. *Idearium español*, in *Obras completas*, I. Madrid: M. Aguilar, 1943, pp. 155, 243-244. (Selections dated October, 1896.)

Cervantes is the greatest of the *conquistadores* for he conquers Spain itself. When he begins to formulate his novel he has a great genius, but outside him there are only figures that move about like divine intuitions. Cervantes seizes these figures and drives them forward like a muledriver drives his mules, encouraging them with loving words mixed with timely blows. Do not seek any other artifice in the *Quijote* than this. The novel is written in prose and is like those rare poems of the mystics which one can read from the end or from the beginning, because each is a pure sensation like a Platonic idea.

All countries have a real or imaginary type in whom they incarnate their own characteristics. Ulysses is the Greek *par excellence*. Our Ulysses is Don Quijote, a purified Ulysses unconcerned with material things. Don Quijote and Sancho did not exist in Spain prior to the Arabs, nor during the Arabic domination. They come into being only after the Reconquest. Without the Arabs Don Quijote and Sancho Panza would have been one man, a copy of Ulysses.

120. Gaos, Vicente. "El *Quijote*: Aproximaciones," in *Temas y problemas de literatura española*. Madrid: Ediciones Guadarrama, 1959, pp. 93-118.

Menéndez Pidal (196) finds that the hero of the early chapters of the *Quijote* is confused and lacking in self-awareness, and that the author was unaware of the depths of the Knight. This is most doubtful. Cervantes *does* see the depths of his hero but deliberately begins by picturing him as uncertain of himself. The same procedure is followed in depicting Sancho. In effect, it would have been artistically improper for Cervantes to begin by picturing complete characters.

What is the function of the interpolated stories? They are there for some reason, other than the fact that they were lying about and available for insertion. Some critics, following Cervantes' remarks, find that the author was merely following the custom of the times when he inserted short stories. But Cervantes never states that the stories have no function; he merely observes that they are *como separadas*. That is, they *seem* to be separate. Furthermore, Cervantes is being ironic in his explanation of the interpolation of the *Curioso* and the *cautivo's* story, just as he is being ironic in downgrading himself and the main plot.

Some state that the interpolations break the unity of the main plot. But plot is not that important in the modern novel (and the *Quijote* is modern). In fact the *Quijote* has no plot to interrupt. There *is* a unity in the *Quijote*, however. It is not in the plot but in the overall psychological truth of the story — a total vision of life. Cervantes, in effect, is attempting to tell us that the main emphasis should not be placed on the adventures of the central characters.

The technique that governs the *Quijote* is irony, and irony becomes extended to the composition itself. If the interpolations interrupt the main plot, Cervantes at times arranges the narration so that the main plot breaks in on the interpolated stories.

121. García Pavón, Francisco. "La Mancha que vio Cervantes." *Anales Cervantinos*, IV (1954), 119-137. [Appreciation is expressed to James Benjamin Tate for his assistance in the preparation of this summary.]

Why did Cervantes choose La Mancha as the setting for his masterpiece? Not out of any desire to satirize a particular Manchegan, as some have contended. Nor because he knew La Mancha better than other regions of Spain. It was because he sought to select the most unexotic location possible. The author's game was to prevent his Knight from seeing anything resembling the stuff of his chivalresque dreams, in order to confront him with harsh reality.

La Mancha was a region admirably suited for such a purpose; and the fact that the title of the novel includes the non-epic name of La Mancha indicates a certain caricature of the flashy titles of chivalry novels with their exotic settings.

In the *Quijote* we have a traveler's view of La Mancha, the same view which the author had had of that area. But Cervantes was not so much interested in setting as in people. He presents many types from his epoch, a human republic of the seventeenth century.

122. Garciasol, Ramón de. *Claves de España: Cervantes y el "Quijote."* Madrid: Ediciones Cultura Hispánica, 1965. Pp. 316.

[In the prologue to his work Garciasol reviews previous interpretations of the *Quijote* and condemns those critics who view Cervantes as having only an average mind and who consider the *Quijote* as having no elevated interpretation of the world.

The first part of this work is devoted to Cervantes' life and the second part to the *Quijote*. Garciasol views Cervantes as a writer who knew how to capture the tragicomedy of life — its beauty as well as its *finitud*. To Garciasol this is the key to the author's intellectual irony, his lyric humor, the eternity of his work.

In Chapter XVII the critic concludes that what had to be said in the *Quijote* was so painful that Cervantes, in order not to make the novel indecent, had to tell his story with poetic grace and with a superior smile. In Chapter XXXIII, "Sabiduría cervantina," Garciasol concludes that Cervantes believed that man is a creature of responsibility and of *antevisión*. Cervantes, the critic states, did not believe in leaving life to chance, for to him that was a sign of inferiority. This idea is echoed in Chapter XXIV where the *Quijote* is referred to as "el ejemplario de la responsabilidad."]

123. Garciasol, Ramón de. "Cinco aspectos de la vida en el *Quijote*." *Cuadernos de Literatura*, III, núms. 8-9 (Marzo-Junio, 1948), 229-246.

Don Quijote is a *caballero*, an archetype taken from the soul of Spain. Dulcinea, who exists in the heart of the Knight, represents the yearning for an ideal. She gives men strength; she causes men to lose their melancholy. Love is a second birth for

Don Quijote, and virtue, in Cervantes' novel, is a creative energy capable of reforming individuals and peoples. The Knight is the exaltation of the individual. He is the perfect demonstration of how the most holy ideal can become invalidated if one does not realize that it must be carried out in a particular environment. The environment, the street as it were, is a corrosive that dissolves the false, and at times even the true.

124. Garrone, Marco A. "*L'Orlando furioso* considerato come fonte del *Quijote*." *Rivista d'Italia*, XIV (1911), 95-124.

The *Orlando furioso* was beyond doubt one of the most important inspirations for the *Quijote*. The idea of satirizing chivalry novels has many passible sources, but Ariosto's poem seems the most likely. In addition, there are reminiscences of *Orlando furioso* in numerous scenes in Cervantes' novel: Andrés, the Biscayan, Marcela, Micomicona, Montesinos, the Knight's Penance, Clavileño, Cardenio, and Ginés de Pasamonte. The tale of the *Curious Impertinent* is taken directly from Ariosto's poem.

In spite of the great influence of *Orlando furioso* on the *Quijote* there are many essential differences between these two works. There is little of the classical in Cervantes' novel, whereas in Ariosto's work it is abundant; in *Orlando* there is a great deal of the impossible, while in the *Quijote* there is little or none; with Ariosto the irony is almost unconscious, whereas Cervantes is deliberately ironic; Cervantes appears to be more moral and religious than the Italian poet; the madness of Orlando is a madness of love, whereas the Knight's folly springs from the excessive reading of chivalry novels; Ariosto chooses a known epic figure as his hero, while Cervantes creates a totally new personality; Orlando goes completely insane, while Don Quijote is mad on only one subject; Orlando is tragically insane because he is an epic figure, whereas the Knight is humorous in his madness; *Orlando furioso* is art for art's sake while the *Quijote* is educative in its social satire; Ariosto is objective and is interested in his characters only from an artistic point of view, while Cervantes is envolved with his figures and at times even appears to become his heroes.

125. Gerhardt, Mia I. *Don Quijote, la vie et les livres*. Amsterdam: Noord-Hollandsche Uitgevers Maatschappij, 1955. Pp. 71.

Books are an essential part of the *Quijote* and literature is the *protagoniste disincarné et omniprésent du livre*. Almost all the characters in the *Quijote* are interested in literature, one way or the other. Sancho is the only nonreader of note, and curiously he is the only one taken in by his master's talk of chivalry. Largely because he is illiterate, the Squire cannot distinguish between the literary assertions and the realistic assertions which the Don makes.

Cervantes contents himself with the role of second author and adopts the fictitious historian technique. This is in part a satire of chivalry novels, but has more subtle purposes. Cervantes, by using this device, gains distance from his work and is also able to anticipate the objections of the reader. In fact he places himself on the reader's side in advance. Although the *Quijote* is supposedly a true history, a chronicler cannot be a *romancier*, and vice versa. Cervantes clearly sees the inverisimilitude of this position.

Don Quijote reads with complete participation and fully identifies with the heroes of the books of chivalry, whom he imitates at times unconsciously, at times with premeditation. He pictures himself as already in a book of chivalry. Don Quijote desires fame, but as a figure of literature. He even pictures the *sabio* historian who will write a history of his exploits, a historian very like the one Cervantes has actually chosen. But since Don Quijote is able to give himself a surname, the *sabio* is not really free to write what he desires. Cervantes thus amuses himself with two parallel fictions: denying the *sabio* this liberty of control over facts just as he denies himself the right to be the true author.

Literature causes Don Quijote to create Dulcinea, and literature tells him what qualities to give her. She is more a myth than a person. From the beginning of Part II Don Quijote states that he has never seen Dulcinea. Thus her identification with Aldonza Lorenzo no longer exists. Here Cervantes sacrifices burlesque possibilities in order to achieve more interesting psychological results.

In the 1615 *Quijote* people recognize the Knight. While this may lessen the spontaneity of Part II, this mirror technique (of Part I becoming a portion of Part II) adds depth to the story. The appearance of the false *Quijote* causes Part II to be filled with unusual episodes after Chapter LIX. Cervantes cannot leave well enough alone, for Avellaneda obsesses him. It is wrong for Cervantes to imply that Avellaneda's Don Quijote was a real person like his own Knight. All in all, Cervantes should have left the false *Quijote* alone.

126. Gillet, Joseph E. "The Autonomous Character in Spanish and European Literature," *Hispanic Review*, XXIV (1956), 179-190.

[Gillet points out indications of the independence of a character from his or her author in medieval and renaissance works. This tendency is quite strong, he notes, in Francisco Delicado's *Lozana andaluza* where several figures suggest their independence of their creator. While fiction overflows its frame in the *Quijote*, Gillet states, reality may suddenly emerge from fiction, and the world of a fictional character may be suddenly transformed into a world of reality where the fictional character is master of his fate. Cervantes, Gillet observes, created two worlds, never clearly separated, and some of his characters are equally at home in either; they often casually cross the fluctuating line between imagination and reality.]

127. Gilman, Stephan. "Los inquisidores literarios de Cervantes." *Actas del tercer congreso internacional de hispanistas celebrado en México, D. F., del 26 al 31 de agosto de 1968*. Publicadas bajo la dirección de Carlos H. Magis. México: El Colegio de México, 1970, pp. 3-25.

What is Cervantes attempting to tell us with his simple declaration about the intention of the *Quijote*? He wishes to call our attention to the deep interrelationship and the interdependence between the critical activity and the creative activity in his art of writing. In the *Quijote*, more than in any other work, there is a systematic, conscious and calculated plan to combine creative invention with critical meditation. Or, expressed in another way, the *Quijote* was written in a continuous act of critical creation and creative criticism.

In the *escrutinio* the priest acts as the District Attorney and the barber as the lawyer for the defense. The priest charges that the *Amadís* was the source of infection in Spain. The barber answers that the *Amadís* founded no sect and that its generative power makes it unique in its kind. If Cervantes chose the image of a book-burning Inquisition, he did it not for what it has of violence but as an analogy to show us his own critical point-of-view. Others had attacked chivalry novels as sinful and scandalous (Alemán, Avellaneda). Cervantes judges them as works of art. There is here a hidden attack on the Inquisition, for the author subtly implies that the inquisitors do not know what they are talking about. They listen to hearsay evidence and only spare *Amadís'* life for the time being. All in all, Cervantes pictures books as the victims of ignorance, especially that of the niece and the housekeeper. It ought not to surprise us that Cervantes combines a desire to criticize certain books with a satire against those who want to limit the freedom of the reader.

If chivalry novels were a dying genre, why did the author attack them? Because they were being revived in the theatre, as Marco Moriñigo implied in "El teatro como sustituto de la novela" [*RUBA,* II]. In the adventures of the Sierra Morena Cervantes becomes fully aware of the similarity between the chivalry novel and the *comedia*. The priest and the barber change roles, and the novel takes on the aspect of a theatrical farce or masquerade. Fernando is the *burlador* type, and the whole material about Cardenio, Luscinda, Dorotea and Fernando is a complicated honor play. In these episodes Cervantes shows how the reading of chivalresque literature affects the lives of normal people, not merely the life of an eccentric. The lack of reality in their reading corresponds to the lack of authenticity in the social being of these readers. Dorotea is unwilling to be a simple peasant girl, and Cardenio is not willing to be a true gentleman.

Does the Canon of Toledo speak for Cervantes? Did Cervantes want a censor of plays? No! The author was slyly saying, however, that if Spain must have an Inquisition, the Inquisition should help to improve esthetic tastes. Deep down Cervantes knew that the Inquisition was too fanatical to do an intelligent job of esthetic evaluation.

128. Gilman, Stephan. *Cervantes y Avellaneda; Estudio de una imitación*. Traducción del original inédito por Margit Frenk Alatorre. México: El Colegio de México, 1951. Pp. 182.

Cervantes is primarily opposed to chivalry novels because of their lack of artistry, while Avellaneda disliked them because of their immorality and because of their wordly dreams. Avellaneda appears to have thought that Cervantes, after destroying the chivalresque myth, should have gone on to affirm the divine myth. The *Quijote* of 1605 probably appeared to Avellaneda to be a picaresque novel without instruction.

There is a vast difference between Cervantes' hero and Avellaneda's Don Quijote. Cervantes' Knight has an aberration of the will; Avellaneda's Don has an aberration of the intelligence and of the memory. Cervantes' protagonist has a purpose while Avellaneda's does not. Nor does the false Sancho truly resemble Cervantes' Squire. With Avellaneda he is a bestial type who cannot adapt. In short, the false *Quijote* presents a world of negative social values. Cervantes preached virtue while Avellaneda preaches only good manners, viewing the heroes as buffoons lacking in the social graces.

In the second part of Cervantes' *Don Quijote* there are passages very similar to portions of Avellaneda's *Quijote*. Who copied whom? While Menéndez Pidal (196) believes that Cervantes was the imitator, it would appear more likely that Avellaneda heard parts of the 1615 *Quijote* read before a group of Cervantes' friends and drew upon Cervantes' continuation in the preparation of his 1614 version.

129. Goggio, Emilio. "The Dual Role of Dulcinea in Cervantes' *Don Quijote de la Mancha.*" *Modern Language Quarterly*, XIII (1952), 285-291.

There are a number of theories as to the meaning of Dulcinea. Walter Savage Landor, c. 1876, thought that she represented an attack on the worship of the Virgin Mary; Benjumea, c. 1878, believed that Aldonza Lorenzo was the love of wisdom and that Dulcinea was the objective soul of Don Quijote; B. Villegas (314), in 1903, concluded that Dulcinea represented the fatherland. Unamuno (309) in 1905 asserted that she represented glory.

In reality, there are two Dulcineas just as there are two Don Quijotes, and each Dulcinea has a function in accordance with the two purposes of the book: (1) to destroy the vogue of chivalry novels; (2) to bring back the essence of chivalry.

130. Gonthier, Denys Armand. *El drama psicológico del Quijote.* Prólogo de Julián Marías. Madrid: Ediciones Studium, 1962. Pp. 216.

The reconciliation of Christian ideals with pagan wisdom creates the tension which makes the *Quijote* a true psychological drama. In effect, Don Quijote is both Erasmian and tridentine, both a Renaissance courtier and a knight of the Middle Ages.

In the *Quijote* there is created for the first time a complex and dynamic person. For the first time the psychological problem of the human being is expressed. The contradiction which is the basis of the *Quijote* is the same as that of the novels of Flaubert, Dostoyevski and Galdós — the contradiction between what man thinks he is (and wants to be) and what he actually is.

The real lesson of the *Quijote* is not to give up. While some state that the hero of Cervantes' novel dies when he loses his illusions, it is more correct to conclude that he loses his illusions when he dies.

131. Goyanes, J[osé]. *La tipología de el Quijote. Ensayo sobre la estructura psicosomática de los personajes de la novela.* Prólogo del doctor G. Marañón. Madrid: S. Aguirre, 1932, Pp. xvi + 297.

Don Quijote is *leptosómico-atlético* in body type. Perhaps he is Jaensch's type B (Basedowoide), a very emotional person inclined toward impressionability and toward bizarre expression. The Knight is also *esquizotímico* and is insecure in sexual relations. He represses his sexual urges, and this repression leads to his hurling himself out into the world. His basic sexual drives rebel against suppression, but the Knight succeeds in ennobling his rebelling desires.

Sancho is *pícnico* and *ciclotímico*. He is attracted by objects in the real world. (With the Knight objects only serve as stimuli for his subjective state.) The Squire is *medio ciclotímico,* a happy medium between a manic state and depression. He is easy-going. His most notable trait is the fluctuation of his general state of mind between sadness and joy. The Don's strongest characteristic is his tendency to react emotionally (positively or negatively) to a given situation. Don Quijote is an *esquizotímico superior;* he is *hiperestésico,* bordering on *autismo.*

It is impossible to say whether the Knight is truly insane, since he is a fictional character. He appears, however, to be suffering from a form of paranoia characterized by delusions of grandeur. His feeling that highborn ladies are madly in love with him is typically paranoid. The Knight's delirium is further characterized by a desire to achieve glory by bringing justice into the world.

Don Quijote's personality changes during the course of the novel. At the beginning of Part I many adventures befall him simply because he desires them to happen. As the novel moves along, his illusions grow milder. He begins to see inns as inns, not as castles. Sancho changes even more than his mater. The Squire begins as a simple peasant but becomes infected with ideals. Though Don Quijote and Sancho are opposites in their vital structures, they both become elevated to the same spiritual level.

In the *Quijote* there are both comic and tragic elements, and in this novel there is an oscillation between these two attitudes toward existence. The tragic arises from the noble, conscious struggle against powerful forces that act against human existence. Tragedy is not pessimistic; it is deeply optimistic, heroic, a triumph of the spirit over life, an affirmation of the personality. *Don Quijote* is tragic in that the hero suffers physically in order to achieve spiritual values.

There are many comic elements in *Don Quijote.* The comic is a negation, a triumph of the material, the acceptance of one's fate. Cervantes' novel is more serious and transcendentally humorous than comic. The author, for example, makes fun of himself and of his own defects of style. This is true humor.

Don Quijote and Sancho are not drawn from real life. They are almost mythological figures into whom the author has breathed life; and this breath of life makes these figures universal and eternal.

132. Green, Otis H. "El *Ingenioso* Hidalgo." *Hispanic Review,* XXV (1957), 175-193.

The adventures that occur to Don Quijote could have happened only to a choleric type of person. From Huarte's sixteenth-century study of temperaments, we see that Cervantes sought to describe a person in whom yellow bile (choler) prevailed over blood, melancholy (black bile), and phlegm. Due to this chemical imbalance the Knight is by nature a man of great enthusiasm and quick to anger. This enthusiasm causes the Don to develop a passion (for chivalry books), and this passion deprives him of sleep. Not having sleep, his brain dries up, giving free rein to the imaginative and the visionary.

In order for a person to be *ingenioso* he would have to be choleric, under then medical theories. The flow and ebb of *cólera* determine the alternation of Don Quijote's spates of *disparates* with his lucid intervals.

133. Green, Otis H. "Realidad, voluntad y gracia en Cervantes." *Ibérida*, núm. 5 (Junio, 1961), pp. 113-128.

Don Quijote so desires his own continued, conscious survival that he makes it true. At the beginning of the story he desires his helmet to be repaired and declares the job done. In the Sierra Morena episode he asserts that Dulcinea is a creation of his will. At the end of Part I he declares that he is enchanted and will hear no arguments to the contrary. Yet at times he doubts. In fact he knows that part of his existence as a knight-errant is fantasy. He reveals this in Chapter XXXI of Part II where he states that only after his acceptance by the *Duques* did he feel himself a true knight. Later, however, he begins to doubt again, especially about the truth of the events in the cave of Montesinos. Thus in his lucid intervals he will doubt, but in his violent moods, which are simply the result of his choleric sickness, he does not doubt.

Why does the Don wish to falsify truth? To fulfill himself as a superior man, to have the fame of a hero. His fantastic megalomania causes him to distort the truth, and this weakens his idealism. He becomes a danger to society. Chapter VIII of Part II is the first indication of the change that will take place in the hero at the end. Here the Knight speaks of *fama santa* as opposed to *fama infame*. In Chapter LVIII he feels humble when he views the statues of the four saints and seeks to find a better path to glory. From this point on, Cervantes will cause his hero to suffer a series of indignities so that he may become transfigured in two ways: (1) he will lose the *cólera* that caused his madness by going through a series of events which will bring on melancholy, the opposite of *cólera*; (2) he will lose his pride and vainglory and embrace humility. But Don Quijote backslides from time to time and even after his defeat in Barcelona thinks of eternal fame as a shepherd-poet.

At first Don Quijote is ruled by his will. He is not ready for the grace of God. Later, in Chapters VIII and LVIII of Part II, he desires to remove himself from his error. He feels the presence of God but does not see clearly. Only through the mercy of God is he saved. At the end, through "natural" means (sleep and the *frío humor melancólico*) he receives the final mercy.

134. Grierson, Herbert. "*Don Quixote:* Some War-time Reflections on Its Character and Influence." *The English Association,* Pamphlet No. 48 (January, 1921). Pp. 22.

Don Quijote is human, not mystic, not sentimental, not cynical. It is playfully ironic and gives the reader an armor against outrageous fortune. The *Quijote* is the first modern novel for several reasons. It has the proper style; Cervantes seems to take you by the hand and converse with you agreeably on the road — apostrophizing, commenting, digressing. The subject matter of this novel is also modern. It deals with human nature and the ordinary life of men. The characters are real people in a real world. Cervantes poured himself into his creation in a torrent of sympathy and humor and made his hero the perennial symbol of dream-ridden humanity. Don Quijote, the man, is great because he is neither a mere dreamer nor a hateful buffoon like Hudibras, but a man of high character and fine sanity, a gentleman and a scholar. Cervantes inextricably mixes sanity and madness in his hero without any suggestion of unreality or sentimentality such as would inevitably have marred a character drawn on deliberately preconceived lines.

Don Quijote is the happiest of books because it renews our faith in humanity, not only by its sunny but unsentimental picture of normal everyday life and character, but because its twin heroes are of all men the most happy: the idealist whose faith no disappointment can altogether destroy, and the common man who takes life as he finds it.

135. Guillén, Claudio. "Luis Sánchez, Ginés de Pasamonte y los inventores del género picaresco." *Homenaje a Rodríguez Moñino*, I. Madrid: Editorial Castalia, 1966, pp. 221-231.

Although *Lazarillo de Tormes* was published in 1554, it was not really read until the end of the sixteenth century. Its successor, *Guzmán de Alfarache*, 1599, by Mateo Alemán, was very successful and caused a revival of interest in *Lazarillo*. Between 1599 and the appearance of Part I of the *Quijote* the concept of a picaresque novel comes into being. Hence Ginés de Pasamonte's remark about "aquel género" of books. Cervantes saw *Lazarillo* as a new type of literature, but he opposed its pseudoautobiographical nature. Cervantes' rejection of this form had a great effect on the history of the European novel.

136. Guillén, Jorge. "Vida y muerte de Alonso Quijano." *Romanische Forschungen*, LXIV (1952), 102-113.

After the Don's defeat Alonso Quijano cannot go on living; he cannot resign himself to his luck. He could renounce books of chivalry but he could not renounce the vocation of *gran caballero* and still live. Alonso Quijano dies because he does not want to live. It is not a question of his dying for *ejemplaridad moral* like Anselmo *el curioso* or Carrizales, *el celoso extremeño*, both of whom were impertinent. Life is inherently a drama because it is the frenetic struggle to be in fact what we are in potential. For Alonso Quijano the most interesting thing is not the struggle of man with the world or with his external destiny, but the struggle of man with his calling.

137. Gutiérrez-Noriega, Carlos. "La contribución de Miguel Cervantes a la psiquiatría." *Cuadernos Americanos*, XV (1944), 82-92.

Psychiatry as an independent discipline did not exist in Cervantes' time, and thus the author of the *Quijote* does not study mental illness in a systematic or scholarly manner. Nevertheless, some of his works, such as the *Quijote* and the *Licenciado Vidriera*, appear to be true case histories of insanity.

Cervantes is the first to discover the connection between constitutional type and madness. In the *Quijote* he deals with a chronic madness brought on in part by the environment (chivalric ideas) and in part by the hero's *leptosómico* body-type. The Knight is painted as a true schizoid personality. The Squire is described as a *ciclotímico,* even *hipomaniaco,* manic-depressive. The author, however, causes his protagonists to act sanely at times, and this indicates that he meant to symbolize something common to the sane and the insane. The idea that reality and fantasy are not mutually exclusive, but parts of the same thing, is typically Spanish, but this concept reaches its peak in the *Quijote* where Cervantes shows that sanity and insanity are not clearly separable. Sancho, at first, seems perfectly sane, and Don Quijote appears to be quite mad. But there comes a time when the roles are reversed and the reader vacillates in his judgment as to who is sane and who is insane.

138. Gutiérrez-Noriega, Carlos. "La personalidad y el carácter en la obra de Cervantes." *Revista de Neuro-psiquiatría,* X, No. 4 (1947), 516-541.

Cervantes' great contribution to literature is his creation of complex characters in whom there are conflicts between reason and belief, between blind obedience to principles and free will. Cervantes insists on the responsibility of the individual, whereas previous writers had subordinated the individual to cultural values. The author of the *Quijote* saw freedom as an essential quality of man. Cervantes, unlike classical writers, does not emphasize absolute values such as destiny and passion, but instead gives great weight to the unstable, the dynamic, the variable, showing that a thing can be either itself or its opposite.

Cervantes combines the serious and the comic in the same character. This is something new, something not even found in Shakespeare. The humor of Cervantes' characters is in their duality: the Don is both sane and mad; Sancho is both simple-minded and shrewd.

139. Haley, G. "The Narrator in *Don Quijote:* Maese Pedro's Puppet Show." *Modern Language Notes,* LXXX (1965), 145-165.

Cervantes' use of the fictitious author technique is a satire of similar devices used in chivalry novels. However, the author of the *Quijote* was able to make this device come alive, and to show the dynamic interplay of a story, its dramatized tellers and its dramatized readers, all in the process of becoming. Along with the story of Don Quijote and Sancho there is another story: how that story came to be known and set down, a record of that story's written stages. This secondary tale develops its own entanglements and moments of suspense that have nothing to do with the main plot. The characters in this supplementary novel are: (1) the unidentified *I* who begins the story and who surrenders control at the end of Chapter VIII of Part I; (2) the *segundo autor,* who takes over and who describes himself as a frustrated reader of the first eight chapters; (3) the translator; (4) Cide Hamete Benengeli; (5) the shadowhy figure who materializes at the end of Chapter VIII, Part I, to join the first author's fragment to that of the second author, and who reappears in the final chapter of Part I to supply the concluding remarks; this figure is the farthest removed intermediary from the Knight's adventures and the closest to the reader.

Each intermediary acts as a critical reader of a previous version, and none forgets the reader. The interplay of the story, the teller and the reader is repeated in countless variations. The most vivid illustration of this interplay is Maese Pedro's puppet show, because the teller, the story and the listener are all literally dramatized. This puppet show is a climax in a series of dehumanized mimicries: people imitating donkeys, monkeys imitating people, etc. The assistant to Maese Pedro is the narrator. His narrative style overshadows the dialogue. He confuses his tenses, slipping from the present into the imperfect and the preterite. Also, he injects personal comments. The assistant is thus a narrator who is both part of the creative act and also the ideal spectator. Maese Pedro is the author of the play and breaks in to offer a commentary.

He knows the story of Melisendra is fiction, and is not interested in his assistant's claim that it is historically accurate. Cervantes uses a technique kin to Brecht's *Verfremdungseffekt* to keep the reader from falling into the illusion that the story of Melisendra is real. The main plot and the play of Melisendra have a number of similarities. Both have a series of intruding authors. Both are a tissue of ballads. The mock heroic tone of Maese Pedro's assistant is similar to the tone of the main narrative. Melisendra's leaping onto the croup of the horse is quite like the incident in which the enchanted "Dulcinea" does the same.

140. Hatzfeld, Helmut. "Boccacciostil im *Don Quijote*," in *Vom Geiste neuer Literaturforschung. Festschrift für Oscar Walzel.* Herausgegeben von J. Wahle und V. Klemperer. Wildpark-Potsdam: Akademische Verlagsgesellschaft Athenaion, M.B.H., 1924, pp. 113-126.

Boccaccio influenced not only the form of Cervantes' *Novelas ejemplares* but had a deep effect on the Spaniard's style in general. Antithesis and the rhetorical question are common in both writers, as is the use of epithets both open and closed. Boccaccio's prose, based on medieval Latin letters, is characterized by frequent vocatives and by the interweaving of short relative clauses. Cervantes follows the Italian in this type of sentence structure. In fact, the opening line of the 1605 *Quijote* is written in the style of Boccaccio.

141. Hatzfeld, Helmut. *El "Quijote" como obra de arte del lenguaje.* 2nd Spanish ed. revised and extended. Madrid: C. S. I. C., 1966. Pp. xvi + 371. (Based on *"Don Quijote" als Wortkunstwerk; die einzelnen Stilmittel und ihr Sinn.* Leipzig-Berlin: B. G. Tuebner, 1927. First Spanish edition 1949: Madrid, Patronato del IV Centenario del Nacimiento de Cervantes.)

There are eight motifs in the *Quijote:* (1) the chivalresque mission; (2) the praise of Dulcinea; (3) the calm of the Knight of La Mancha; (4) the chivalresque anger; (5) the *cuerdo-loco* theme; (6) the ambition of Sancho to be governor; (7) Sancho's threats to return home; and (8) the enchantment of Dulcinea. The chivalresque mission is a constant idea and has certain set phrases that accompany it. The Dulcinea (inspirer) motif also has many varied expressions that go with it, and Sancho twists these phrases just as he does the chivalric verbiage. Motif (3), the Knight's calm, carries a number of set expressions such as "con mucho sosiego." Anger, motif (4), is the counter-motif to calm, and there are graded variations between them, ranging from slight annoyance to rage. The *cuerdo-loco* motif is especially strong in Part II. It reflects the central tone of the novel — *ambiguity*. It is this factor which allows so many interpretations of the *Quijote*. The ambiguity arises from the fact that the line between sanity and madness is unstable. Sancho's motifs are secondary and are counterpoint motifs. These follows the calm-anger characterization of Don Quijote and do not have an independent existence.

The *Quijote* contains many contrasts or antitheses: Don Quijote-Sancho; *cuerdo-loco; sosiego-cólera; gobierno-vuelta a casa*. There are others which arise from the hero's madness: inn-castle; flock-army; mills-giants. The Don Quijote-Sancho contrast undergoes many stylistic shades. At times there is hardly any contrast at all.

Cervantes saw that chivalry novels were a loose string of events, and sought to bring unity to his own work. The enchantment motif is protracted until the end of the novel in order to bring about this unity. Sansón is also a unifying element. He bridges the gap between Part I and Part II by his references back to the earlier part. There is a *vinculación continua* in the *Quijote*; characters often reappear: Andrés, Tosilos, Ricote, Ginés de Pasamonte. Also, the foretelling device adds unity. At times there is a spiritual *enlace*. For example, Sancho's falling into a ravine is related to the Knight's descent into the cave of Montesinos.

The spirit of the Counter Reformation in the *Quijote* is obvious. Cervantes is a devout Catholic, and is not sanctimonius or hypocritical in his references to the Church. Cervantes' remark about freedom of conscience in Germany is neither a condemnation of Spain nor or a praise of Germany.

142. Hatzfeld, Helmut. "Das Stilproblem bei Cervantes." *Spanische Philologie und Spanischer Unterricht*, No. 6 (1926), pp. 1-8.

One cannot speak of the development of Cervantes' style from idealistic toward realistic and then back to idealistic. Idealism and realism accompany the author during his entire literary career and continually enrich his style.

The pastoral style is not just a fad with Cervantes. It gives him an opportunity to use classical speech. In general he does not poke fun at the pastoral style, nor does he mock the chivalry-novel style as such, merely the bad chivalry-novel style. The Italian style, such as that found in the *Curioso*, is characterized by the abundant usage of analogies, and Cervantes cannot altogether escape this technique. The realistic or picaresque style in the *Quijote* begins with the appearance of Sancho, and the episode of the galley slaves constitutes a miniature picaresque novel. The humorous style often involves the use of plays on words; and the syntactical joining of incongruent elements can often have a comic effect. The religious style in Cervantes' works, as in Part II of *Don Quijote,* is, in reality a baroque re-doing of the chivalresque and pastoral style.

143. Hatzfeld, Helmut. "Thirty Years of Cervantes Criticism." *Hispania,* XXX (1947), 321-328.

Impressionistic critics see Cervantes as apart from the limits of his epoch. Other critics view the author as a reactionary, while still others, such as Américo Castro (63), consider him a non-conformist. Castro supposes a Cervantes in whom an intellectual relativism is manifested by the motif of the *engaño a los ojos;* in whom a world relativism disguises sin by the euphemism *error;* in whom aristocratic idealism is symbolized by Don Quijote *el sabio,* full of contempt for the gregarious, vulgar spirit of Sancho *el necio,* representing the masses of the people. Jean Cassou (61) believes that Cervantes' novel is a poetic though tragic vision of the modern world erected on the débris of the Middle Ages. Thomas Mann (190) emphasizes Cervantes' political relativism, believing that the Spaniard is hypocritical when his loyalty towards Spain and his personal feelings are supposedly at odds — as in the Ricote episode. Joseph Bickermann (38) develops an anti-superman school of thought and concludes that the Knight is a reprehensible extreme.

A psychologist school is represented by J. Goyanes (131) and José V. Castro Silva (76). The former sees the Knight as a schizothymic and the Squire as cyclothymic. Castro Silva regards the two parts of the *Quijote* as different techniques in bringing the hero back into society.

A Communist school of interpretation has Pavel I. Novitsky (221) as one of its representatives, a critic who believes that Don Quijote and Sancho represent the tragic dualism of a bourgeois-class civilization hesitating between an aimless dream of spiritualism and a well-planned policy of money-making, without the courage to choose between the two.

Cervantes is embued with the Renaissance and its Erasmian attempts to combine Christian standards with Humanism, but he is writing at a time when Erasmian harmony had given away to radical, theocentric Christianity. Is Cervantes renaissance or Baroque? This is quite difficult to say. Ludwig Pfandl (235) sees him as typically renaissance and anti-baroque. Aubrey Bell (31) also views Cervantes as renaissance, but in a very different way — as a man who harmoniously adapts to the Council of Trent.

Mario Casella (60) concludes that Don Quijote represents the essentials of the Augustinian-Thomistic tradition in metaphysics, esthetics, and ethics. To Casella, the Knight is struggling to set up the City of God on earth. Cervantes, under this school of thought, is the last of the Medievalists.

A "Baroque Man" school has been developed by Marcel Bataillon (29) and Joaquín Casalduero (58), the former examining the baroque subject matter in Cervantes' works and the latter studying their baroque form.

144. Hatzfeld, Helmut. "Results from *Quijote* Criticism since 1947." *Anales Cervantinos*, II (1952), 129-157.

Prior to 1947 *Don Quijote* criticism was paralyzed by two myths: (1) that Don Quijote represented idealism, the prototype of a Spaniard who did not care about external success (Unamuno); (2) that Cervantes was a non-conforming Erasmian, a Platonic thinker, a hater of the Counter Reformation [Américo Castro's *Pensamiento* (63).] Both approaches appear to be wrong. It is a mistake to think of Don Quijote as another Ignatius Loyola, as

Voltaire, John Bowle, D'Alembert and Unamuno (309) do. It is also wrong to view Cervantes as a wise fool, scoffing at the ideals of his epoch and his nation, as a sceptic with hypocritical protestations of orthodoxy, as Américo Castro does (63). *Don Quijote*, as Toffanin (300) revealed in 1920, is a product of the Baroque in style and content, and has nothing to do with Enlightenment. Cervantes was an anti-Humanist ascetic. Liberals are disturbed by Cervantes' open anti-Semitic, anti-Negro, anti-Protestant remarks, and this group of critics mistakenly attempts to show that such remarks were feigned.

145. Hatzfeld, Helmut. "¿Don Quijote asceta?" *Nueva Revista de Filología Hispánica*, II (1948), 57-70.

Don Quijote is convinced that he possesses great virtue, even as much virtue as a saint. But this Don Quijote is based only on his own words. There is, however, another Don Quijote — proud, fearful of his life, irascible. This Don is not really interested in serving others; he primarily desires fame.

Don Quijote seeks to be an *asceta*, the highest form of morality in the Golden Age. In practice he fails. What does this mean to Cervantes? Just that illusions make man fall below the ideals to which he aspires.

If we only look at the Knight's conduct, we might well conclude that Cervantes is an existentialist, a vitalist. But this overlooks the Don's ever-recurring defeats and his conversion at the end. This repentance is not a beatification but the logical, Christian reorientation of a soul fallen into error.

146. Hatzfeld, Helmut. "Artistic Parallels in Cervantes and Velásquez," in *Estudios dedicados a Menéndez Pidal*, III (1952), 265-297.

A generation separates Cervantes from the painter Velásquez, yet they are similar in several of their techniques. Both poetically uplift daily life; neither is purely realistic nor completely idealistic. There is a great feeling of time and space in the works of both of these geniuses. Each uses an impressionistic technique in the portrayal of characters. Cervantes and Velásquez have a penchant for grotesque characters, and both employ a *chiaroscuro* technique at times. In addition, these two masters take an equally ironic view of mythology, and both use self-criticism as part of their artistic style.

147. Hatzfeld, Helmut. "The baroque of Cervantes and the baroque of Góngora exemplified by the motif 'las bodas'." *Anales Cervantinos*, III (1953), 87-119.

There are two types of baroque: (1) manneristic, a late renaissance development; and (2) impressionistic or tridentine. El Greco and Góngora are manneristic, while Cervantes and Velásquez are impressionistic. Both Cervantes and Góngora are baroque in that they attempt to cope with the tensions of life which are, after the Renaissance, seen again in their Christian depth. Cervantes approaches these tensions with humor, while Góngora makes a conscious flight into a wake-dream of incarnate *piropos*. Cervantes is moral; Góngora is amoral. While both deal with the motif "las bodas," Cervantes uses decaying renaissance forms merely to underline the grandiose or to add irony. He creates a new view on life with all its accepted Christian tensions, in full appreciation of post-tridentine dignity, and replaces the wanton decorations with a solid new content which makes the renaissance tradition almost unrecognizable. Cervantes thus creates out of a new philosophy the real Baroque, the Spanish, the Velasquian, the impressionistic, the fertile Baroque.

148. Hatzfeld, Helmut, ed. *Don Quijote: Forschung und Kritik*. Darmstadt: Wissenschaftliche Buchgesellschaft, 1968. Pp. 499.

[Professor Hatzfeld gathers together the following excellent essays, all written since 1947 and all rendered in German: A. F. G. Bell's "The Wisdom of Don Quijote" (32); A. A. Parker's "El concepto de la verdad en el *Quijote*" (230); Amado Alonso's "Las prevaricaciones idiomáticas de Sancho"; Guillermo Díaz Plaja's "La técnica narrativa de Cervantes" (93); a selection from Joaquín Casalduero's *Sentido y forma del Quijote* (58); Dámaso Alonso's "Sancho-Quijote, Sancho-Sancho" (5); Rafael de Balbín Lucas' "Lo trágico y lo cómico mezclado: Nota al capítulo XXXV de la primera parte del *Quijote*"; Eleanor O'Kane's "The Proverb: Rabelais and Cervantes"; Erich Auerbach's "Die verzauberte Dulcinea" (14); Helmut Hatzfeld's "Artistic Parallels in Cervantes and Velásquez" (146); Emilio Goggio's "The Dual Role of Dulcinea in Cervantes' *Don Quijote de la Mancha*" (129); José F. Montesinos' "Cervantes Anti-novelista" (207); Jorge Luis Borges' "Análisis del último capítulo del *Quijote*" (49); Richard L. Predmore's "La función del encantamiento en el mundo del *Quijote*"; a selection from Harald Weinrich's *Das Ingenium Don Quijotes* (317); Manuel Criado de Val's "*Don Quijote* como diálogo" (84); Otis H. Green's "El ingenioso hidalgo" (132); J.-J. A. Bertrand's "La naissance du chef-d'œuvre" (37); Alan S. Trueblood's "El silencio en el *Quijote*" (305); Raymond Immerwahr's "Structural Symmetry in the Episodic Narratives of *Don Quijote*, Part One" (158); Martín de Riquer's "Estilo del *Quijote*" (253); and the final chapter of E. C. Riley's *Cervantes' Theory of the Novel* (248). In his *Einleitung*, Hatzfeld comments briefly on each of the essays included in this collection and notes the increased interest since 1947 in the existentialistic and stylistic elements in the *Quijote*.]

149. Hazard, Paul. *Don Quichotte de Cervantes. Étude et analyse.* Paris: Mellottée, 1931. Pp. 378.

Many types of prior literature had a great influence upon the *Quijote:* the chivalry novel, the pastoral, the ballad, the picaresque, the Italian *novella*. There is also a great deal of renaissance mockery in Cervantes' masterpiece. This *burla*, a social art in the Renaissance, achieves, in the author's hands, a place of honor, even epic proportions.

The *Quijote*, besides provoking laughter, poses many irritating questions, such as the limits between sanity and insanity. The general attitude of the novel, however, is to laugh goodnaturedly at life, to advise the reader to mind his own business. Though Don Quijote cannot adapt to this, we should not necessarily want him to. The world would perish if there were no Don Quijotes among us. The Don awakens admiration in us, little by little. After reading the *Quijote* we feel adhesion to life, even though the novel is a critique of life.

150. Hendrix, W. S. "Sancho Panza and the Comic Types of the Sixteenth Century," in *Homenaje a Menéndez Pidal: Miscelánea*

de estudios lingüísticos e históricos, II. Madrid: Edit. Hernando, S. A. 1925, pp. 485-494.

Menéndez y Pelayo, in *Orígenes de la novela* (200), concluded that the squire in *Cifar* was the only known ancestor of Sancho Panza, but the evidence is not conclusive that Cervantes was acquainted with that work. However, he *was* familiar with the sixteenth-century drama and dialogued novel, both of which contained comic types similar to Cervantes' Squire. There were two types of comics in sixteenth-century plays and dialogued novels: stupid ones and clever ones. Sancho has characteristics of both. Furthermore, a number of these pre-Cervantine works contained abundant proverbs and "asides," both of which are devices used by Sancho. All in all, Cervantes did *not* really need to know of *Cifar* in order to create Sancho.

151. Herrero-García, Miguel. "Cervantes," in *Estimaciones literarias del siglo XVII.* Madrid: Editorial Voluntad, 1930, pp. 353-420.

Bonilla in his *Cervantes y su obra* (44), 1916, is incorrect in concluding that Cervantes' contemporaries considered him *discreto, con decoro e invención.* It is undoubtable that professional critics were adverse to him, for they considered *Don Quijote* to be non-transcendental and lacking in substance and seriousness. Gracián indicated that the *Quijote* was a waste of time, and Juan Valladares de Valdelomar, in 1617, reached a similar conclusion. No one among his contemporaries considered the *Quijote* as anything but a book of entertainment. In the late seventeenth century Cervantes' masterpiece declined in esteem, and is not even mentioned by Saavedra Fajardo in his *República literaria,* 1696.

However, if the *Quijote* is only a work of *invención discreta, escrita con decoro,* why is it referred to so often by writers of fiction (as opposed to moralistic critics)? Creative writers of the seventeenth century saw the *Quijote* as an imposing work. How did they picture Don Quijote? Some saw him as self-sacrificing. Others saw him as Christian. Some pictured him as dauntless, others as arrogant. Some considered him largely laughable, others as insane. Sancho is pictured as loyal, brainless, gluttonous, materialistic, of low aspirations, or cowardly. [Herrero-García discusses many adaptations of the *Quijote*. He further studies the conflicting views of Menéndez Pidal (196) and Cotarelo y Mori (83) in regard to the supposed influence on the *Quijote* of the *Entremés de los romances*.]

152. Hilton, Ronald. "Four Centuries of Cervantes: The Historical Anatomy of a Best-Selling Masterpiece." *Hispania*, XXX (1947), 310-320.

The interpretation of the *Quijote* reflects the history of Western intellectual thought from the seventeenth century to the twentieth century. During that time Cervantes' novel has acquired a rich harmony of overtones. We still, however, do not know the author's original intention in writing his masterpiece, and we probably never will. In recent years the *Quijote* has declined in popularity. Critics who believe that present-day youth enjoys the *Quijote* are wrong. Our youth is practical, and even the most idealistic are overwhelmed by material, political, and international problems. They want something clear and succint, and the *Quijote* is neither.

153. *Hispania*, XXX, No. 3 (August, 1947). *Cervantes Quadricentennial Number*.

[This issue contains eleven articles on Cervantes or his works. The following deal in whole or in part with the *Quijote:* (1) "Four Centuries of Cervantes: The Historical Anatomy of a Best-Selling Masterpiece" (152), by Ronald Hilton; (2) "Thirty Years of Cervantes Criticism" (143), by Helmut Hatzfeld; and (3) "A Travestied *Don Quijote*," by Joseph Fucilla.]

154. Howells, William Dean. "Cervantes," in *My Literary Passions*. New York and London: Harper and Brothers, 1910, pp. 17-24.

The *Quijote's* free and simple design, where event follows event without the fettering control of intrigue, but where all grows naturally out of character and conditions, is the supreme form of fiction. If we ever have a great American novel it must be built upon such large and noble lines.

Don Quijote is always heroic and beautiful; he has a sublime nature. It seems strange that both his noble qualities as well as the indignities that befall him could both flow from the same mind.

155. Hume, Martin. "The National Significance of *Don Quixote*." *The Fortnightly Review*, LXXXII, new series (1907), 652-665.

To understand the *Quijote* we must understand the Spanish race. We must also realize that all great works are the culmination of racial, social or political events. The Spaniard is proud by nature and desires to be mystically selected. He views himself as the center of the cosmos, as uncontrolled. He needs fame in order to avoid extinction. The desire for fame sends Don Quijote forth; the desire for fame caused Cervantes to write his masterpiece.

Under the Catholic rulers the Spaniards became convinced of their superiority and attempted to live up to the impossible, even when living in squalor. A period of disillusionment set in during the sixteenth century. A thirst for realism grew, and *Lazarillo* reflects this thirst. Cervantes saw the greed around him, the cult of sacrificing, the decadence. There are hints as early as the *Galatea* that Cervantes saw a true picture of his country. However, it is doubtful if Cervantes deliberately intended the *Quijote* to be the mouthpiece of a national trend toward realism, though this is possible. The fact is that the Knight's chivalresque madness had also been Spain's madness.

In addition to being national, Cervantes' masterpiece has universal qualities, since it deals with primal human passions. For example, the desire to do good without judgment has been a recurring phenomenon since the beginning of man. In short, the *Quijote* is universal because it is human; it is Spanish because it is founded on the racial instinct to enforce the assertion of the ego by suffering, and voices the great national disillusionment of a ruinous popular obsession.

156. Ibáñez, Jaime. "Cervantes y la novela moderna," in *Miguel de Cervantes Saavedra; homenaje de Insula en el cuarto centenario de su nacimiento, 1547-1947* (202), pp. 223-229.

The system of two simultaneous actions is easy to observe in the *Quijote*, not as a central theme but as an indication of what today has been adopted successfully by several contemporary writers, such as Faulkner.

Both in the *Quijote* and in the present-day novel there is also an anguish over time, a profound separation between real time and psychological time. For the Knight one time is that of his own world; another time is that of real beings. In Huxley one notices this same rupture, this same separation, the existence of two worlds which are united only by subtle threads, and which at times in Joyce are found completely separated.

The interior time determines a series of very individualized special relations, and one of these relations is the orientation which is given exterior events. Each person has to resolve, within his time, the interior importance which a given event has. Don Quijote reduces phenomena to a determined interior state, which is precisely the means by which he unites himself to the social conception of the world. This fact, which apparently is not made specific in the *Quijote,* is made clear in modern works; and this very important factor in the modern novel is drawn from Cervantes.

There is one basic distinction between the heroes of modern novels and Cervantes' Knight. The modern protagonist tends to have the mental characteristics of his social class, whereas the Don's state of mind is permanent in nature. For that reason he is universal.

157. Icaza, Francisco A. de. *El "Quijote" durante tres siglos.* Madrid: Renacimiento, 1918. Pp. 229.

Eighteenth-century England caused anti-Cervantes Spain to re-examine Cervantes' great novel. England had penetrated the Spaniard's deep irony, and had, with Coleridge, seen his pity of human weakness. Some English criticism, however, is quite silly. For example, Sir Walter Scott once remarked that Spaniards in battle saw the Knight of La Mancha in their midst.

Although there were many French translations of the *Quijote* during the seventeenth and eighteenth centuries, that novel was not appreciated in France until the nineteenth century. In fact, it was regarded at times with hostile curiosity, though Saint-Evremond, in 1671, regarded it as the book he would most like to have written.

Although Germans were well aware of the figure Don Quijote in the early seventeenth century, there was no special influence of Cervantes' novel in Germany until the late eighteenth century with Lessing. Romantics, such as Friedrich Schlegel and Schelling, saw Cervantes not as just another satirist, but as a force apart in literary creation.

In Italy the *Quijote* was well-known in spite of the small number of Italian editions. Much of Italian *Quijote* criticism, until recently, has dealt with two matters: (1) comprehension of the text; and (2) a comparison of *Don Quijote* and *Orlando furioso*.

[The last part of this work is entitled *El "Quijote" en su tercer centenario* and is divided into three short chapters. Here Icaza concludes that Cervantes does not have to be annotated to be enjoyed, for the most important thing is the work itself. After a discussion of recent Italian *Quijote* criticism the critic attacks certain students of the *Quijote* as parasites. The original parasitic criticism of the *Quijote*, he states, considered the novel to be a satire on Charles V, the Duke of Alba, or Medinaceli, while recent parasitic criticism amounts to subjective wanderings. Icaza next criticizes those who quibble about the place where the *Quijote* was written. At pages 215 and 223 the critic examines Ortega's (223) assertion that Cervantes is waiting for someone to understand him. Icaza concludes that this statement is erroneous and that there has *not* been a general incomprehension among the readers of the *Quijote*.]

158. Immerwahr, Raymond. "Structural Symmetry in the Episodic Narratives of *Don Quijote*, Part One." *Comparative Literature*, X (1958), 121-135.

There are seven inserted narrations in the 1605 *Quijote*. The first (Marcela episode) and the last (Eugenio's tale) are pastoral. Between Marcela and the *Curioso impertinente* are two stories, Fernando-Dorotea and Cardenio-Luscinda. The denouement of these two tales is postponed until after the reading of the *Curioso* and just prior to the tale of the *Cautivo* (5th narration) and the following episode of Luis and Clara (6th narration). The latter two stories are tied together, since Clara's father is the captive captain's brother. Furthermore, the tale of Clara's father, the judge, and that of the captive tie in with the previous Arms and Letters lecture by Don Quijote, since the judge represents the man of letters and the captive the man of arms. The seven interpolated narrations are like a series of mirrors symmetrically placed around the main action, so as to reflect from different angles the general relation of literature to life. In the first and the last of the episodes (Marcela and Eugenio) love is left unfulfilled; in the center *(El curioso)* a happy marriage is destroyed. On either side of the center, however, love is fulfilled. When one compares the successful love episodes prior to the *Curioso* with the successful love stories after it, one notes a dynamically progressive symmetry, since Clara, for example, is resolute while Luscinda is weak in will. There is also a kind of thematic progress from the three stories preceding the *Curioso* to the three after it. The first three present a general renaissance milieu in which Don Quijote is active, while in the last three interpolated narrations the hero is passive and the characters are participating in the actual affairs of Spain, in its wars and in colonization.

159. Kayser, Wolfgang. "Origen y crisis de la novela moderna." *Cultura Universitaria* (Caracas), núm. 47 (1955), pp. 5-47. [Translated from the German by Aurelio Fuentes Rojo; based on *Entstehung und Krise des modernen Romans*. Stuttgart: J. B. Metzler, 1955. (Sonderdruck aus *Deutsche Vierteljahrsschrift für Literaturwissenschaft und Geistesgeschichte*, XXVIII, Heft 4.)]

Until late in history the narrator of the novel did not enter in contact with the reader nor take part personally in the narrated events, so that his figure becomes lost for us in some inaccesible place. The earlier novelist spoke coldly and anonymously and limited himself to knowing and evaluating. For this reason the novel was not regarded as poetic, but as a work of pure entertainment, until the middle of the eighteenth century with Fielding and others. Fielding states that *Joseph Andrews* was written "in imitation of the manner of Cervantes." Is he referring to the presence of a pair of heroes, or to Cervantes' characters in general? No! It is more likely that Fielding is referring to the Spaniard's technique. This conclusion is confirmed in part by the fact that the

Quijote had been reinterpreted in the mid-eighteenth century. Previously the Knight had been regarded as a fool, a model of incorrect behavior, a figure whose collisions with reality were designed by the author to provoke laughter. With the new interpretation the Don becomes regarded as amiable and natural, as well as ridiculous. He is considered a victim of his own illusions, like the rest of humanity. Besides this, the critics of the mid-eighteenth century believed that Cervantes recognized the hero's noble qualities and that he presented them in a personal way. Cervantes' multitude of perspectives, the multiple stratification with its "disillusion of the disillusion" constituted for Fielding the peculiar aspect of Cervantes' literary technique, an aspect which Fielding renewed and developed in his own way.

The change which was carried out in the interpretation of the *Quijote* can be expressed in a formula: previously considered as a comic novel (in which the comic and the ridiculous depended upon the object), it came to be a humorous novel, because in humour the comic note of things becomes incorporated into the conception of an observer who, one way or the other, adopts a positive attitude. Thus the personal narrator is an indispensable condition of the humorous novel.

These are the distinctive and the original features of the style of Cervantes, Fielding and Wieland: (1) the appearance of a completely personal narrator who intervenes as a mediator and whose activity presents multilateral aspects; (2) the position of the narrated material at the intersection of various perspectives so that the language reaches a peculiar depth; (3) a common bond between the narrator and the reader (in spite of all the narrator's surprises), which common bond is caused by a mutual belief in the naturalness of the story, the naturalness of all the errors of the heart and soul.

Not what is narrated but the spirit of the narrator is, according to Schiller, the special element, the poetic element in a work. Because of their use of this narrative technique, Cervantes and Sterne were regarded by Friedrich Schlegel as supreme artists. As later literature has confirmed, Cervantes, Fielding and Wieland were the creators of the modern novel.

160. Ker, W. P. "Don Quixote," in *Collected Essays of W. P. Ker,*
II. Edited and with an Introduction by Charles Whibley.
London: MacMillan and Co., Limited, 1925, pp. 28-44. (Addressed to the Royal Philosophical Society of Glasgow, 31st of Jan., 1908.)

Don Quijote, to begin with, is a literary burlesque; not a satire on chivalry but a gibe at the ridiculous style and the poor commonplace invention of the degenerate prose romances. It is not a modern democratic assault on the gentle castles of romance. The *Quijote* is one of the largest and roomiest books in the world, a book that has been, to many readers, a revelation of everything that is meant by imaginative freedom; the delightful power of bringing real people before the mind.

Don Quijote is the most careless great work in literature. Part I is not merely a medley of adventures, it is a confusion of styles and literary ideals. No great work was ever so casual as the *Quijote* of 1605. Cervantes was a great humorist and therefore could think of several things at one time. Many commentators see only one intention of the author when he is really working on a number of different meanings all at once.

Cervantes, like Shakespeare, plays fast and loose with the old romantic motifs, and tries to make the best of both worlds. The Marcela episode is the same double game with regard to Arcadia. Marcela opposes the conventional literary theory of the martyrs of love. But the mischief of Marcela's reasonable argument is that it is part of an episode where the pastoral conventions, instead of being exploded, are used by Cervantes as thoroughly and with infinitely greater effect than in his *Galatea.* Cervantes is different from other men of genius. He is much less free than Chaucer, Rabelais or Shakespeare. He is taken in by the solemn pretenses of the learned schools of literature; he believes in the dignity of certain established forms, such as the pastoral and the Greek prose romance. This is the true irony of *Don Quijote* and of the spirit of the age and of the world in which it was written. The author sets out to make fun of books of chivalry; and all the time he is himself in the grip of a delusion as absolute as that of his hero: the authority of the most vacant and pithless of classical superstitions, the phantoms of arcadian romance.

161. King, Willard F. "Unamuno, Cervantes y *Niebla*." *Revista de Occidente*, XVI, 2ª época (1967), 219-231.

Unamuno began, about 1904, to attack Cervantes as a creator by accident, as a man who falsified the manner of the death of his hero. Nevertheless, Unamuno's theory of the *nivola* is heavily indebted to Cervantes. The *nivola* was to have four basic characteristics: (1) an undetermined plot that would develop spontaneously; (2) characters who would create themselves; (3) limited description of setting; (4) an abundance of dialogs and monologs. The *nivola* was also to be tragicomic; it would treat serious matters comically, and comic matters seriously, thus confusing the reader. It would be a constant mixture of "burlas con las veras." This is an exact description of the *Quijote*. In fact, Unamuno must have had Cervantes' masterpiece in mind when he wrote *Niebla*. In both works the problem arises as to who is the real author. Unamuno, less subtly than Cervantes, even enters his own novel. The hero in *Niebla*, Augusto Pérez, is a spiritual twin of Don Quijote. He has little pre-history and becomes alive only when he meets and begins to idealize Eugenia. At the end of both novels the hero dies peacefully.

162. Kommerell, Max. "Humoristiche Personifikation in *Don Quijote*." *Die Neue Rundschau*, IL Jahrgang, Band I (1938), 209-232.

Many types of humor are found in the *Quijote:* the anachronism, the hero's seeing himself differently than others see him, his seeing outside reality differently from others. Also, Cervantes uses the "zwei Deutende" technique, having two viewpoints given: Don Quijote's and Sancho's. It is also comical for Sancho, from time to time, to become part of his master's insanity, and for him to go through all levels of belief and disbelief. Another comic device is the reversal of roles which takes place during the enchantment of Dulcinea. Here Sancho becomes the creator of illusions and Don Quijote the doubter.

The *Quijote* is not a book that has a hidden meaning, for Cervantes is interested in inventing and in building, not in imparting conceptual meanings. Generally speaking, Cervantes is a true son of the Church, and the disillusionment of the hero at death amounts to the overcoming of his tragic *hubris*.

163. Krappe, Alexander Haggerty. "La vrai philosophie du *Don Quijote*." *Bulletin Hispanique*, XXXVI (1934), 129-136.

In his masterpiece Cervantes preaches the quiet life. This is in conflict with the spirit of his times. In effect, Don Quijote is a man of the Renaissance, full of limitless optimism, who seeks the new immortality of personal glory first preached by Petrarch. This optimism of the early sixteenth century gave way to the pessimism of *Lazarillo* well before the end of that century. Cervantes continues this pessimstic trend, satirizing the unbridled optimism of his hero by leading him into numerous absurdities. The basis of Cervantes' pessimism was the events in his own life, his wounds, his slavery in Algiers, the corruption and decadence he saw around him on his return to Spain.

164. Krauss, Werner. *Miguel de Cervantes. Leben und Werk*. Neuwied and Berlin: Luchterhand, 1966. Pp. 253.

There were two opinions of Cervantes in the seventeenth century. Most readers loved the *Quijote,* and a number of playwrights adapted it to the stage. The intellectuals looked down on the *Quijote,* however. Suárez de Figueroa condemned Cervantes for being too autobiographical and self-praising, and Gracián even indicated that Cervantes showed intellectual poverty in his work. Tamayo de Vargas referred to him as a lay genius, which observation misled subsequent critics into believing that Cervantes was a purely spontaneous writer unaware of the rules of art. In eighteenth-century Spain Maruján and García de la Huerta viewed Cervantes as being full of bitter resentment, an opinion that was challenged by the masses of that country. In 1780, Vicente de los Ríos opened new avenues to investigation when he concluded that the *Quijote* was a source of poetic laws, not merely a fine example of them. At the end of the eighteenth century Cervantes came to be regarded as a man who had been mistreated by critics, but true *Cervanteskunde* did not really begin until 1818 with the publication of Martín Fernández de Navarrete's biography of Cervantes.

In Germany Bodmer (*Von dem Charakter des Don Quijote* — 1740) found that the charm of the Knight lay not in his insanity, but in his mixture of foolishness and reason. To Bodmer, viewing such a character brings out a perverse pleasure in the reader, who delights in seeing in persons he admires a strong element of nonsense. The Romantics, unlike Schiller and other Classicists, placed their emphasis on subjectivity. To the Romantics, Sancho was only a function of Don Quijote. The Knight, to them, typified creative consciousness which in romantic irony (i.e., in the self-destruction of a self-created world) enjoyed its own self-destruction. [Krauss next touches upon Hegel and his followers, on the *Jungdeutschen* and on the idea of E. Dühring and others that Cervantes' hero was a social revolutionary. Karl Marx's view that the *Quijote* was a true picture of Spanish historical development is briefly examined. The critic next turns his attention to the movement of *krausismo* in Spain at the end of the nineteenth century.] *Krausismo* is based on Immanuel Kant's philosophy, and there are two generations of *krausistas* in Spain. They generally view the complementary relationship between the idealistic and mystical Knight and the sensual Squire as a starting point for the building of a new Spain. Between these two generations of *krausistas*, however, falls the Generation of '98, which is heavily influenced by Maurice Barrès and his *ichkult*. With Barrès, each country is viewed as having its own internal dynamic force. Unamuno (309), for example, sees in Don Quijote the great power of a folk myth. All in all, for the Generation of 1898 Cervantes becomes only a medium, not a creative force in himself. After this generation, the new *krausistas* (or *institucionalistas*) arise. Ortega y Gasset (223), a neo-Kantian educated at Marburg, views the *Quijote* as a critique of culture carried out by confronting ideals with reality and resulting in disillusion. Ortega raises the question of Cervantes' culture, and Toffanin (300) continues this subject, concluding that the author of the *Quijote* was affected by the literary theories of his times in creating his masterpiece.

[The critic also discusses the views of Américo Castro (63), Mario Casella (60), and others.]

165. Krauss, Werner. "Cervantes und die moderne Welt." *Beiträge zur Romanischen Philologie,* Sonderheft, c 1967, 1968. (Das literarische Werk von Miguel de Cervantes), pp. 10-18.

Cervantes belongs to that group of writers whose lives become incorporated objectively in their works. He is also a writer who reaches his peak only in his later years. Cervantes is neo-Aristotelian in his outlook and sees that fiction must be distinct from history. However, he realizes that the writer of fiction must give his work the appearance of truth and probability.

Cervantes' work is, in a sense, realistic, but it is a critical realism. While the author does not hesitate to enter the picaresque world, he does so with a critical consciousness that allows him to keep his distance. A critical consciousness of prior and contemporary literature is another characteristic of Cervantes' writing.

166. Kruse, Margot. "Ariost und Cervantes." *Romanistisches Jahrbuch,* XII (1961), 248-264.

Ariosto viewed *Orlando furioso* as a serious continuation of the classical epic, and Cervantes so regarded Ariosto's work. At first blush there appears to be little similarity between *Don Quijote* and Ariosto's *Orlando.* For example, in the Italian work almost equal weight is given to several protagonists, whereas in the *Quijote* attention is fixed upon the Knight and the Squire. But Cervantes follows Ariosto in several matters: sudden interruptions for comic relief; stating at the end of a chapter that matters are postponed until the following chapter; interpolated short stories; the borrowing of material for the plot (*El Curioso impertinente* is quite similar to Ariosto's Canto XLIII, even as to the name of the protagonist, Anselmo). More important, however, is Cervantes' use of Ariosto's technique of tying interpolations to the main plot. In *Orlando furioso* and in the *Quijote* the hero will first hear a story about a person; then there will be a long digression; then the hero will meet the person about whom the story has been told. The Marcela episode, for example, is closely akin structurally to the story of Ginevra in *Orlando furioso.*

167. Krutch, Joseph Wood. "Miguel de Cervantes," in *Five Masters: a Study in the Mutations of the Novel*. New York: Cape & Smith, 1931, pp. 63-105.

Boccaccio's style of story-telling was too simple, presenting only a duality of flesh and spirit, and choosing flesh. He was not interested in abstractions. Cervantes' world was more aware of the intellectual implications of the Renaissance. By that time, however, the Counter Reformation had set in, and the Council of Trent cast its shadow over Spain during all of Cervantes' effective life. Whereas practical paganism had previously been tolerated, after Trent even Boccaccio was placed on the Index. Spain, which had never had a joyous adolescence, accepted the Counter Reformation passionately. Hence Cervantes saw life in sombrer colors than the Italian had seen it, and his problem was one far more complicated than that presented to Boccaccio. The central problem of the Renaissance, the ideal versus the real, had to be solved, but not in such simple terms as Boccaccio had used (flesh accepted to the exclusion of the spirit).

Don Quijote represents the essential method and spirit of the modern novel. Cervantes broke with literary tradition by not conforming to any previous pattern. (In the epic the hero never sank; in the picaresque he never rose). Cervantes brings unity under impossible conditions. Humanism was quite complicated; it was an attempt to realize the implications of the fact that life is led upon two levels — the human and the natural — which intersect but do not coincide. It attempted to determine where the assumption that man was merely a shrewder sort of animal was fruitful and where it was not, and *Don Quijote* is a statement of this problem in comic terms.

Cervantes discards simplicity of narration in favour of a more complicated form capable of suggesting this emotional ambiguity of life. We see the world through two sets of eyes, those of the Knight and those of the Squire. Their viewpoints do not contradict one another; they fuse. And out of that fusion comes a sense of solidity in the moral realm which is utterly new in Cervantes.

Cervantes had strong romantic tendencies and at times slips back into the primitive *novella* form. His interpolated tales seem flat in comparison to the main action. It would be fantastic to suppose that he wrote these minor tales deliberately to call attention by contrast to the virtues of his great work, but certainly they can be made to serve that purpose.

The author reserves his affection for those who are willing to act as though the mind and the imagination were the supreme realities. The hero embodies everything which the background is not, and this glaring contrast between the realism of the setting and the fantastic poetry of the central character contains a harmonious whole for the simple reason that its existence in the form of the present contrast between fact and aspiration is the thing of which our experience in living makes us most persistently aware.

Cervantes advanced the art of story-telling more than anyone else in literary history. He states the chief intellectual problems of his times and paints the realistic details of everyday life with a hitherto unapproached fidelity. But his main contribution is three-dimensional fiction, which is purely a modern contribution to narration. The power to suggest the emotional and intellectual complexity of any series of events is the very essence of the art of the modern novel.

168. Krynen, Jean. "Don Quijote, ejemplar poeta." *Anales Cervantinos*, VII (1958), 1-11.

Don Quijote's madness is a poetic madness, for he wants to bring Aristotle's poetic truth into the real world. Cervantes satirizes this attempt; he does not praise poetic madness. The tendency of the modern writer of fiction is not to be a craftsman but to be a revealor of deep psychic reality. This, however, runs the risk of making literature an absolute of life, a means for conquering the divine. Modern writers could profit by Don Quijote's failure to do just this. The Knight sought to live fiction. He ignores the distinction between historical truth and spiritual truth. In the end he destroys the poetic work of art by trying to find the reality of life in it. The Knight's madness goes through three phases: (1) pathological aggression; (2) sublimation (in Chapter XXV, Pt. I); (3) true enlightenment (after Chapter L, Pt. II). In his sublimated schizophrenia the Don tries to unite in Dulcinea the ultimate reality, a mixture of the highest ideal state and the most concrete presence (Aldonza Lorenzo). Dulcinea, however, is not an end in herself to Don Quijote. She is the means by which he seeks to bring about a mythic universe.

In the Cave of Montesinos the poetic world and the real world separate. This is the culmination of a tendency already existing in the early portion of Part II, where the ideal Dulcinea and the wretched, peasant-girl "Dulcinea" created by Sancho existed side by side. In the cave episode the Don, deep in his imagination, sees his error. At the end of the story Alonso Quijano comes to understand what the poetic madness confuses: literature and mysticism. He no longer confuses the esthetic experience with the religious experience. Like Juan de la Cruz, he ceases to confuse poetry and the real world.

1969. Lascaris Commeno, Constantino. "El nombre de Don Quijote." *Anales Cervantinos*, II (1952), 361-364.

Cervantes did not have to invent the word "quijote." It was an actual surname used by several men who lived prior to Cervantes' times. The word *quixote* also meant thighplate, and had already been used by Juan Álvarez Gato, in a symbolical sense, for erotic desire. Finally, Dámaso Alonso (3) has suggested that Cervantes chose the word *quijote* to rhyme with the name "Camilote" from the *Primaleón*.

170. León Máinez, Ramón. *Cervantes y su época, con un prólogo del excmo. sr. Eduardo Benot*. Jerez de la Frontera: "Litografía jerezana," 1901. Pp. 572.

[In Chapter III the critic concludes that only one other writer of the Golden Age can be compared to Cervantes for beauty of style: Fray Luis de León. The *Quijote*, León Máinez continues, is a moral work: Those who transgress are severely punished. In Chapter VIII the critic discusses Part II of Cervantes' *Quijote* and concludes that the characters in this part are better portrayed than in Part I, that the hero becomes less obstinate, less insane, and more reposed, and that Sancho is better presented. In Part II of the *Quijote*, the critic concludes, monotony is avoided; variety, discretion, and inventiveness abound.]

171. Levin, Harry. "The Example of Cervantes," in *Contexts of Criticism*. Cambridge, Mass.: Harvard University Press, 1957, pp. 79-96. [Reprinted in *Cervantes: A Collection of Critical Essays* (219), pp. 34-48.]

In the Ginés de Pasamonte episode we read that this rogue had written a book which he believed would outdo *Lazarillo de Tormes*. This is the "fiction within a fiction" device. This technique can show up the book mentioned thereby sharpening the realism of the book that does the mentioning. This is what Ginés does for his own work at the expense of *Lazarillo*, and what Cervantes is doing for the *Quijote* at the expense of the *Amadis*. Ginés also brings out the limitations of fiction; it cannot cover all of life, Cervantes tells us. Life itself is infinitely larger than any artistic medium. However, by revealing the limitations of their medium, writers like Cervantes heighten our consciousness of what existence means.

Characterization of the protagonist gains in depth as he passes through the levels of the characters who surround him, in their assumed roles, with their recounted adventures — sometimes tales within tales. As in Chaucer's *Canterbury Tales*, the story-tellers take on an extra dimension against the formal backdrop of their stories. The effectiveness of the play-within-the-play device lies in making the main drama more convincing. One way of achieving this effect is to make the theatrical figures unconvincing. Hence, among the many stratagems that Cervantes employs against the romance, none is more sharply conceived nor more skillfully executed than Maese Pedro's puppet-play.

The use of the fictional narrator technique has several advantages. Since the author presents himself as editor, assuming the intervention of a Spanish translator from the Arabic, the text stands at three removes from ourselves, enriched with afterthoughts like a palimpsest. This procedure has the advantage of enabling the author to digress more freely, to blame his source for indiscreet remarks, and to cultivate an air of authenticity. But authenticity is deeply called into question on one problematic occasion, when the whole trend of the book is reversed, turning back from pragmatic demonstration to metaphysical speculation. That adventure takes place in Montesinos' Cave. Here we are tempted to believe that Don Quijote's descent into the cave is a return to the deep well of the past, the unconscious memory of the race, and that the mythical heroes sleeping there personify the ideals he struggled to practice, the ideology of the Golden Age. Yet the simple and brutal alternative persists that he may have been caught in a lie and have become a party to the general imposture.

172. Lewis, D. B. Wyndham. *The Lion and the Fox: The Role of the Hero in the Plays of Shakespeare.* London: Methuen & Co., Ltd., 1966, pp. 215-227. (First published in 1928. London, Grant Richards, Ltd.)

The fact that Don Quijote does not have a ceremonious pathos and only fights phantoms does not make him any less a hero. He is a lonely figure and in that respect corresponds to one of the chief requirements of tragedy.

The humor of Falstaff achieves the same result as Don Quijote's chivalric delusion; it makes him immune from accidents. The contrast between these two figures is a contrast in two unrealities, two techniques for turning the world into something else by means of enchantment. Falstaff is a negation; Don Quijote a positive inspiration. Falstaff is too wide awake; Don Quijote is dreaming. But both, in effect, direct their efforts at defeating reality.

173. Lewis, D. B. Wyndham. *The Shadow of Cervantes.* New York: Sheed & Ward, 1962. Pp. ix + 197.

The ranks of Cervantes' interpreters, speaking more languages than one, include as usual what might be called without offence the professional tumblers performing in the rear, as in the wake of a Russo-Byzantine wedding procession: the psychologists, pre-Freudian, Freudian, and post-Freudian; the Pirandellists, the Symbolists, the Kafkarians, the Imagists, the Cabbalists, spying a cryptogram in Cervantes' every other sentence. There is an infinite amount of bargain-sale rhetoric about the New Renaissance Man, a splendid fellow freed from medieval chains and facing a glorious destiny with roars of joy. To the left of this group marches the "secret rebel" group, waving a top hat, among whom we recognize, with mild surprise, our own stentorian Walter Savage Landor.

[On page 125 the critic refers to Landor's theory (that the figure Dulcinea is a satire on the Virgin Mary) as an "engaging absurdity".]

There are spots on every masterpiece. Homer nods, Dante turns at times into a sour Ghibelline politican, Shakespeare's occasional glissades from the heights have made many a pedant's holiday. Cervantes' lapses are remarkably few and, with one exception, insignificant; any author is liable to overlook a chain-gang guard's missing firelock or the temporary absence of an ass. More willful is the interpolation of a long elaborate romance, quite irrelevant, like *La Novela del Curioso Impertinente*. It was a labor-saving device of the period, and even of the century following — see Fielding and Smollett — to pad out a novel with stories from the Italians.

174. Lida de Malkiel, María Rosa. "De cuyo nombre no quiero acordarme..." *Revista de Filología Hispánica,* I (1939), 167-171.

Since Cervantes states in the prologue to the 1605 *Quijote* that his story is something engendered in a jail, popular tradition has construed "de cuyo nombre no quiero acordarme" to mean that the author was imprisoned in a given town such as Argamasilla de Alba and there began his masterpiece. However, opening lines such as "de cuyo nombre no quiero acordarme" had been used by numerous writers prior to Cervantes: Herodotus, Marie de France, Juan Manuel and Torquemada. Such an opening line is also found in the tale of *Aladin's Lamp.* Therefore, it is most doubtful that Cervantes' voluntary forgetfulness is connected with any event in his real life. Casalduero (56) states appropriately that Cervantes sought to make his protagonist's story as unheroic sounding as possible. What better way to do so than with an opening line from a folktale! Spitzer (288), in 1936, considers "de cuyo nombre no quiero acordarme" to be a mere stylized negative construction, without noting that such openings were traditional. [For a later opinion by Spitzer on this point *see* "Linguistic Perspectivism in *Don Quijote*" (289), fn. 33, where he concludes that "no *quiero* acordarme" exalts the freedom of the artist *qua* artist.]

175. "Das literarische Werk von Miguel de Cervantes." Deutsche Akademie der Wissenschaften zu Berlin (Sept. 29-Oct. 1, 1966).

A SELECTIVE ANNOTATED BIBLIOGRAPHY 155

Beiträge zur Romanischen Philologie (Berlin). (Sonderheft, c 1967, 1968.)

[This volume contains the following articles on Cervantes and his works: "Cervantes und die moderne Welt" (165), by Werner Krauss; "Exégesis esotérica y análisis de intenciones del *Quijote*," by Marcel Bataillon; "Cervantes und seine Auseinandersetzung mit Avellaneda," by Werner Bahner; "Die Pikareske als Formproblem bei Cervantes," by Horst Baader; "Nuevas consideraciones sobre la temática y estructura de *Las novelas ejemplares*," by Karl-Ludwig Selig; "Cervantes und die Tradition der Ehebruchsgeschichte: Zur Wandlung der Tugendverfassung," by Hans-Jörg Neuschäfer; "Die zweifache Präsenz des Dichters in der Novella *La Gitanilla*," by Walter Pabst; "Bemerkungen zum Thema 'las armas y las letras'," by Ulrich Ricken; "Quelques particularités du style du roman *Don Quichotte* de Cervantes" (287), by Nina Snetkova; "Die Insula Barataria, die Insula Firme, und das Schloss Chambord," by Hans Sckommodau; "Sobre el tipo del 'Labrador rico' en el *Quijote*," by Noël Salomon; "El caballero cervantino, juez ejemplar," by Francisco Olmos García; "Don Quijote arbitrista: Sobre la *reformación* en tiempos de Cervantes," by Jean-Pierre Vilar; "Zur Wirkungsgeschichte der Literatur des Siglo de Oro in der deutschen Frühaufklärung," by Kurt Schnelle; "Montalvo und Cervantes," by Adalbert Dessau; "Don Quijote arquetipo nacional: Sobre algunos rasgos de la autocrítica nacional en la España moderna," by Karlheinz Barck; "Sobre algunas interpretaciones del *Quijote* en la España del siglo XX (209) by Ioana Terterian; "Sobre el *Quijote* y la modernidad," by Carlos Rincón; "Sobre Don Quijote: Meras notas de lector," by Iorgu Iordan; "Lo cotidiano y lo perenne en el teatro de Cervantes," by Ileano Georgescu; "Un eco cervantino en la poesía de Mihail Eminescu," by Olga Tudoricá; "Los 'desgarrados' y la picaresca," by Silva Viscan; "Don Quichotte et l'Espagne de 1600: Les fondements historiques d'un irréalisme," by Pierre Vilar.]

176. Lledó Iñigo, Emilio. "Interpretación y teoría de *Don Quijote*." *Anales Cervantinos*, VI (1957), 113-122.

Some novels describe reality. Others, like the *Quijote*, not only described it but interpret it. However, Cervantes' novel does not examine reality sociologically or historically. It reflects on it, and out of this reflection comes light. Descartes said "cogito ergo sum," but Don Quijote had already given a similar basis to all his speculations: life is the representation which *I* have of it. Don Quijote accepts reality but regards it as pure phenomena, not the essence of things. His quixotic will seeks to keep the essence alive. The idea of enchantment serves to keep his *yo* supreme. No matter how we interpret the ideology of the *Quijote*, the figure of the Don impresses itself on us. He is the most sustained and energetic affirmation of the *yo* that man has ever created.

177. Lloréns, Vicente. "Historia y ficción en el *Quijote*." *Papeles de Son Armadans*, Año VIII, tomo XXVIII, núm. LXXXIV (March, 1963), 235-258.

There is a background of reality in the *Quijote*, which was not true in the chivalry or pastoral novel. The cities and battles to which Cervantes refers are real, as are characters such as Roque Guinart. The expulsion of Ricote too has an historical basis, as does the ironic reference to the recent lineage of Dulcinea (most of the inhabitants of El Toboso were *moriscos*).

178. Lloréns, Vicente. "La intención del *Quijote*." *Revista de Occidente*, XVIII (1967), 143-158.

Cervantes' attack on the dead genre of chivalry novels ties in with his discussion of the contemporary theatre. It is not basically a question of both genres having a lack of unity and verisimilitude; the principal fact is that both the chivalry novel and Lope's theatre were seeking to bring the heroic ideals of a bygone age into a totally new society. This, to Cervantes, seemed a reprehensible anachronism. The madness of the Knight is not in believing the exploits of chivalry books to be historically true, for the innkeeper is also guilty of this absurdity. The Don's true madness is in seeking, like Lope, to restore chivalry in a new and different age.

Cervantes did not hate the past; he loved it. He did not hate the chivalresque ideal, for he appears to prefer the medieval chivalresque to the renaissance pastoral. He also prefers the chivalresque ideal to the Christian-Epicurean ideal of the Caballero del Verde Gabán. Nevertheless, Cervantes saw that the chivalresque ideal belonged to a different and bygone age and felt that attempts to restore such an ideal would only lead to failure.

179. Lollis, Cesare de. *Cervantes reazionario.* Rome: Fratelli Treves, 1924. Pp. ii + 241.

Don Quijote is a book of unexpected modernness, but it is not at all revolutionary. Basically it is a destructive book in its first intention. The function of the *Persiles* was to rebuild. Lope wrote to amuse the masses; he loved romantic material. Cervantes is more a preceptist, unfortunately: Cervantes ebbe il torto di non sentire a pieno la singolare e privilegiata condizione del suo paese davanti al problema di una litteratura, la quale, anzichè di classe, fosse di tutti e per tutti.

[De Lollis refers to Cervantes the preceptist as mediocre, but as redeemed by his artistic temperament. The influence of the Council of Trent on Cervantes, with its emphasis on didacticism, is brought up from time to time, and dealt with especially in Chapter III.]

180. López Navío, José. "Génesis y desarrollo del *Quijote*." *Anales Cervantinos,* VII (1958), 157-235.

A number of critics have suggested that the *Entremés de los romances* was the source for Chapters I-IX of the *Quijote*: Adolfo de Castro, in 1874; Pí y Molist, in 1886; as well as Millé y Giménez (203) and Menéndez Pidal (196). Millé also concluded that this *entremés* was anti-Lope. Blanca de los Ríos (251), at the end of the nineteenth century, concluded that Cervantes' novel was anti-Tirso.

There *is* a great deal of the anti-Lope and the anti-Tirso in *Don Quijote.* Lope is represented by the Knight and Tirso by the Squire. Dulcinea is an anagram for Lucinda, a name that Lope gave to Micaela Luján, a chubby illiterate like Aldonza Lorenzo. The purpose of Cervantes in attacking chivalry novels was to forestall their use as plots for *comedias.* There was no need to drive out these books as such, since they were already a dying genre.

Don Quijote's body type was the same as that of Lope de Vega: tall, thin, *leptosómico,* active, strong-willed, imaginative and somewhat paranoid. Lope was a megalomaniac on the subject of his ancestors and at times was subject to fits of melancholy.

181. Madariaga, Salvador de. "Our Don Quixote." *Hispania*, XI (1925), 91-118.

Don Quijote is a case of self-delusion. He does not trust reality; instead he leaps at reality before it has the opportunity to give him the lie. Yet as mad as he is, he cannot completely kill the voice inside him that tells him that all his ideas are vain imaginings. In essence, the Knight is a blend of self-delusion and self-knowledge, and Montesinos' Cave is an episode symbolic of his double state of mind. This adventure is a kind of harmonic of the whole novel, a delusion within a delusion. It is one of those passages in which Don Quijote touches the fringe of reality and appears half in the sun of sanity and half in the shadow of folly.

Sancho appears to be the antithesis of his master, but in reality is a replica of the Don at a different level. The Squire and the Knight are a case of parallelism. Both can be reasonable; yet at times each has delusions. The Don's self-delusion is glory (symbolized by Dulcinea); the Squire's self-delusion is material power (symbolized by the island he has been promised). Sancho, like his master, searches for reasons to believe. He is fascinated by his master's theoretical imagination and culture. Sancho seeks in the Don what he feels he himself does not possess.

182. Madariaga, Salvador de. *Guía del lector del "Quijote." Ensayo psicológico sobre el "Quijote."* Buenos Aires: Editorial Sudamericana, 1967. Pp. 206. (First published between June, 1923 and February, 1925, as a serial, by *La Nación* in Buenos Aires. English title: *Don Quixote; an Introductory Essay in Psychology.* Oxford: Clarendon Press, 1935.) [Appreciation is expressed to Angela Miller for her assistance in the preparation of this summary.]

Don Quijote, Sancho, Don Juan, Hamlet and Faust are the five great men who were created by men. Each generation interprets these figures, and in the case of Cervantes' two protagonists the many opinions regarding them are due to the depth of their souls. Sancho and Don Quijote are not simple, clear-cut figures. It is not a question of a brave man versus a coward, an idealist versus a materialist. They exert great influence on one another and grow alike. Their relationship resolves itself into a delicate and complex parallelism, the development of which is one of the marvels of the story.

Don Quijote's fall is slow and subtle, and is handled by Cervantes with consumate artistry. At the beginning of Part II the hero is not as sure of himself as he was during his first two sallies. With the enchantment of Dulcinea, the Knight enters into a full decline. He becomes skeptical and depressed. He even accepts Sancho's advice. After the episode of the Knight of the Mirrors and that of the lions he revives and appears to take over his usual function. Yet he is disturbed. The episode of the cave of Montesinos is symbolic of the hero's spiritual decay. The Knight's attitude toward this adventure is complex. Though he talks about it jokingly, coldly and irreverently, his faith is no longer intense.

183. Madariaga, Salvador de. "Cervantes and His Time." *The Virginia Quarterly Review*, XXXVII (1961), 229-249.

Consciously Cervantes was perhaps a faithful child of the Church. But he is a free thinker like Shakespeare. At times sly and ironical, Cervantes is foreign to rigid orthodoxy. For example, the *Ricote* episode is a concealed protest against the cruelty of the expulsion. What should we make of Cervantes' mocking attitude toward the clergy, his hardly veiled hints about the Inquisition, his protest against the expulsion of the Moors, and by way of implication, of the Jews, his irony toward the Old Christians? Perhaps the time may have come to direct research toward a possible Sephardi origin of Cervantes.

The three great spirits of Europe are Rabelais, Montaigne and Cervantes. Rabelais, still medieval, ends and liquidates the Middle Ages. Montaigne, a critical rather than a creative mind, draws the chief lines of the human spirit with an objectivity free from the fetters of time. Of the three, Cervantes is the most genuine herald of our time, the true forerunner of modern man. In its creative impulse *Don Quijote* springs up with a vertical vigor similar to that which animates the immense work of Rabelais. In both cases we are struck by a similar volcanic independence from social and moral layers deposited by the past; a similar primitive force of a creation flowing from deeper levels and rising to higher levels than those of ordinary, everyday life.

184. Maeztu, Ramiro de. *Don Quijote, Don Juan y La Celestina; ensayos de simpatía*. Madrid: Espasa-Calpe, 1963, pp. 11-69. (First published in 1926: Madrid, Calpe.)

Don Quijote is a decadent work, both melancholy and desillusioned. It is the voice of a tired race that seeks rest after its work. The *Quijote* is not only a satire against books of chivalry but against the chivalresque ideal. Both Shakespeare and Cervantes are against their leading characters, Hamlet and Don Quijote. Hamlet's speaking in short sentences causes the audience to want him to act; Don Quijote's speaking in long sentences causes the reader to want to stop him and send him home. There is an irony here. When Spain produced a work that recommended repose, it governed an empire; when England produced a work urging action, it was hardly a power in the world.

There are two types of disillusionment in the *Quijote:* (1) cosmic, eternal, independent of time and place; (2) the personal disillusionment of the hero. Cervantes' life is woven into his masterpiece. He conceived his great novel when disillusioned and bankrupt. His masterpiece is not an esoteric work; every page rings with his own life, his dreams and his misfortunes. The author identifies with his hero on every page, saying: "If I had not been good, I would not have gotten into trouble."

[At p. 55, Maeztu, who views Don Quijote as a product of "hispanidad," pictures Cervantes as saying: "Laugh at my phantasms, reader, as I laugh at my own disillusion, and remember as you laugh that you dreamed along with me, for all Spain has been Don Quijote."]

185. Maldonado de Guevara, Francisco. "El niño y el viejo: desmitologización en el *Lazarillo* y en *El Quijote*." *Anales Cervantinos*, VIII (1959-1960), 241-260.

The essence of the modern novel is an irreverent attitude toward the myth, as Ortega (223) has observed. In the case of *Lazarillo* and *Don Quijote* the myth envolved is that of the eternal child, *puer aeturnus,* who has a supernatural birth, accomplishes great feats, and usually fades away mysteriously at the end. Cervantes creates a *viejo-niño* in Don Quijote. Like a child-hero he yearns for the eternal feminine until his death. The child in the *viejo-niño* is *andancia;* the old man in the *viejo-niño* is *angustia.* The old man cannot be a myth. He is a conscious literary creation. Cervantes has an irreverent attitude toward the myth, but he is not cynical. With Cervantes this irreverence acts as a *fuerza componente* in a complex human being. The *desmitologizador* Don Quijote is actually full of mythology. To understand the *Quijote* we must see both the author and the hero as old men. Only then can we understand the final renunciation of chivalry and of madness.

The niece in *Don Quijote* represents the eternal feminine at the end of the story. After Dulcinea has been de-mythicized, the niece reappears as the eternal feminine to concern herself with her dying uncle.

186. Maldonado de Guevara, Francisco. "Del *Ingenium* de Cervantes al de Gracián." *Anales Cervantinos*, VI (1957), 97-111.

Astuteness in madmen is a well-known fact, but a clever clinical madman who imitates madness will always feign a madness other than his own. Don Quijote, however, imitates his own madness. He does this creatively and consciously, as in the Cave of Montesinos adventure. Hence the Knight's madness is not clinical but transcendental. The Knight knows how to cure himself; the clinical madman does not. Don Quijote is the only humble madman in history, and his humbleness is what permits his recovery.

Ingenium originally meant a generating force, like nature, but it was an ambiguous word that became confused during the Renaissance with *entendimiento, sensibilidad,* or *imaginación.* Don Quijote's *genio,* the basis of substance of his mind, is his insanity. His *ingenio* (not *genio*) is revealed to us in the intervals during which he fictionalizes (without pretending) his own madness. This *vía media* of fictional *ingenio* makes possible his continuity, and permits the transition toward lucid intervals, which, at the end of the story, impose themselves in the renunciation of chivalry and of madness.

187. Maldonado de Guevara, Francisco. "Dos estudios cervantinos." *Anales Cervantinos*, IX (1961-1962), 45-96.

[The first note is entitled "Poética, poesía y personaje."] A number of critics are taken in by Cervantes' trick in Part II of making the hero aware of his prior history (Part I). They conclude that the Knight acquires a separate existence. This is not so. This play-within-a-play device is old, for Odysseus arrives at the palace of Alcinoo (like the Don arrives at the estate of the *Duques*) preceded by his reputation. But basically there are two types of plays-within-plays: (1) the functional type where the play is part of the plot and reinforces and complicates the main theme without modifying it, as in *Hamlet*; (2) the *intrínseco* or *tensional* type of play-within-a-play. This type is more revolutionary. It denies the author (first negation) and claims that the characters *espiritizan* in the actors and that the actors *encarnan* in the characters (second negation). Examples of this type of play-within-a-play are Calderón's *El gran teatro del mundo*, Pirandello's *Six Characters in Search of an Author*, and Unamuno's *Niebla*. The *Quijote* does not belong to this revolutionary type, for there is no dialogue between Cervantes' characters and the author himself. Don Quijote and Sancho, in Part II, *do* confront Cide Hamete but only the Cide Hamete of Part I. Cervantes does not attribute the same reality to the fictional knights of chivalry as he does to the Cid. Don Quijote does this, and he is insane when he does so. The innkeeper also confuses real and fictional characters, and he represents the attitude of the average reader of Cervantes' day. It is not that Cervantes seeks to confuse real and fictional characters, or give his characters a separate identity. It is simply that Cervantes knows how to create a *sensación histórico-biográfica*, as Velásquez is able to create an *éxtasis temporal* in his paintings.

[A large portion of this first note is dedicated to a critique of Luis Rosales' *Cervantes y la libertad* (261), with which work Maldonado strongly disagrees, particularly with Rosales' tendency to remove the melancholy element from the Knight's personality. What to Rosales is a *teatro de la felicidad* (mixture of reality and illusion) is to Maldonado *desengaño* and *desmitologización*, the beginning of the Don's conversion. A significant portion of this first note is also devoted to the question whether Cervantes maintains decorum in the presentation of his hero's personality. Except where the author drags his hero into a dispute with Avellaneda, Maldonado concludes, decorum is preserved.]

[The second note is entitled "Ociosidad y Sanchoquijotismo," first published in 1947 in the *Boletín de la Biblioteca Menéndez Pelayo de Santander*.] Don Quijote is, above all, idle, for idleness is basic to *hidalguía*, as opposed to *burguesía*. *Faust* is an epic of the bourgeoisie; it praises activity. *Don Quijote* is the epic of pure spirit in the age of the last aristocracy. The hero believes in absolute (mystic) activity. Yet Cervantes does not praise idleness. He is openly contemptuous of the Duke and Duchess and does not hold in high esteem the Knight of the Green Cloak, who is content in his idleness.

The story of Sancho's government is literarily kin to the motif of *somnium vitae humanae*, a Central European theme, in which a peasant dreams that he is king. The Don's advice to his squire is a mixture of elements from various sources. Cervantes, however, humorously omits bravery from the list of virtues usually considered to be needed by a ruler.

188. Mañach, Jorge. *Examen del quijotismo*. Buenos Aires: Editorial Sudamericana, 1950. Pp. 151.

If the setting of the *Quijote* is real, the hero is not. He is a strange outgrowth of Alonso Quijano who goes insane out of a will to power but with no way to use it. Cervantes employs the insanity device not primarily to justify the extravagant behavior of his hero but to reveal the soul of Alonso Quijano, to put quixotic conduct under an ambiguous light.

All literature from the classical epic to the Byzantine novel tended toward the extravagant. Medieval times inherited this irreality but added naturalistic touches. Thus a dualistic literature arose, part realistic, part idealistic. By 1600 in Spain, idealism and naturalism had still not been integrated by the Renaissance. But in the *Quijote* the crude antithesis of idealism and naturalism found in *La Celestina* ripened into its deepest and most ambiguous expression.

Don Quijote identifies reality with preconceived ideas and images. He replaces direct experience with imaginative experience. He replaces life with culture. In the *Quijote* idealism never really triumphs. We should not, however, view Cervantes as a pessimist. He merely satirizes his hero's imposing his *a priori* values on the world without first ascertaining what the world is really like. The fact that Cervantes grows to love his hero does not mean that the author accepts the Don's ideas. The *Quijote* is ambiguous. It praises yet mocks heroism. This anguished contradiction is found in all true humor, and beneath the satire on contemporary Spain Cervantes' novel contains a pathetic humor that yearns for unity between idealism and realism.

189. Mandel, Oscar. "The Function of the Norm in *Don Quixote*." *Modern Philology*, LV (1957-1958), 154-163.

Since the eighteenth century *Don Quijote* criticism has been divided into two schools. The "soft" school sees the Don as a hero, and the normal people in the novel as the butt of Cervantes' satire. Some critics in the "soft" school emphasize the Knight's invencible sublimity; others make Don Quijote a Christlike figure. The "hard" school views Cervantes as favoring the status quo in society. Hegel, for example, considered the Knight an anachronistic struggler agains legally constituted authority.

After the first several chapters Cervantes gives his hero extra dimension. But this transformation of the Knight into a cultured gentleman is not due to character development but to the schoolmaster in Cervantes. The author splits his hero in two (part reasonable, part mad), and the story moves from a satire on pure madness to a satire on noble madness.

The classic comic pattern is to set up a series of values (a norm) and to have the comic hero depart from the pattern. The norm does not have to be acceptable to the reader. What is Cervantes' attitude toward the norm? The Romantics say that he sees it as shabby. However, Don Quijote really belongs to the family of error-stricken comic heroes whose destiny is to reenter the company of the sound and the normal; they enjoy their moment of *anagnorisis*, and then the story ends. The centers of normal behavior are the priest, the barber, Sansón Carrasco, and the Canon of Toledo. They and Cervantes supply the element of sound reason. Cervantes nearly always favors the norm, and his obvious dislike of the chaplain at the palace of the *Duques* is an exception to the rule.

In essence we should love Don Quijote but should not approve of him from an intellectual point of view. Cervantes wants us to respond to his hero with affectionate reprobation.

190. Mann, Thomas. "Voyage with Don Quijote," in *Essays of Three Decades*. Translated from the German by H. T. Lowe-Porter. New York: Alfred A. Knopf, Inc.; London: Martin Secker & Warburg Limited, 1957. [As reprinted in *Cervantes: A Collection of Critical Essays* (219), pp. 49-72. Original German title "Meerfahrt mit Don Quijote," in *Leiden und Grösse der Meister:* Berlin, Fischer, 1935.]

[Thomas Mann, like Ricote, has been exiled from his native country. In the summer of 1934, he records his impressions of the *Quijote* as he makes his way to his new home in the United States.]

Don Quijote is a unique monument. It is more conditioned in its taste by its time than the deliberate satire against that taste would indicate. The whole spirit of the work is sycophantic in its protestations of loyalty; yet how its creative genius, critical, free, human, soars above its age. The false *Quijote* is the work of a bungler, but it did induce Cervantes to write Part II to rehabilitate the success of Part I. The second part of Cervantes' masterpiece no longer has the happy freshness and carelessness of the first. In the 1615 *Quijote* Cervantes labors to bring out clearly and consciously the depth and diversity of the main characters.

Cervantes demonstrates great epic wit in basing Part II on an already historical Part I. Nowhere else in literature has a hero lived on his own fame, upon the reputation of his reputation. It is a romantic illusion, a trick with an ironic undertone. This device of trick mirrors runs the risk of leading to an ironic dissolution of form, as does every technique that seeks to combine the humorous with the realistic.

Cervantes' intemperate cruelty toward his hero is appalling. Despite his identification with the Knight, the author puts his hero into many humiliating pitfalls. There is something sardonic and desperately funny in such inventions. Yet the author loves his hero. Does not this cruelty look like self-flagellation, self-revilement, castigation? Yes, but this grim coming to terms with reality is actually the definition of humor.

The scenes in the *Quijote*, like those in the late-classic novel, are striking in their inherent oddness and lack of motivation. It is significant that they are in the second, intellectually more ambitious part of the book. Ancient writers loved scenes like Camacho's wedding. For example, Achilleus Tatius' *Leucippe and Cleitophon* has a fake death scene. Do I deceive myself, or do this blood-filled gut and the trick dagger in *Don Quijote* come from the same school? Let the scholars decide whether Cervantes received these episodes directly from classic Roman literature or by way of Italy.

The Ricote episode is arresting and significant as well as a shrewd mixture of professions of loyalty and of the author's strict adherence to the Church, his blameless submission to the great Philip III — and the most lively human sympathy for the awful fate of the Moorish people. Cervantes' compassion for Ricote the Moor and his indirect criticism of the state's harsh attitude are much more powerful and intellectually significant *after* he has expressed the submission which with him is a matter not of hypocrisy but of actual intellectual conditioning.

The death of Don Quijote is weak and artificial. Cervantes had a fixation against all unwarranted literary exploiting. Don Quijote's death is a literary death born of Cervantes' jealousy, but this only shows Cervantes' identification with his hero. Don Quijote's return to sanity does not make us rejoice. It leaves us cold; we even regret it to a certain extent. We share the hero's defeat though we know it had to be. If *Don Quijote* were only a book that condemned chivalry novels, the hero's death would be simple. But since everything was expanded beyond the fundamental idea (undermining chivalry novels), the possibility of a satisfactory ending was destroyed. Cervantes could not kill off the Knight in a foolish adventure; this would be too jarring. Nor could he allow him to live after his return to sanity; that would be to make the husk survive beyond the soul; would be a degradation of the character below its lofty height. It would have been neither Christian nor edifying to let him die in his delusion, yet in despair over his downfall. It was certainly imperative to save Don Quijote's soul to sanity before he died. But in order that his salvation might be more after our hearts, the author should have made his unreason less lovable.

191. Marasso [Rocca], Arturo. *Cervantes: La invención del Quijote.* Buenos Aires: Biblioteca Nueva, [1943]. Pp. 254.

[Marasso views the *Quijote* as a work highly influenced in its episodes by the classics, particularly by the *Iliad,* the *Odyssey,* and the *Aeniad.* He is careful to note that previous critics had already observed parallels between certain episodes in the ancient epics and those in the *Quijote.* In general, Marasso regards the 1605 *Quijote* as a kind of disordered *Iliad,* in that the hero allows himself to be dragged along by the road. The 1615 *Quijote* is, to Marasso, more like the *Odyssey* and the *Aeniad.* Numerous similarities between the episodes of Cervantes' novel and the ancient epics are observed: for example, the stay of the Don at the home of Diego de Miranda is compared to the "City of Helen" episode in the *Aeniad,* and the sojourn of the Knight at the palace of the *Duques* is seen to be influenced by Aeneas' arrival at the court of Dido; the episode of Altisidora's "death" is viewed by Marasso as a satire on the death of Dido, while the galley-slaves adventure is said to have its source in the *Aeniad* VI.

As Marasso points out, Martín Fernández de Navarrete, in 1819, had already found a parallel between Don Quijote's descent into Montesinos' cave and Ulysses' and Aeneas' descent into hell.]

192. Maravall, José Antonio. *El humanismo de las armas en Don Quijote.* Prólogo de Ramón Menéndez Pidal. Madrid: Instituto de Estudios Políticos, 1948. Pp. xv + 305.

The Knight of La Mancha's primary interest and his deepest yearning is to perfect himself from within. Thus Bickermann (38) is mistaken in placing the major emphasis of the Don's reforming zeal on its effect on others. Don Quijote is greatly influenced by the renaissance concept of *fama.* He believes that glory arises from virtue. His social and political mission is based on the interworking of three factors: (1) the Knight's disaccordance with his times; (2) his yearning to reform; (3) the ideal of the Golden Age. For any of these factors to be produced it was necessary for a man to have gone through the experience of the Renaissance. A typical medieval knight had no conception of reform, and Don Quijote, thus, is much more than medieval.

Don Quijote's transformation of the world is, first of all, a product of his will, a renaissance will. He is not so much insane as arbitrary. At the end, Cervantes causes his hero to lose his arbitrariness and reenter the fold. But the Don's capricious recreation of the world had an object: the making possible of his mission of interior perfection through individual bravery. Since the Renaissance and the modern bureaucratic state with modern weapons made this individual valor virtually impossible, the Don seeks to annul existing reality. Only by doing this can he carry out his enterprise.

The Age of Gold concept is an ancient idea, found for example in Ovid's *Metamorfosis*. In medieval times there was, too, a yearning for a better state. But this was a matter either of the hereafter or the stuff of dreams. The Knight, however, seeks to bring into reality this Golden Age. This urge of his had a precedent in sixteenth-century utopistic literature. In Spain, however, the *utopia* took a different form — the *Quijote,* a human drama, not an abstract treatise. As in utopistic literature, the *Quijote* presents a discordance with the times coupled with a great urge to perfect reality.

193. Márquez Villanueva, Francisco. "Sobre la génesis literaria de Sancho Panza." *Anales Cervantinos,* VII (1958), 123-155.

There has been a certain attempt to find a real-life model for Sancho Panza, but the search for literary models has been more intensive and more rewarding. For example, Menéndez y Pelayo in Chapter V of his *Orígenes de la novela* (200) suggests the squire Ribaldo of *Caballero Cifar* as Sancho's forerunner. Menéndez Pidal (196), however, is of the opinion that Bandurrio, the squire in the *Entremés de los romances,* is the prototype for Cervantes' Squire. W. S. Hendrix (150) concludes, instead, that Sancho springs from the pre-Lope comic figures of the sixteenth-century *comedia,* such as the part serious *bobo* in Sebastián de Horozco's *Historia de Ruth.*

194. Medvedev, P. N. *Formalny metod v literaturovedenii. Kriticheskoye vvedenie v sotsiologicheskuyu poetiku,* "Priboi," 1928. [As cited by, and based on a summary of, Ludmilla B.

Turkevich in *Cervantes in Russia,* Princeton, N. J.: Princeton University Press, 1950, pp. 220-221. (This item could not be located in its original form).]

Despite Shklovskii (284), the formalist critic, unity in the *Quijote* is not the result of external devices, but of internal coordination. Otherwise Cervantes' masterpiece would be a mere collection of *novelas.* There is a unifying element in the *Quijote* — the hero himself, who is the thematic element as well as the unifying element. He is valuable *per se,* not because his madness is needed to motivate the adventures. The Don and the Squire, as a contrast, represent the basic thematic concept of the story, and all the episodes, speeches, and *novelas* evolving therefrom are subordinated in importance to the main figures.

195. Meier, Harri. "Zur Entwicklung der europäischen Quijote-Deutung." *Romanische Forschungen,* LIV (1940), 227-264.

In the seventeenth and eighteenth centuries the French regarded Cervantes as a modern satirist. Rapin saw the *Quijote* as a satire on Lerma. Saint Pierre interpreted the novel as an attack on the Spanish aristocracy. Montesquieu, however, considered the *Quijote* a satire on the whole Spanish nation. In general, the French viewed Cervantes as anti-pedantic and anti-fanatical. As early as 1698 the *Bibliothèque universelle* viewed the *Quijote* as an attack on Loyola, a point-of-view later shared by d'Alembert, Holbach, Voltaire, and Diderot. Thus, if Cervantes were an enlightened man, his hero must represent a fanatic and a bigot. This interpretation by the French reverses the earlier idea that the Don was merely a good-natured but silly fellow.

The English had a vastly different conception of humor from the French. Samuel Johnson praised Cervantes as a true humorist. Motteux went so far as to say that we are all Quijotes in part, a view echoed by Fielding, who considered the Knight's madness to be different only in type from the madness of the other characters in the story.

In Germany there are seven threads of *Quijote* interpretation: (1) the satirical approach; (2) the activistic approach; (3) the national character or realistic school of thought; (4) the non-literary, political approach; (5) the literary-aesthetic interpretation;

(6) the idealistic approach; and (7) the historical-philosophical understanding of the *Quijote*. These approaches are by no means chronological, and at times two or more threads are intertwined.

The satirical approach dominates *Quijote* criticism until the nineteenth century. The activistic approach went through several phases: *Aufklärung, Spätromantik,* and *Junges Deutschland.* At the end of the eighteenth century, and the beginning of the nineteenth, Herder, Eberhardt and others view the *Quijote* as pro-reason and anti-fanatic. Later activistic critics like the "Young German" Notter, view Don Quijote as a friend of the oppressed, and Rosencranz, a "Young Hegelian," considers Cervantes a reformer.

The realistic-national character approach was developed in the eighteenth century by Herder and Humboldt and followed in 1812 by Friedrich Schlegel, the Romantic, who thought all literature should be national.

The literary-aesthetic approach to the *Quijote* was developed by the Romantics. Tieck considered the novel a non-logical product of fantasy. The interpolated portions of the masterpiece came to be regarded by this group as highly poetic. Friedrich Schlegel compared the structure of the *Quijote* to a painting while his brother August Wilhelm compared it to a musical composition.

The idealistic (or symbolical) interpretation of the *Quijote* is derived only in part from the Romantics. Actually, Schiller is the important developer of this approach. In his *Über naive und sentimentalische Dichtung* he raised the difference between satire and humor to a philosophical level. Schiller regarded Cervantes as the great uplifter of satire, as the man who brought satire into the realm of the pure aesthetic without surrendering the awareness of the tension between reality and the ideal. Schiller also noted the conflict between the noble character of Don Quijote and the non-understanding world that surrounded him, and further contrasted the idealist with the realist.

The historical-philosophical approach to the *Quijote* seeks to place Cervantes in a particular epoch of thought. Friedrich Schlegel considered him medieval. Tieck saw him as a product of the turbulent sixteenth century in which moral rigidity was no longer regarded as a virtue. Critics of our century continue this discussion, Américo Castro (63) considering Cervantes a late product of the Renaissance, Toffanin (300) and Hatzfeld (141) regarding him as a Counter-Reformation man, and Pfandl (235) judging him to be essentially anti-Baroque.

196. Menéndez Pidal, Ramón. "Un aspecto en la elaboración del *Quijote*," in *De Cervantes y Lope de Vega*. Madrid: Espasa-Calpe, 1964, pp. 9-60. (Discurso leído en la inauguración del curso 1920-1921 del Ateneo Científico, Literario y Artístico.)

Even in the Middle Ages a comic element had appeared along with the heroic in chivalry literature. The Renaissance accentuated this comic element. Pulci and Boiardo, at the end of the fifteenth century, could still take the medieval epic with some seriousness, but Ariosto in his early sixteenth-century poem *Orlando furioso* presents Roland as tragicomic.

In addition to the comic element in the French epic and in Italian epic poetry, there is a folk tradition of the idealistic madman recorded by Sacchetti in the last half of the fourteenth century. Sacchetti describes one Agnolo di Ser Gherardo, a seventy year-old monomaniac who attended jousts where tricks were played on his mount, similar to those played on Rocinante in Barcelona. There is also a folk tale of a student at Salamanca who suffered illusions as a result of his reading chivalry novels.

The *Entremés de los romances* was of definite influence on the first chapters of Part I of the *Quijote*. In this one-act farce, or *entremés*, a poor farmer named Bartolo reads too much of the *Romancero* and goes out into the world as an epic warrior, along with his squire Bandurrio. His adventures are very similar to the early adventures of Don Quijote. Also, Bartolo, after his beating, believes that he is Valdovinos. There is, in addition, a similarity between Bartolo's return home and the first return of Cervantes' hero. In general, Cervantes is excessively impressed by the *entremés* in his early chapters. Later he changes his satirical emphasis to chivalry novels, rather than ballads. The first real switch from the ballads to the bringing back of knight-errantry occurs in Chapter VII. Here begins the grand purpose of the *Quijote*, the noble ideal that fails. Using Bartolo as a model at first, Cervantes begins to create *el loco cuerdo*. The *desvaríos* of Bartolo become the ideals of perfection of Don Quijote, a matter that attracts our sympathy.

Avellaneda in his false *Quijote* falls back on the *Romancero* and relies on the *Entremés de los romances*. His hero thinks he is many people, whereas Cervantes abandons this idea of multiple identities after the early chapters. Avellaneda's novel, in spite of its grossness, did inspire Part II of the *Quijote,* even portions prior to Chapter LIX where the false *Quijote* is first mentioned by Cervantes. Part II is unquestionably better than Part I. Here the use of *romances* reappears, but not in a form to disparage Don Quijote. Savi-Lopez (278) is incorrect in asserting that Part I is comic while Part II is grotesque, for the opposite is true. The episode of Montesinos' cave is comic, while the Marqués de Mantua episode in Part I (where Don Quijote is confused about his own identity) is grotesque.

In a sense the story of Don Quijote is related to the myth of Ajax, who, in a fit of insanity, kills sheep thinking that they are his enemies. Later Ajax, seeing that it was all an illusion and that he had made himself utterly laughable, kills himself in shame. Don Quijote, whose madness is from his own sick soul, dies of sadness when he sees that reality is inferior to his expectations.

[Menéndez Pidal also discusses the theory, to him incorrect, that the *Quijote* was first intended to be a short story.]

197. Menéndez Pidal, Ramón. *Cervantes y el ideal caballeresco.* Madrid: Patronato del IV Centenario del Nacimiento de Cervantes, 1948. Pp. 29.

The most disputed problem in *Don Quijote* criticism is Cervantes' true attitude toward medieval epic poetry. The first understanding of the novel was that it was a humorous satire of the abnegation and nobility of character found in chivalry novels. Later, in the nineteenth century, some began to mix a tear with a smile and concluded that *Don Quijote* satirized all generous instincts: Byron, Saint Hilare, Gautier. But Cervantes saw chivalry as noble. To understand his burlesque tone we must put ourselves in the author's times. Critics had long attacked chivalry novels on moral or esthetic grounds. At times the *Romancero* even parodied the chivalresque legends. But Cervantes never goes to the gross extremes of Góngora and Quevedo in his satire of epic figures. Only in the Belerma episode in Montesinos' cave is he crude in his parody of the chivalric myth. Actually he only touches the surface of the myth, not its basis.

198. Menéndez y Pelayo, Marcelino. "Cultura literaria de Miguel de Cervantes y elaboración del *Quijote*," in *Estudios y discursos de crítica histórica y literaria*, I. Edición preparada por Don Enrique Sánchez Reyes. *Edición nacional de las obras completas de Menéndez Pelayo*. Dirigida por D. Miguel Artigas, VI. Madrid: C. S. I. C., 1941, pp. 323-356. (Discurso leído en el Paraninfo de la Universidad Central en la solemne fiesta de 8 de mayo de 1905.)

Cervantes' basic talent is as a novelist, not as a poet or dramatist. He produced a new kind of prose narration, human, transcendental and eternal like the great epics, and at the same time domestic, familiar and accesible to all. But there are two novelistic Cervantes: (1) the continuer of old tradition *(Galatea)*; and (2) the innovator, the creator of a new type of extraordinary beauty *(Coloquio de los perros)*. Cervantes' *Novelas ejemplares* are a transition from the sketchy and fragmentary *Don Quijote* of 1605 toward the serene, perfect and balanced *Quijote* of 1615. Part I is ingeniously inspired; Part II is divinely reflective. The *Quijote* is a complete poetic world; it includes all the types of previous novels in such a way that all prior imaginative literature could be reconstructed from it. The greatest single influence on Cervantes was Boccaccio, but he affected the Spanish author's formal style only, not his *prosa familiar*. Cervantes was not an idiotic genius who was lucky only in one moment of his life. All his writing, even the weakest, shows culture and good sense.

Part II of the *Quijote* was written slowly, not with *genial precipitación* as some assert. Cervantes is at his best in dialogue, which was influenced by Lope de Rueda's *pasos* and by Rojas' *Celestina*, the latter, in turn, having been influenced by the Arcipreste de Talavera's *El corbacho*.

199. Menéndez y Pelayo, Marcelino. "Interpretaciones del *Quijote*," in *Estudios y discursos de crítica histórica y literaria*, I.

Edición preparada por D. Enrique Sánchez Reyes. *Edición nacional de las obras completas de Menéndez Pelayo*, VI. Dirigida por D. Miguel Artigas. Madrid: C. S. I. C., 1941, pp. 303-322. [Discurso leído en la Real Academia Española, el 29 de mayo de 1904, contestando al de recepción de don José María Asensio (9).]

The *Quijote* is not a work of antithesis, of dry and prosaic negation, but of purification and completion. Cervantes did not come to kill an ideal but to transfigure and enoble it. The *Quijote* is thus the last of the chivalry novels, the perfect and definitive one.

One of Cervantes' greater strokes of genius was leaving indecisive the boundary between sanity and insanity, and presenting the greatest wisdom through the mouth of a fool. By doing so, however, he did not intend to mock human intelligence or to scorn heroism in the *Quijote*, only the inadequate and anachronistic way in which the hero seeks to carry out an ideal which is good in itself. What unhinges Don Quijote is not his idealism but his anarchistic individualism. A false concept of activity is what disturbs him and drives him mad, what puts him in a terrible struggle with the world and makes sterile all his virtue and his effort. In the conflict of liberty with necessity Don Quijote succumbs because of his lack of adaptation to the means, but his defeat is no more than apparent because his generous aspiration remains whole and will be fulfilled in a better world, a fact revealed in his sane and calm death.

If Don Quijote is a symbol, and to a certain extent he is, he was not a symbol to Cervantes, but a living being, full of spiritual beauty, the prodigal son of his romantic fantasy. Cervantes did not compose the *Quijote* as an allegory; he *saw* Don Quijote with the sudden illumination of genius, followed his footsteps bewitched by him and produced a symbol without looking for it.

200. Menéndez y Pelayo, Marcelino. *Orígenes de la novela*. 4 vols. Madrid: Bailly-Bailliere e Hijos, 1905-1915.

[Chapter V of Volume One of this masterpiece deals with the chivalry novel in Spain. Don Marcelino, at page cxcviii, concludes that Ribaldo, the proverb-quoting squire in *Cifar*, is the only known literary ancestor of Sancho Panza. The critic, however, notes that Cervantes never mentions that work. In this same chapter Menéndez y Pelayo discusses Cervantes' judgment of *Tirante el Blanco* and mildly suggests that the author meant to say that Martorell "hizo tantas necedades de industria," instead of "no hizo tantas necedades de industria." The critic takes issue with Juan Calderón's atempts, in *Cervantes vindicado*... [Madrid, 1854, pp. 19-27], to rewrite Cervantes' judgment of that novel. At pages cclv-cclvi Menéndez y Pelayo disagrees with J. M. Warren [*A History of the Novel Previous to the Seventeenth Century*, 1895, p. 175] who concludes that *Tirante el Blanco* is a satire of chivalry novels. At page cclxvi the critic indicates that an episode in the *Palmerín* is the likely source of the lion adventure in the *Quijote*. At page ccxcviii Don Marcelino repeats his earlier observation in "Interpretaciones del *Quijote*" (199), that Cervantes' novel is a work of purification not of negation.

In Chapter VIII, which deals with the pastoral novel, Menéndez y Pelayo concludes that Cervantes probably took the name "Dulcinea" from Antonio de Lofrasso's *Los diez libros de la fortuna de amor*, Book VI, where the names Dulcineo and Dulcina appear.

In Chapter I of Volume III Don Marcelino briefly notes Cervantes' judgment of the *Celestina* and points out the great effect of that work on the author's habitual style.]

201. Merejkowski, Dmitri de. "Cervantes." *Hispania* (Paris), IV (1921), 97-124.

Cervantes devotes little attention to nature in his works, for he is far more interested in the human element. To him, unlike Byron, Shelly, Goethe and Shakespeare, nature has no power in and of itself.

Don Quijote, though a proud individual, loves the simple life. He is a forerunner, in this respect, of Jean-Jacques Rousseau. Both condemn the faults of modern culture. Sancho is the antithesis of the Knight, just as Mephisto is the opposite of Faust. The Squire and his master represent the eternal conflict between good sense and enthusiasm, realism and idealism. Sancho is a child of the Church. He is a monarchist and a confirmed conservative. The

Knight and the Squire represent the attraction of opposites, and they are inseparable until death.

There is a serious irony hidden in the *Quijote*. The protagonists are eccentric, foolish and idle dreamers. But are their scoffers more reasonable? No! Cervantes goes to great lengths to show the heartlessness and foolishness of such normal people as the Duke and Duchess.

202. *Miguel de Cervantes Saavedra; homenaje de Insula en el cuarto centenario de su nacimiento, 1547-1947.* [Madrid]: Insula, [1947]. Pp. 229. (*Cuadernos de Insula*, I).

[This collection contains fifteen articles on Cervantes and his works. The following deal with the *Quijote:* (1) "La palabra escrita y el *Quijote*" (73), by Américo Castro; (2) "La composición del *Quijote*," by Joaquín Casalduero; (3) "Un Quijote inglés," by William J. Entwistle; (4) "El *Quijote* de don Antonio de Sancha," by A. Rodríguez Moñino; (5) "Cervantes en la obra de Mark Twain," by Stephan Gilman; and (6) Jaime Ibáñez' "Cervantes y la novela moderna" (156).]

203. Millé y Giménez, Juan. *Sobre la génesis del Quijote.* Barcelona: Araluce, 1930. Pp. 219.

[A great deal of this work is devoted to the animosities between Lope de Vega and his contemporaries. Also, much attention is given to the various editions of *romances* at the end of the sixteenth and the beginning of the seventeenth century. Discussing *El entremés de los romances* Millé concludes (p. 89) that while it is not a great work, it is not altogether to be despised. In Chapter XIX the critic notes the similarities between Lope de Vega and Bartolo, the hero of the *entremés*: for example, both were married only a short time before going off on adventures. In Millé's opinion the *Entremés de los romances* is clearly a satire on Lope and even has a resemblance to an earlier play by Lope, *Belardo furioso*. In addition, notes Millé, the name Bartolo was apparently chosen because it had a sound similar to the name Belardo. In Chapter XXIV Millé concludes that the *Entremés de los romances* was written about 1588. In Chapter XXVI he presents a summary of other opinions on the question of the date of the *entremés* and whether it was a model for, or imitation of, the *Quijote*. In Chapter XXVII the critic refers to Avellaneda's remark about the "sinónimos voluntarios" used by Cervantes in place of real names. To Millé this indicates that Don Quijote was supposed to represent Lope de Vega, both figures being incorrigible idealists and mad on the subject of nobility. This appears to be the case, he adds, since the earlier chapters of the *Quijote* strongly resemble the *Entremés de los romances* and the *entremés* is definitely a satire against Lope.]

204. Monroy, Juan Antonio. *La biblia en el Quijote*. Madrid: V. Suárez, 1963. Pp. 176.

PART I

Although Cervantes refers to theology as the queen of the sciences, he is no theologian. Nevertheless he was an assiduous reader of the Holy Scriptures, as is particularly revealed in the *Quijote*.

The *Quijote* is by no means equal to the *Bible*, and they should not be compared. Nevertheless, there are certain parallels between them. The Bible is the history of the world as told by God; *Don Quijote* is the history of the world, told in a mundane way, by a great man. Both works are a mixture of history and poetry, artistically interwoven. Both are humanly profound. The difference is that the *Quijote* limits itself to analyzing our human condition, whereas the Scriptures, after analyzing our state through God's scrutinizing eye, offer us the solution: the blood of Christ is our redemption. The Bible and the *Quijote* are both widely circulated, universal works that have been of great influence on their readers. Both are sincere, and neither obscures human defects. These two works are also books that can only be understood when approached in the proper spirit, and there are portions in each which cannot be understood by mortals. The Bible and *Don Quijote* reveal a love for mankind. If the Bible is a manifestation of the love of God toward fallen man, the *Quijote* is the revelation of the love that an ill-treated man feels for his fellow human beings. In the pages of the Bible Cervantes learned to love God, and also learned to orient his love downward toward man, as the Holy Book counsels us.

Part II

[In this portion of his work Monroy sets forth, in order of their appearance in the *Quijote*, Cervantes' references to matters found in the Bible. Some such references are clearly biblical, such as the mentioning of Adam, Samson, Goliath, the belly of the whale, Sarah and Lot. Others are of a generally biblical flavor. Monroy cites the book, chapter and verse of the Bible that Cervantes appears to have drawn upon, and offers a brief comment on each reference. At the end of this work Monroy includes an index of the books of the Bible with citations to the chapter of the *Quijote* where passages in such books are referred to.]

205. Montero, Lázaro. "Dulcinea." *Anales Cervantinos*, IX (1961-1962), 229-246.

Don Quijote is a Platonist. For him things cease being what they are in order to correspond with the ideas he demands of them. Names are of great importance to him. His choice of "Rocinante" and "Quijote" are of simple derivation, but Dulcinea is harder to explain. Menéndez y Pelayo (200) believes that Cervantes drew upon Antonio Lefrasso's *Los diez libros de la fortuna de amor;* Clemencín and Lapesa conclude that Dulcinea is based on the word *dulce;* and Lubino states that Dulcinea comes from *Dulcis Ane, Ane* being *Ana Zarco* who supposedly jilted Cervantes in favor of Rodrigo Pacheco.

But Dulcinea is the pure creation of Don Quijote's imagination. She is born of the logical consequence of his love. Is she a symbol? Some view her as such. To Unamuno (309) she is glory, while to Suarès (295) she is liberty. Some view her as poetry, while others view her as Spain.

206. Montero Díaz, Santiago. *Cervantes, compañero eterno.* Madrid: Aramo, 1957. Pp. 200.

Turgenev saw Don Quijote and Hamlet as poles apart. This is not correct since Hamlet was capable of action and Alonso Quijano was at times melancholy. To Dostoyevsky the Don was sublime, the highest expression of human thought, yet a man filled with inner doubts, who yearned for reality. Cervantes and Dostoyevsky both suffered, but suffering had a different effect on each. Cervantes reacts with dignity; Dostoyevsky does not. Cervantes is a true Catholic; the Russian is anti-Church. Their two heroes, Don Quijote and Myshkin, are not at all alike.

[In his chapter "La idea de la muerte en la obra de Cervantes" Montero Díaz finds that death is *not* the center of Cervantes' works. Cervantes, Montero concludes, is very much oriented toward life.]

207. Montesinos, José F. "Cervantes Anti-novelista." *Nueva Revista de Filología Hispánica*, VII (1953), 449-514.

In the eighteenth century the novel had no status because critics were generally more interested in philosophical thoughts than in a story. Few in the eighteenth century considered the *Quijote* to be a novel, or *Roman*. Many thought that the novel should be an epic about the distant past. This idea continues into the nineteenth century, for an article in *El Censor*, dated May 16, 1822, concluded that the *Quijote* was to be highly valued because it was amusing, *not* because it was a novel.

208. Montoliu y de Togeres, Manuel de. *El alma de España y sus reflejos en la literatura del siglo de oro*. Barcelona: Editorial Cervantes, [1942]. Pp. 752.

The *Quijote* is a cruel book, for in it the chivalresque figure of old is brought into the real world and mocked. Yet Cervantes' novel merely follows the ironic current of literature applied to chivalresque matter, a current begun in Italy. In the *Quijote* this ironic attitude is applied to the *Amadís*, a Spanish work. Thus the material of the novel is Spanish, while the form (the interpretation of the Knight) is Italian.

The classical interpretation of Cervantes' masterpiece is that it is the last and greatest of the books of chivalry, a tearful goodbye to the medieval world. This is not a correct interpretation.

The *Quijote* was, instead, engendered and illuminated in a picaresque world, not a chivalresque world. What Cervantes does is uplift the picaresque genre, giving his rebelling hero the ideal of a redeeming end. To do this the author makes use of the chivalresque genre, which he never intended to continue, much less rejuvenate. In his hands the astute young vagabond becomes a part-sane wise man obsessed with the idea of becoming a model of chivalry. But the environment of the novel is essentially picaresque — highly realistic and basically pessimistic.

Cervantes' *Quijote* was first regarded as a burlesque novel. Later it came to be viewed as a satire on the struggle of reason against overimagination. With the early Romantics attention became focused upon the symbolical meaning of the two protagonists. The figure of the Knight, surely intended to be a burlesque figure, came to be the living and eternal image of the romantic soul, the great martyr of idealism.

After the early Romantics the satirical interpretation revives, but now the *Quijote* becomes with Heine, Byron, Grillparzer and others, a satire against all ideals, not merely a satire against books of chivalry. Many dispute this interpretation, and Unamuno (309) is the very antithesis of the view of Lord Byron and the other pessimists.

The concept of the dualism of an idealistic hidalgo and a realistic squire already existed in *Lazarillo*. Cervantes merely gives this idea amplification and transcendence. He confronts these two attitudes, these two worlds, the chivalresque and the picaresque. He does not prefer the one to the other, but uses the one to illuminate the other.

The noble function, the great mission, of the *picaro* is to confirm the Knight in his faith, to inculcate in him the full awareness of his lofty mission. In the *Quijote picaros* defeat the noble Knight. This is the supreme adventure of the Spanish *picaro*. Cercantes' masterpiece is thus not only a picaresque novel but the most basically picaresque novel of all, a superpicaresque novel. Don Quijote's return to sanity at the end is a victory of the picaresque; it is a picaresque incident. The fact that Cervantes causes his hero to regain his sanity shows that the author is basically anti-heroic.

The essential difference between the *Quijote* and the picaresque novel is that in Cervantes' work the hero is not a *picaro*, but a victim of *pícaros*. The style of the *Quijote*, however, is that of a picaresque novel. The hero has no internal evolution, though his viewpoint changes. In addition, there is a series of adventures without any cause and effect relationship between them. The *Quijote* can be defined as the only picaresque novel in literature that is written with a feeling of pity. But this pity is concentrated on the humble people who make up the picaresque environment. This contrasts with the author's cruelty toward the Knight, not as a human being but as a representative of a bygone age discredited by the victorious current of the Renaissance.

Cervantes' life indicates his Stoic character, but the *Quijote* is far from a Stoic work. The Knight, however, is Stoic in the sense that he seeks justice and reason on earth, but his self-seeking desire for fame prevents his being a true disciple of Stoicism. Certain Stoic ideas are, nevertheless, expressed by Cervantes in his masterpiece: that liberty is the basis of happiness and dignity; that conquering oneself is the first virtue; that each person creates his own destiny. The Don's death, however, is not truly stoic. It is simply a Christian death.

209. Montoliu y de Togeres, Manuel de. *Tríptico del "Quijote". Edición homenaje con motivo del IV centenario del nacimiento de Cervantes*. Barcelona: Editorial Cervantes, 1947. Pp. 244.

The four-point basis of the *Quijote* is made up of: (1) the chivalry novel; (2) the pastoral novel; (3) the byzantine novel; and (4) the picaresque novel. The chivalry novel was dying; the pastoral and byzantine genres were exhausted. The picaresque novel, however, was just beginning, and it is this genre that gives the *Quijote* its essentially realistic basis. In effect Cervantes' masterpiece is an original combination of the spirit of books of chivalry and the spirit of the picaresque novel.

Sancho and his master are complementary parts of one complete human soul, complete in its excellence and in its miseries. Both protagonists are philosophers; both have proverbs based on justice and fairness; each always ends by understanding the other, though their common philosophy has a different manner of expression in each.

The marvel of the *Quijote* springs from the same moral, psychological and social depths that produced the picaresque novel.

In both, the hero is unable to adapt. Neither the Don nor the *pícaro* knows any law but his own individuality. What Cervantes succeeds in doing is to bring the *pícaro* out of his vulgar struggle for existence and give him an ideal.

210. Morel-Fatio, A. "Le *Don Quichotte* envisagé comme peinture et critique de la société espagnole du XVIe et du XVIIe siècle," in *Études sur Espagne*, I. Paris: E. Bouillon, 1895, pp. 295-382. (Lecture fait à l'Institut Taylor d'Oxford, le 21 Novembre, 1894.)

Cervantes was not well educated. He uses faulty reasoning, and his ideas are poorly expressed and confused when he attempts to be philosophical. Contrary to a number of critics, Cervantes was not an advanced thinker on religion and politics; nor was he a universal genius as some contend. He was a very able storyteller *et un honnête homme*.

The *Quijote* was begun as a satire on chivalry novels but grew to become the great social novel of Spain, a novel that reflected Spain's passions, prejudices, customs and institutions at a precise moment in history. Cervantes pictures priests, bureaucrats, Moors, noblemen, hidalgos, soldiers, jurists and other types. His work is not a critical review of social classes like Quevedo's *Sueños*. Instead it is a fantastic voyage through Spanish society guided by Cervantes' capricious imagination. Some types are not pictured in the *Quijote*, especially certain city types. But those who are chosen are portrayed with such great relief and life that, if the *Quijote* were the only work to survive, we would have an excellent idea of its author's epoch.

[Morel-Fatio concludes on pages 340 and 341 that the *Quijote* is basically a disguised attack on the plague of Spanish society, *hidalguismo*. This criticism of *hidalguismo*, Morel-Fatio continues, is especially effective since it is never actually formulated; it is even disguised by the fact that the hero is endowed with lovable traits of character. Cervantes, states the critic, undertook to kill off *hidalguismo* by causing the reader to laugh it out of existence.]

211. Morel-Fatio, A. "Le troisième centenaire de Cervantes." *Revue des Deux Mondes*, CCLIV (1916), 590-619.

[Morel-Fatio traces the question whether the *Quijote* destroyed the concept of honor in Spain, and the opinions of William Temple, Juan Maruján, Lord Byron and others are discussed. The critic regards Cervantes' masterpiece as a social novel, not a *roman à clef* or a symbolical work. But if forced to find symbols in the two protagonists, Morel-Fatio would contend that the Knight represents the heroic individualist who disdains the day-to-day life, and that the Squire symbolizes the materialistic, submissive, domestic type governed largely by fear.

Other matters discussed in this article are the reception of the *Quijote* in Spain, France and England, and the generally unfavorable attitude of seventeenth-century Spanish critics toward Cervantes. As in his prior work (210) Morel-Fatio finds the *Quijote* to be *antihidalguismo*.]

212. Moreno Báez, Enrique. "Arquitectura del *Quijote*." *Revista de Filología Española*, XXXII (1948), 269-285.

The *Quijote* began as a short story, but Cervantes added extraneous matter grouped around a discourse on Arms and Letters. In Part I Cervantes is occasionally uncertain and makes several changes in plans. For example, the author first states that Fernando and Dorotea will accompany the Knight to his village; then he decides instead that the *cuadrilleros* are to escort him home. Part II of the *Quijote* is more compact, though it too contains side episodes. The purpose of the episode of the *Duques* is to avoid the monotony of a series of adventures; but the pranks at the ducal palace become quite boring. In general, however, Part II is better planned, there are fewer breaks in the action, and the denouement is preconceived.

Platonism denied the reality of sensations, and Being was considered to be ideas received through reflection. The early Renaissance is Platonic. However, in the middle of the sixteenth century thinkers turned to Aristotle, who believed that there were no ideas without concrete forms. The Baroque era is Aristotelian; it emphasizes the concrete and does not avoid ugliness. Cervantes is at the crossroads of the Renaissance and the Baroque. He grew up a Platonist but later accepted the Aristotelian Baroque. However, Cervantes does not use Platonism as a mere ornament or as a disguise for his true attitudes. He genuinely believed in the superiority of ideas.

In Part I Don Quijote is Platonic and gives form to his preconceived ideas. The other characters seek to bring him into the world of Aristotelian forms. In Part II others attempt to keep the Knight within the world of Platonic ideas. In Part I the fantastic and the real worlds are distinct, whereas in Part II they cross each other permitting more complicated attitudes.

213. Moreno Báez, Enrique. *Reflexiones sobre el Quijote.* Madrid: Editorial "Prensa Española," 1968. Pp. 181.

[This work consists of twelve chapters. Chapter I is an elaboration of Moreno's previous artcile (212) on the structure of the *Quijote*. Chapter II is concerned with the history of chivalry novels, which Cervantes attacked not as a moralist, the critic states, but as an artist. In the third chapter Moreno discusses the author's attitude toward chivalric ideals and concludes that in the *Quijote* Cervantes was spoofing his early idealism. Cervantes' soul was split on the question of ideals, the critic concludes — he makes fun of pastoral idealism yet yearns to finish the *Galatea*. The fourth chapter of this work is an analysis of Madariaga's (182) concept of the *quijotización* of Sancho and the *sanchificación* of Don Quijote. Religion is the topic of Chapter V. Here Moreno reaches the conclusion that Cervantes was a product of the Counter Reformation and not a man who supported *libertad de conciencia* as we understand the term today. Though two of Cervantes' passages were later censored (making a rosary out of a shirttail and criticizing half-hearted works of charity), Moreno concludes that Cervantes' anti-clerical remarks were typical of his times.

In Chapter VI, "El *Quijote* y la España de los Felipes," the critic warns the reader not to worry about the geography and chronology of the *Quijote,* and not to be concerned about the fact that several of the characters may have been based on real-life figures. In Chapter VII Moreno Báez asks what *verdad* meant to Cervantes, and concludes that he was referring to artistic truth, or verisimilitude. Discussing the structure of the *Quijote,* Moreno concludes that Cervantes saw the advantage of writing his story at various levels of fiction, for this added a certain depth to the story, a depth characteristic of baroque literature. In the following chapter Moreno continues his examination of baroque elements in the *Quijote,* finding that the series of contrasts in the novel is typically baroque. Chapter IX deals with the *dinamismo* of Cervantes' novel, another factor which, to Moreno, indicates its baroque structure. The following chapter discusses baroque *manierismo* which, to a certain extent, Moreno finds to be present in the *Quijote.* Chapter XI deals with the humor in Cervantes' novel — the puns, the anachronisms, the new words, etc. The final chapter discusses Cervantes' renaissance desire to amaze the reader with strange events, his search for variety and suspense.]

214. Murillo, Luis Andrés. "Cervantic Irony in *Don Quijote:* The Problem for Literary Criticism." *Homenaje a Rodríguez Moñino,* II. Madrid: Editorial Castalia, 1966, pp. 21-27.

In English criticism of the eighteenth century Cervantes had been regarded as a writer of grave irony. Romantic, subjective criticism was aware of the dialectical opposites which became reconciled by the author of the *Quijote.* Historical criticism saw the conflict of Cervantes with his times, and biographical criticism concluded that the author's life was likely to lead him to an ironic view of idealism. Menéndez y Pelayo, in his *Orígenes de la novela* (200), is the first in Spanish criticism to view Cervantes as a benevolently ironic writer who in a kindly way sought to destroy previous genres. Theretofore in Spain Cervantes' *ironía* had been regarded not as kindly but as *burla fina.* Actually, Menéndez y Pelayo's concept of Cervantine irony is a synthetic composition of nineteenth-century Cervantine criticism: esthetic, biographical, historical.

215. Navarro González, Alberto. "La locura quijotesca." *Anales Cervantinos,* I (1951), 273-294.

Don Quijote can behave sanely, but superior forces compel him at times to act insanely. The essential characteristics of his madness are: (1) his belief that chivalry novels are real; (2) his tendency to deform reality (windmills become giants); (3) his inclination at times to transfigure reality, to see things as they are but to interpret them differently from others (*Galeotes* and enchanted Dulcinea episodes).

What did the Don accomplish, other than injuring several people? He did not bring peace, but war. Viewed from the outside, he gained nothing. But viewed from the inside, he was able to present himself before God and history with his personality developed to the maximum and as a supreme model of heroic sacrifice ("desvivir") in pursuit of something considered as objectively superior to his own existence.

216. Navarro González, Alberto. "El ingenioso Don Quijote en la España del siglo XVII." *Anales Cervantinos,* VI (1957), 1-48.

It is a cliché nowadays that he seventeenth century did not see the deeper side of Don Quijote. This is incorrect. The Knight from La Mancha, due to the many facets of his character, provoked varied reactions. True, some such as Francisco de Ávila, saw only his silly side. However, Juan de Burgos, in his *Gracioso romance* did not dwell on the Don's ridiculous aspects, and Guillén de Castro pictured the Knight as patient, courageous, and more a Christian than a knight-errant.

Some erudite critics of the seventeenth century considered Don Quijote a purely burlesque figure: Nicolás Antonio, Mateo de la Bastida. Yet with Padre Moret in 1666, the Knight becomes a symbolic type.

217. Navarro González, Alberto. "El ingenioso Don Quijote, caballero andante cristiano y santo." *Anales Cervantinos,* VI (1957), 49-95.

Cervantes did not seek to portray Don Quijote as a perfect, exemplary knight of the seventeenth century. Nor did he intend to picture his hero as completely ridiculous. Cervantes gives the Don certain virtues, but does not grant him the means for carrying out his ideals. To the author the Knight was both sublime and ridiculous, a much more human figure than Amadís and other fictional knights-errant. Though Cervantes pictures his Don as practicing basic Christian virtues, he does not intend for the hero to be considered a saint, for the Knight is clearly not even an exemplary Christian. Don Quijote has too many faults: he is proud; he has an exaggerated devotion to Dulcinea; he neglects prayer.

The idea that Don Quijote is similar to Ignatius Loyola goes back to 1688. The belief that the Knight is related to Teresa de Ávila arises somewhat later. While all three are similar, they differ sharply in a number of respects. All read chivalry novels, but with differing intensity. All three seek to bring back an older way of life and thereby save Christianity. But the older way of life which each searches for is vastly different, and their means of accomplishing their goal vary markedly. While Saint Teresa and Saint Ignatius have quixotic qualities (reforming zeal and self-sacrifice), they are serious, humble and reasonable. Don Quijote, though he moves partially along the path of sainthood, becomes vain, violent and anarchistic.

218. Navarro y Ledesma, Francisco. *El ingenioso hidalgo Miguel de Cervantes Saavedra*. Buenos Aires - México: Espasa Calpe Argentina, S. A., 1944. Pp. 350.

Part I of the *Quijote* is like Part I of Goethe's *Faust*. But the German failed in his continuation while the Spaniard succeeded. Cervantes, in 1615, knew how to resolve all difficulties and to leave man consoled. The hero dies happy. Goethe would have disenchanted Dulcinea and brought Aldonza Lorenzo to the dying Knight's bedside. Cervantes admirably portrays the deathbed scene. Only Shakespeare could have equalled it for only these two geniuses could turn a tear into a smile and a smile into laughter, and at the end, convert laughter into a smile and a smile into a tear.

219. Nelson, Jr., Lowry, ed. *Cervantes: A Collection of Critical Essays*. Englewood Cliffs, N. J.: Prentice Hall, 1969. Pp. x + 176.

[In his introduction Nelson traces the general history of the interpretation of the *Quijote*. He warns against trying to type Cervantes as a humorist, for, like Shakespeare, he resists classification. Nelson also suggests that the reader of the *Quijote* exercise restraint in using that novel as a textual ground for expansive speculation on large philosophical and existential issues. Included by the editor in this work are the following ten articles, all rendered in English: Gerald Brenan's "Cervantes" (50), Harry Levin's "The Example of Cervantes" (171), Thomas Mann's "Voyage with Don

Quixote" (190), W. H. Auden's "The Ironic Hero: Some Reflections on Don Quijote" (13), Leo Spitzer's "On the Significance of *Don Quijote*" (290), Erich Auerbach's "The Enchanted Dulcinea" (14), E. C. Riley's "Literature and Life," Carlos Blanco Aguinaga's "Cervantes and the Picaresque Mode: Notes on Two Kinds of Realism" (30), Edwin Honig's "On the *Interludes* of Cervantes," and an excerpt from William J. Entwistle's *Cervantes* (100), entitled "Ocean of Story."]

220. Neuschäfer, Hans-Jörg. *Der Sinn der Parodie im Don Quijote*. Heidelberg: C. Winter, 1963. Pp. 119.

Don Quijote is still worth studying as basically a satire on the extremes found in books of chivalry, for the author's satire against such works is not mere window dressing in that novel. The *Quijote* is a culmination of tendencies already found in the better chivalry novels, such as *Tirant lo blanc*. This work, quite a realistic story, contains a critique of the self-inflicted agonies of courtly love. The idea for chivalry ideals to move into the fantasy of one person is the culmination of a long historical process. *Amadís* is the great forerunner of the *Quijote* in this respect, though courtly love was still accepted by society in the *Amadís*. The power of the lady-love had grown stronger from the *Artusroman* to *Erec* and on to the *Amadís*, and the hero Amadís' complete belief in Oriana is a step towards Don Quijote's imagined fantasy of complete devotion to Dulcinea. Furthermore, in *Palmerín*, Floramán's intense devotion to his dead lady-love is not far removed for Don Quijote's love for the fantasized Dulcinea.

In the *Artusroman* the hero's deeds benefit society. This is no longer true in *Amadís*, and becomes even less true in the *Quijote*. Ariosto is an important stage in the development of the *Quijote*. In *Orlando furioso* the epic world is still present, but the story of the typically insane lover is told with ironic distance. In the *Quijote* the epic world is no longer there, and the insanity of the hero becomes the real motivation of the plot.

Don Quijote's being a foolish idealist is only part of the picture. A goodly portion of the hero's insanity is a moral problem. The *Quijote*, Américo Castro's *Pensamiento* (63) notwithstanding, is *not* a critique of reality. Cervantes is on the side of reality. His hero's return to reason is a return unto himself and a recognition of his true self.

Weinrich (317) asserts that the irony of the *Quijote* is that the hero goes insane and yet achieves higher spiritual capabilities. This is incorrect, for the true irony is that the Knight becomes insane yet keeps his reason. Luis Rosales (261) asserts that *quijanismo* is based on giving reality to *quijotismo*. This is not correct, for the opposite is true.

221. Novitsky, Pavel I. *Cervantes and Don Quixote: A Sociohistorical Interpretation*. Translated from the Russian by Sonia Volochova. New York: The Critics' Group, 1936. Pp. 32. Russian version "Don Kikhot Servantesa," in *Khitroumny idalgo Don Kikhot Lamancheski*. Moscow-Leningrad: Academia, 1929, pp. v-xxxvii. [A portion of this work is presented as "Thematic Design" in *Cervantes Across the Centuries* (112), pp. 249-255.]

The *Quijote* is not structurally perfect. The interpolated material is not convincingly linked to the basic theme, for the novel was in its beginnings with the *Quijote*. Yet the appearance of Cervantes' masterpiece proclaimed the victory of the new artforms that reflected the new socio-cultural modes. It marked the beginning of the naturalistic novel in the history of literature. The unity of the *Quijote* was achieved not through superficial, external means, but through the unity of the age itself. The explanation for its organic completeness is to be found in the unity of its thematic design which not only governs the general structure, but also governs the individual parts of the composite whole.

Cervantes' novel was directed against the literature of the period. The *Quijote* ridiculed the novels of chivalry, their authors and their readers, for they were attempting to escape reality. Cervantes showed how such books could befog life. But he does not limit himself to exposing the harmful influence of such works. His book has a more profound and more far-reaching purpose. It lampoons the aristocratic culture of the nobility. It reveals the cynicism of Ducal courts, the uselessness of certain groups, the greed of the merchants. The *Quijote* is not merely a satire on the Spanish gentry of the sixteenth century; it is a record of a culture centuries old.

Heine saw that the *Quijote* was an attack on misdirected enthusiasm, but failed to distinguish between reactionary utopianism and revolutionary utopianism. Thus Heine left no outlet for life and struggle.

The Knight lacks a feeling for reality. He has slept through the fall of feudalism. The Don ignores his environment. To him reality is a world of dreams. He is aimlessly mad, for his madness lacks direction.

Cervantes needed protagonists, not only for the sake of maintaining the dialogue and burlesque technique of the novel, but also to enable him to give the fullest and most profound solution of the fundamental thematic problem of his composition. His two protagonists symbolize the tragic dualism of a vast class-culture that hesitates between negating the reality of the external world (spiritualism) and championing materialism and sober reckoning.

222. Olmedo, Félix G. *El Amadís y el Quijote; Soneto famoso al túmulo de Felipe II; El Persiles.* Madrid: Editora Nacional, 1947, pp. 1-148.

Many readers took the feats of Amadís and Esplandián literally. The Don does so and fails because he does not see the true spirit of these two stories. Montalvo sought to correct this tendency toward a literal reading by revealing the true moral of his *Amadís* and *Esplandián*: that they were designed to show that virtue, when accompanied by prudence, was a powerful force. The battles in these stories were symbolical, and the miraculous cures of the heroes illustrated the superiority of spirit over matter, of virtue over vice. In the *Esplandián,* the continuation of the *Amadís,* Montalvo even criticized chivalry novels, which criticism later became crystalized in the *Quijote*. Thus Cervantes' masterpiece is not truly a parody of the *Esplandián* but an ingenious interpretation of it. In both of Montalvo's chivalry stories there appears a spirit of disillusionment, a feeling that life is a vanity of vanities. This same air pervades the last chapter of the 1615 *Quijote*. In fact, Cervantes follows the *Amadís* and the *Esplandián* in numerous ways, though he pretends to be mocking them. The lion adventure and that of the army of sheep are drawn from the *Amadís,* as is the Don's letter to Dulcinea; and the advice of the Knight to

Sancho is similar to Amadís' counsel to his squire Gandalín. From Chapter XCIX of the *Esplandián* Cervantes appears to have drawn the episode of Montesinos' cave, for both deal with a sleeping protagonist who has a subterranean adventure. The opening chapters of Part II of the *Quijote* are like Book IV of the *Amadís* where King Lisuarte spends ten days in bed surrounded by chatting friends, and Chapter XCVIII of the *Esplandián* may well be the source of the Clavileño episode. But the greatest similarity between the *Quijote* and these two prior works is in their spirit and style, and the critique of chivalry novels in Chapters XCVIII and XCIX of the *Esplandián* may well be the very genesis of the *Quijote*.

There is one basic difference between the attitude of Montalvo and that of Cervantes: their portrayal of clergymen. With Montalvo priests are very conscious of themselves and their mission. Cervantes, however, takes the same ironic view of men of the cloth that he takes of laymen, though he does not go to the extremes found in *Lazarillo*. In general, the author avoids theology for he does not feel qualified in this area. In no sense is Cervantes a follower of Erasmus.

223. Ortega y Gasset, José. *Meditaciones del Quijote*. Comentario por Julián Marías. Madrid: Revista de Occidente, 1966. Pp. 367. (First published in 1914: Madrid, Imprenta Clásica Española de Madrid.)

The secret of an ingenious work of art does not admit itself to intellectual invasion, and Cervantes is sadly seated in the Elysian fields waiting for a descendant who can understand him.

Cervantes is typically Mediterranean or Latin in his ability to picture things before our eyes. The North European Goethe does not have this ability. The *Quijote* is ambiguous, and previous investigation is of little value. Is the author making fun? What is he making fun of? Is making fun necessarily a negation? The *Quijote* gives few clues as to how it is to be interpreted. Cervantes is no ideologist. But isn't this perhaps his supreme gift? Is the author serious about his book being an attack on chivalry novels, or is this a cover-up like his calling his short stories *exemplary*?

Cervantes can not picture the world as simply as did the Greeks and the medieval writers. He looks at the world from the height of the Renaissance. During that epoch psychology became important. The interior world, the subjective, became of ever increasing interest. The *Quijote* is the product of these tendencies. The reality of the adventure is saved but its saving involves the sharpest irony. The reality of the adventure is reduced to the psychological.

How can reality convert itself into poetic substance? We must take it obliquely as a destruction of the myth. The myth is always the point of departure of all literature, including realistic literature. Only that in realistic literature we accompany the myth in its fall.

There are two ways of looking at the hero — tragically or comically. He is a hero, but not an epic figure. A tragic figure is half unreal. To take the tragic hero and eliminate the unreal element is to convert him into a comic character. The comic lives upon the tragic like the novel upon the epic. Don Quijote is converted into a comic figure, and the novel is on the point of becoming simply a comedy. The novel is *tragicomedia,* a synthesis of the tragic and the comic. The *Quijote* is pessimistic, but not perversely so like nineteenth-century pessimism. In a sense the *Quijote* is a sad parody of a more divine Christ, a Gothic Christ created by a heartsick imagination that has lost both its innocence and its will.

224. Osterc, Ludovik. *El pensamiento social y político del Quijote.* Mexico: Ediciones Andrea, 1963. Pp. 280. (Colección Studium, vol. 40.)

Previous criticism of the *Quijote* is wrong to consider that novel as purely an imaginative work separate from its times. The author's repeated assertions that his story is only an attack on chivalry novels is merely a smokescreen for an attack on dying Medievalism and rising Capitalism. Morel-Fatio (210) and others are wrong to consider Cervantes as purely a man of his times. He was by no means typical of the prejudices of his era. Cervantes not only describes his epoch; he takes a position about his environment and its institutions. From the viewpoint of renaissance Humanism the author of the *Quijote* criticizes the social, political, and religious institutions of the rotten feudal system of Spain. He condemns the rising capitalists, the clergy, and the idle, parasitic nobles. But the author is subtle in his attacks, for he could not afford to be open and frank. Cervantes symphathizes with the humble. His heroes rise up against the powers that be in such episodes as that of the galley slaves. The *Quijote*, in essence, is the first great social-philosophical novel in universal literature.

225. Palacín Iglesias, Gregorio B. *En torno al Quijote (Ensayo de interpretación y crítica)*. Madrid: Leira, 1965. Pp. xv + 261.

Prior to the *Quijote* reality was not considered a proper matter for poetic treatment, but Cervantes makes it an integral part of the novel. The author reveals the tragic sense of life, but at the same time shows a sense of humor. This conscious duality, coupled with observation, makes Cervantes' novel a full picture of humanity.

[Palacín's work presents a history of the chivalry novel and also a very general summary of the criticism of the *Quijote* from the seventeenth to the twentieth century.]

226. Palacín Iglesias, Gregorio B. *El Quijote en la literatura universal*. Madrid: Leira, 1965. Pp. 70.

[In his first chapter Palacín quotes the opinions of numerous critics about the *Quijote*: William Godwin, Victor Hugo, William Dean Howell, and many more. He also raises the question whether Cervantes' masterpiece is a difficult work to understand, and concludes that it is not. Chapter II deals with the diffusion of the *Quijote*, its translation, and its influence on both literature and on art. Chapter III continues the examination of the effect of the *Quijote* on later writers: Fielding, Sterne, Smollet, Jean Paul, Flaubert and others. Chapter IV discusses the influence of Cervantes' novel in North America on such writers as Washington Irving and Mark Twain. The fifth and last chapter of Palacín's book studies the *Quijote* as a work of consolation, stimulation, and of human solidarity.]

227. Palacios, Leopoldo Eulogio. "La significación doctrinal del *Quijote*." *Revista de Filología Española*, XXXII (1948), 307-318.

There is a double intention in the *Quijote*: (1) what is said by Cervantes (to discredit chivalry novels); (2) the hidden meaning. There are two schools of thought: (1) those who take Cervantes literally; and (2) those who, in their search for a secret meaning, go beyond the confines of time and space.

All human action has two levels, the ends and the means. Don Quijote has good intentions but poor means, whereas Sancho is the opposite. The Knight is the symbol of doctrinairism (doing good through abstract principles). Sancho is practical, but at the same time greedy and opportunistic. Neither of them is a complete man; together they would form a perfect man — a prudent man.

228. Parker, A[lexander] A. "*Don Quijote* and the Relativity of Truth." *The Dublin Review*, XLIV (1947), 28-37.

Is Don Quijote a saint, as Sir Herbert Grierson (134) contended? No! A truer reading of Cervantes' novel reveals that though the Don may have the courage of a saint, he does not pursue the aims of a saint; that his conception of right is disturbed by wrong; that his moral error, not his virtue, makes him mad.

It is also mistaken to view the *Quijote* in terms of philosophical idealism (i.e., that each man is the moulder of reality) as Américo Castro does in *El pensamiento de Cervantes* (63). Though this approach makes the novel infinitely suggestive, it confuses the human issues at stake. If one views the *Quijote* realistically (if reality is what it is, and if human actions are seen to conform or go counter to reality because of motives which the actors conceive rightly or wrongly to be in their own interest), then the novel makes sense. It is true that the Knight's ideal is noble, and his tenacity is admirable, but the essential point is that a vainglorious conceit distorts the ideal and stultifies it in practice. The *Quijote* is not a consoling book in the way that Grierson (134) thought, for the hero is so pathetic that the novel is deeply tinged with irony. It seems to impress a not too comforting conclusion on us: that men, for a variety of selfish reasons, are all too prone to pervert the truth and to jest with life, but that there is a final reality not easy to trifle with.

229. Parker, Alexander A. "A Revaluation of *Don Quijote*." *The Listener*, XLV (March 22, 1951), 509-510.

The Romantics notwithstanding, Cervantes' hero does not represent the idealist, the noble madman, battling vainly against a commonplace world. Instead, Don Quijote is a man who must be delivered from untruth; and Cervantes accomplishes this in stages. The hero is caused to sink from his quixotic pride and to rise to truth. While we take the hero's side against the forces of frivolity and derision, we do not side with him against the forces of reason and sanity.

230. Parker, Alexander A. "El concepto de la verdad en el *Quijote*." *Revista de Filología Española*, XXXII (1948), 287-305.

Américo Castro (63) believed that truth is very important in the *Quijote* and felt that the Knight was entitled to his own view of truth. Castro, more subtly than Unamuno (309), reinforced the romantic conception of the Don — a sublime madman with every right to be one. Don Quijote, said the Romantics, was more sane than those around him. The Romantics, however, were *not* the first to understand the *Quijote*, for Cervantes had a subtle appreciation of his own novel.

The concept of truth in the *Quijote* is that everything and every person has its own inalterable identity, but the human mind has to interpret this identity. The senses do not deceive a person, but men do. In the *Quijote* nearly everyone lies. Don Quijote falsifies truth to gain fame when he insists that the basin is a helmet. He becomes vain, and his vainglory corrupts his high ideals. The Knight becomes a danger to society for he thinks that altruism is all that is needed and that results are unimportant. The hero must be purified of his egoism. The recovery of sanity at the end of the novel is not merely a conventional end to satisfy the requirements of literary satire, nor is it the signal of defeat by breaking the hero's will. The regaining of sanity is a logical culmination; Don Quijote needs to know reality. He recovers his mental faculties when he repents morally. The problem in the *Quijote* is the struggle with self-deception and with the lies of others. In spite of the fact that truth and lies become confused in the novel, there is an antithesis between them. While no doubt the *Quijote* underlines the difficulty of learning the truth, the major problem in the story is moral, not sensorial.

231. Parker, A[lexander] A. "Fielding and the Structure of *Don Quijote*." *Bulletin of Hispanic Studies*, XXXIII (1956), 1-16.

Fielding's *Joseph Andrews*, like the *Quijote*, is rambling, whereas *Tom Jones* is coherent and carefully planned. In the latter work Fielding changed his style. He no longer appreciated the structure of the *Quijote*, referring to it in 1752 as "loose and unconnected," and stating that the adventures in Cervantes' masterpiece could be read in any order. But, was Fielding right? No! The 1605 *Quijote* is a progressive unfolding of a pattern dependent upon the sequence of the adventures. There is no cause and effect progression here but a progression from one motif to a closely related motif. Don Quijote passes from injuring the innocent (funeral cortege) to aiding the guilty (galley slaves). The penance episode is brought in to show the inner side of the hero's madness. Here Don Quijote *deliberately* imposes his imagination upon his will, and here he reaches an inner nadir which the previous adventure of the galley slaves had touched upon in his social world. With the reappearance of the priest and the barber illusions are now created for Don Quijote by others — a logical progression. Don Quijote, having given free rein to his imagination in the penance episode is now without protection against the imagination of others. There are thus five phases to the hero's career: (1) he imposes his will on others: (2) he imposes his imagination on the external world; (3) he imposes his imagination on his own conscious will (penance); (4) others (priest, barber, Dorotea, et al.) impose their imagination on Don Quijote; and (5) others impose their will on Don Quijote (cage). Thus a kind of circular pattern emerges whereby the theme is inverted in the middle and the end returns to the beginning.

Part Two of *Don Quijote* has a unified design, and is a progression from Part I. The purpose of the 1615 *Quijote* was to restore the hero's sanity by bringing forward his good qualities that had been distorted by megalomania. From the start Don Quijote is less arrogant and impetuous. The main difference in Part II is that the Knight is exclusively deceived by others. His responsibility for his madness will grow less and less, and his patience, bravery and magnanimity will come to the fore. The theme of deception shows a progressive graduation from the well-intentioned lies at the close of Part I to the purely selfish and frivolous deceptions aimed at deriding Don Quijote. Responsibility is thus shifted from the hero to others, and as their stature declines, Don Quijote's rises, until he finds salvation.

232. Peers, E. Allison. "Aportación de los hispanistas extranjeros al estudio de Cervantes." *Revista de Filología Española,* XXXII (1948), 151-188. [Translated into English as "Cervantes Criticism Outside Spain," in *Santa Teresa of Jesus and Other Essays and Addresses.* London: Faber & Faber, 1951, pp. 265-290. (Originally read before the Asamblea Cervantina de la Lengua Española, April 17, 1948.)]

[This work traces the various leading interpretations of the *Quijote* from the seventeenth century to the middle of our century. Non-Spanish critics such as Duffield, who saw Cervantes as a crusader, are discussed, and the allegorists, such as André Suarès (295) are noted. Peers disagrees with J. Bickermann (38), who considered the Knight a would-be superman who sought to impose his will on society. Morel-Fatio (210) is criticized for being a *simplista* when he stated that Cervantes was no genius, just a man of his times. The question of Erasmus' influence on Cervantes is discussed, and the opinions of Américo Castro (67) and M. Bataillon (29) are studied.]

233. Pemán, José María. "La 'armazón de cauallería' de Don Quijote (Apuntes sobre el capítulo III de la primera parte)." *Boletín de la Real Academia Española,* XXVII (1947-1948), 7-19.

Cervantes' satire of a knighting ceremony in Chapter III, Part I, is brutal and merciless. In particular it is a parody of the knighting of Esplandián in Chapter LII, Book IV of the *Amadís,* a passage which had inspired Ignacio de Loyola to stand watch over his own arms.

The knighting ceremony was a religious ceremony, but Cervantes' satire of it does not make him a disciple of Erasmus. The author of the *Quijote* is for realism, for modern humanism, for true heroism; he is opposed to both medieval idealism and ancient, epic idealism.

234. Petriconi, H. "Kritik und Interpretation des *Quijote.*" *Die Neueren Sprachen*, XXXIV (1926), 329-342.

The great change in *Don Quijote* criticism appears to have taken place when certain readers began to feel sympathy for the hero instead of laughing at him. Samuel Johnson, in the mid-eighteenth century, is a great exponent of this new attitude.

In the nineteenth century, Spanish criticism of the *Quijote* and other works of Cervantes becomes excessively detailed, and the author comes to be regarded as an expert on almost everything — medicine, geography, military science, etc.

235. Pfandl, Ludwig. "Der Ritter als Narr," in *Geschichte der spanischen Nationalliteratur in ihrer Blütezeit*. Freiburg im Breisgau: Herder & Co., 1929, pp. 289-296.

There are, in general, two groups of Cervantes critics: (1) the subjective-symbolical group; and (2) the literal-minded group that views the *Quijote* as purely a satire against chivalry novels. Each person has not only a right but a duty to interpret the *Quijote* as he sees it. In general, the *first* sally is against chivalry novels. With the addition of Sancho, however, the novel grows beyond the original sketch. The hero is no longer a complete fool. Like his cousin the Glass Licentiate he has lucid intervals. Cervantes, a man of the Renaissance who opposed the degeneracy of baroque literature with its extremes of illusionism and naturalism, creates *Don Quijote* to make the Spain of his times aware of these extremes. The Knight represents illusionism, the Squire materialism (naturalism).

Don Quijote has much in common with Loyola and Teresa de Ávila. All three, late in life, set out to lead people to higher goals. Why must the hero be a fool in Cervantes' novel? Cervantes wants to teach, and the more serious his message, the funnier the story must be. It is part of the "Scherz mit Wahrheit" concept, that seriousness had to be amusing in order to be heard. Avellaneda's Don Quijote is a fool without ideals, and the false *Quijote* is strictly an attack on chivalry novels. Cervantes' *Quijote* is much more.

Why does the hero regain his sanity at the end? Because the hero (and the author) sees that the struggle in behalf of Spain has been in vain.

236. Predmore, Richard L. "La apoteosis de Don Quijote." *Revista de Filología Hispánica*, I (1939), 262-264.

After the Romantic exaltation of Don Quijote in the early nineteenth century, the fame of Cervantes' novel spread to many countries. Turgenev in his "Hamlet y Don Quijote," 1879, came to view the Knight as a Christ-like figure, trampled by the pigs of this world. Enrique Rodó continues this tendency to deify the Don in his "El Cristo a la jineta" (257), calling him "Cristo guerrero" and "Cristo militante." Unamuno, especially in his "Don Quijote en la tragicomedia europea contemporánea" (307), also finds a divine element in Cervantes' hero and concludes that the *Quijote* is a national Bible, a work in which Spaniards might learn the heroic way to withstand mockery.

[Rubén Darío's *Letanía de Nuestro Señor Don Quijote*, 1905, (89) is also noted by Predmore as an example of the tendehcy to deify the Knight of La Mancha.]

237. Predmore, Richard L. "El problema de la realidad en el *Quijote*." *Nueva Revista de Filología Hispánica*, VII (1953), 489-498.

The problem of reality in Cervantes' novel has been overemphasized by Castro (63) and other literary critics who are overanxious to show Cervantes' philosophical modernness. This approach overlooks many episodes in the *Quijote*. Actually, with Cervantes the problems involved with reality are in a man's head, not in reality itself. Cervantes always shows us what the reality of a situation is. If characters become confused, Cervantes does not become confused, nor does he allow the reader to do so. Nevertheless, this does not mean to say that reality is easy to interpret. Far from it. The problem is that Cervantes' characters misread reality because they fashion illusions for themselves. The hero seeks to escape reality and fills his head with chivalresque misconceptions. He insists that things correspond to his needs.

Cervantes did not want to plant the philosophical problem of reality, as Américo Castro asserted in *El pensamiento de Cervantes* (63) in 1925, nor did he wish to show reality as part of each man's vital experience, as Castro (73) contended in 1947. Instead he wished to show man's tendency to distort reality out of self-interest.

238. Predmore, Richard Lionel. *The World of Don Quixote.* Cambridge, Mass.: Harvard University Press, 1967. Pp. 133. (Based on *El mundo de Don Quijote.* Madrid: Insula, 1958.) [Appreciation is expressed to Susan Little and Zuleyka Benítez for their assistance in the preparation of this summary.]

It seems clear that Cervantes was able to explore the relationship of reality to human experience by setting literature in contrast to life. This, then, is another and not improbable way of describing the function of literature in *Don Quijote*. But since everything in the *Quijote* is literature, this relationship of literature to life is an artistic illusion achieved by establishing two fictional levels so separated that the difference which separates them seems to the reader to be the difference between literature and life.

There are two ways of looking at literature in the *Quijote*: (A) as an essential feature of the world in which Cervantes causes his characters to live, for the hero and others are deeply influenced by what they have read; (B) as a device for the achievement of an artistic illusion — by presenting Don Quijote and Sancho as distinct from whatever has been, is, or may be written about them.

What do the adventures in Cervantes' novel tell us about that world in which they occur? They suggest that in reality in a given moment in their existence people and things may allow more uses than their past ever seemed to promise. Even prostitutes minister unto the hero and attend his knighting just as if they were the illustrious ladies of his imagination. Sancho even becomes a part of his master's world for a time.

One characteristic of the world of Don Quijote is its susceptibility to varied interpretations. Little by little, Cervantes works toward this idea, starting with an adventure (windmills) where only Don Quijote could be mistaken, and working toward more complicated, ambiguous situations (fulling mills) where anyone could go astray.

Enchantment is the main book-acquired element of chivalry found in *Don Quijote*. It is a major feature of his world, and the instances of enchantment either represent the apparent fulfillment of the hero's expectations or interpret phenomena otherwise difficult to explain, or both. There is much to be said for the notion that enchantment is the principle by which Don Quijote accounts for the (to him) disturbing fact that people and things so often assume the appearance of what they really are.

Many are puzzled by Don Quijote's madness. What is its function? Cervantes succeeds in presenting Don Quijote's madness as authentic human experience, but nothing we have said is meant to suggest that his madness is not also an instrument of parody. If there is, as some critics seem to believe, any incompatibility between the two functions, it does not apply to Cervantes. In this, as in so many other things, he is one of those rare artists who, as the Spanish saying goes, are able to ring the church bells and walk in the procession too.

239. Prjevalinsky Ferrer, Olga. "Del *asno de oro* a *Rocinante*." *Cuadernos de Literatura*, III, núms. 8-9 (Marzo-Junio, 1948), 247-257.

Cervantes and Apuleius have the same conception of the comic and of the ironic. Both use the same style, motifs, and rhythm. Apuleius' ass-hero and Cervantes' hero-knight convert their own humble condition into material for irony. In both the *Quijote* and the *Golden Ass* the humor arises from the contrast between what the reader expects and the simple rusticity of what happens.

Piteas, one of Apuleius' characters, is a righter of wrongs who, like the Knight, always fails. He also leaves his friend Lucio to pay the bills. Thus Piteas is perhaps a model for Don Quijote.

Both writers add thieves cant and funny details. The happening of events in the *Quijote* and in the *Asno de oro* produces an effect of rapidity, yet this effect, in both works, is tied in with a certain slowness in description. Both Apuleius and Cervantes use the same stereotyped formulas in describing such things as the dawn.

In the *Quijote* there are other echoes of the *Golden Ass*: there is a wineskin episode in both works, and Rocinante's unsuccessful attempt to romp with the mares is very similar to Apuleius' asshero's efforts to do the same.

240. Puyol y Alonso, Julio. *Estado social que refleja "El Quijote."* Madrid: Imp. Asilo de Huérfanos del S. C. de Jesús, 1905. Pp. 108.

[Puyol divides his work into four chapters. The first discusses the various social classes in Cervantes' time: *caballeros; hidalgos;* merchants, priests and soldiers; *el pueblo,* consisting of such types as muledrivers, innkeepers, artisans and lackeys; and *la gente maleante,* the plague of the epoch, consisting of thieves, thugs, beggars and other parasites. Chapter Two deals with national life, and touches upon such matters as foreign and domestic affairs, the heavy taxes, the declining trade, the dangers of travel, and the administration of criminal and civil jurisprudence. The third chapter is concerned with the ideas of the times regarding such matters as religion, superstition, and the protection of women. The final chapter discusses the culture of the epoch and the system of education at the universities. Some attention is devoted here to the trying steps involved in publishing a book; and the status of literature in Cervantes' times is touched upon briefly. To illustrate his points Puyol, from time to time, cites passages in the *Quijote.*]

241. Quilter, Daniel Edward. "The Image of the *Quijote* in the Seventeenth Century." Unpublished Ph. D. dissertation, University of Illinois, 1962. Pp. 327. [Appreciation is expressed to Katherine West for her assistance in preparing this summary.]

The popularity of *Don Quijote* should not be exaggerated. The fact that it went through six editions in 1605 is nothing extraordinary. One should note that there was only one further addition prior to 1614, and that there was a second lacuna between 1675 and 1700. There were, however, thirty-two works in the seventeenth century that were inspired by the *Quijote.* Twenty-two are dramatizations in verse.

Interpretive evaluations of the *Quijote* are relatively rare in the seventeenth century, and most appear prior to 1621. During the seventeenth century there are four broad attitudes toward *Don Quijote*: (1) general praise; (2) praise for ridding Spain of chivalry novels; (3) criticism against Cervantes for adopting the same immoralities found in chivalry novels; and (4) praise of *Don Quijote* as an entertaining and moral work. Diego Suárez Montañés belongs to group (3) above (*Historia de Tremecén y Orán*, 1608). Marqués Torres, in the *aprobación* to Part II, praises the moral worth of the *Quijote*, and is echoed by several writers. All in all, however, the *Quijote* was not considered a serious work. In view of the decline in the demand for the *Quijote* after 1620, it could not be said to be overwhelmingly popular in the seventeenth century, and it was consistently overshadowed by the appearance of new literary works. Its greatest appeal was among the lower classes, since a number of learned scholars thought that it lacked moralizing and that it resembled a book of chivalry.

[Chapter IV discusses the various dramatic imitations of *Don Quijote*, including two *comedias* by Guillén de Castro, an *entremés* by Francisco de Ávila, and a play of uncertain authorship. Chapter V discusses nondramatic imitations of the *Quijote*, including Avellaneda's false *Quijote*, Quevedo's poem *El testamento de Don Quijote*, and two of Salas Barbadillo's stories, *El caballero puntual* and *La peregrinación sabia*. Quilter concludes that the influence of the *Quijote* on nondramatic literature is decidedly less extensive than on the theatre. Part II of this dissertation deals with the influence of the *Quijote* on Europe outside of Spain. Chapters VI through VIII discuss the *Quijote* in France, England and other European countries. Quilter's work contains several tables showing the number of editions of the *Quijote* and other works in various countries. "Appendix A" presents a listing (alphabetized by author) of allusions to the *Quijote* in Spain in the seventeenth century. "Appendix B" is a chronological list of such references. "Appendix C" is an alphabetical list of imitations of the *Quijote* in seventeenth-century Spain. Pages 309-326 contain a bibliography.]

242. Ramón y Cajal, Santiago. *Psicología de Don Quijote y el quijotismo*. Discurso leído por el autor en la sesión conmemora-

tiva de la publicación del *Quijote,* celebrada por el Colegio Médico de San Carlos el día 9 de mayo de 1905. *Obras literarias completas.* Madrid: M. Aguilar, 1947, pp. 1277-1296.

Don Quijote is overflowing with will-power and energy and is guided by a blind faith, a faith characteristic of the great conquistadors. But Cervantes adds pathological traits to his hero's personality. Why does he do this? So that the Don will do marvelous things. In addition, madness adds a pathetic tone to the story.

When a genius creates a great character, that character expands beyond the frame of the book and invades real life, marking the people of his nationality with an indelible stain. But all Spaniards are not Quijotes, and in many eras Spain has suffered from the lack of such figures. *Quijotismo,* purified of nonsense and ignorance, has in presentday Spain a wide field in which to exercise itself. In science *quijotismo* is particularly needed in our times.

243. Real de la Riva, César. "Historia de la crítica e interpretación de la obra de Cervantes." *Revista de Filología Española,* XXXII (1948), 107-150.

[Real de la Riva presents a general survey of the various attitudes toward Cervantes' works (especially the *Quijote*) from the early seventeenth century to the date of his article. Not only are Spanish opinions examined, but also those of non-Spaniards. The ideas of many English writers are summarized — such as Samuel Johnson, Daniel Defoe, and Jarvis; and the views of Lessing, Wieland, Herder, the Schlegels, Tieck, Schelling and other Germans are also set forth. Among the Spaniards of the eighteenth century, states Real de la Riva, Mayáns seemed to see Don Quijote and Sancho as symbols, and several Spaniards compared the *Quijote* to previous works: Mayáns noted similarities between Cervantes' novel and the *Iliad*; Pellicer compared the *Quijote* to Apuleius' *Golden Ass*; Lampillas saw the influence of Ariosto and noted the mixture of the real and the imaginary in the *Quijote,* a hint at the later dualism concept of Vicente de los Ríos. Real de la Riva observes that the idea that Cervantes destroyed chivalry appeared in an anonymous poem in 1750, and that it was later taken up by Byron. The true precursor of Spanish *Cervantismo,* the critic states, is Benjumea, who concluded that Don Quijote's madness was a thirst for immortality. Opinions of other leading Spanish critics of the nineteenth and twentieth centuries are briefly set forth.]

244. *Realidad, Revista de Ideas,* II, núm. 5 (Sept.-Oct., 1947).

[This volume contains Américo Castro's "La estructura del Quijote" (70), Marcel Bataillon's "Matrimonios cervantinos," Francisco Ayala's "La invención del *Quijote* como problema técnico-literario" (19), Joaquín Casalduero's "La composición del segundo *Quijote,*" Francisco Romero's "Don Quijote y Fichte" (259), Jorge Luis Borges' "Nota sobre el *Quijote*" (47), Max Singleton's "El misterio del *Persiles,*" Harry Levin's "*Don Quijote* and *Moby Dick,*" Edwin Knowles' "Cervantes y la literatura inglesa," Jorge Romero Brest's "El Quijote y los ilustradores," Guillermo de Torre's "Cervantes anecdótico y esencial," and Julio Caillet-Bois' "El *Persiles,* versión barroca."]

245. Riegner, Helene I. "Humanitas cervantina." Unpublished Ph. D. dissertation, Radcliffe College, 1942. Pp. [x] + 271.

[In her introduction Miss Riegner concludes that Cervantes is a man of the Counter Reformation, in spite of his use of many renaissance themes. In effect, she states, he is socially an enlightened conservative.

Part One of this work deals with Cervantes' personality and seeks to show how the events in his life affected his works. To Miss Riegner, Cervantes was ennobled, not crushed, by his many adversities.

Part Two of this thesis discusses Cervantes' thought and analyzes how the author adapted and modified various renaissance themes, bringing them in line with the ideas of the Counter Reformation. Cervantes' social attitude, the critic here asserts, originated in an ideological defense of the hidalgo class, and to that end he adopted certain Stoic ideas on the dignity of man, irrespective of his social class. However, Miss Riegner adds, Cervantes did not really reject the idea of class distinction. The author of the *Quijote,* she continues, also modified the Platonic concept of love, following the Counter-Reformation idea that the goal of love is marriage. Cervantes' ideas on fate, honor, and nature are examined here also, as are his notions on truth and reality. Miss Riegner disagrees with Américo Castro's belief [*Pensamiento* (63), p. 375] that Cervantes is truly a skeptical perspectivist like Pirandello. The latter portion of the second part of this work is devoted to the influence of Erasmus on Cervantes' thought, and the similarities between these two figures are listed and discussed in detail.

Part Three of this dissertation deals with the poetic world of symbols and forms. Here Miss Riegner asserts that Cervantes saw literature as part of life and morality, not as separate from them. His genius, she states, transferred the problems of everyday life into poetic matter and by doing so created in the *Quijote* a new literary type, the modern novel. By poetic transformation, she continues, the author: (1) brought about a new relationship between poetry and life; (2) took idealistic literature out of its isolation, combining it with the realistic genre; (3) democratized literature by founding it on the ideal of human dignity; and (4) restored the union of realism and symbolism.

The problem of existence is also examined in this portion of the dissertation, and Cervantes' solution to it is studied. The author of the *Quijote* suggests, the critic asserts, that reality is good, harmonious and beautiful, but that these qualities are hidden from most men by their own imperfections, and revealed only to the virtuous. Cervantes, she concludes, respects reality and expresses it in poetic symbols; he does not distrust reality, nor does he seek to over-idealize it. The last portion of this third and final part is concerned with Cervantes' literary technique, which Miss Riegner analyzes in detail and finds to be baroque rather than renaissance.

In her conclusion, the critic finds that Cervantes' humor is due to his unshakable faith in humanity, and that, therefore, the discordance in his work loses its grimness. He is not tragic, Miss Riegner concludes; and in spite of his use of the classical motif of fate, he essentially believes in free will and the grace of God.]

246. Riley, E. C. "Who's Who in *Don Quixote?* Or an Approach to the Problem of Identity." *Modern Language Notes*, LXXXI (1961), 113-130.

Philosophical skepticism was in the air in Cervantes' times, and he breathed some of the same air as did Francisco Sánchez, Montaigne, Descartes and Hobbes. In 1581, Sánchez, in his *Quod nihil scitur*, observed that one cannot get at the nature of things through language. This assertion is beautifully illustrated by Don Quijote's explanation for breaking up Maese Pedro's puppets: he thought the puppets were actually what their names suggested.

There are numerous names given for Cervantes' hero, and this confusion is plainly deliberate. In some degree it parodies the historians, who cannot even get his name correct. Also, to a certain extent, it reflects "onomastic vacillations," as Spitzer (289) asserts. More importantly, as a few scholars have pointed out, this confusion underlines the indeterminate nature of the main character before he went mad and became Don Quijote — that is, his almost total lack of pre-history. There are, of course, precedents for name changes in chivalry literature. In that genre the name change was calculated but the characterization was essentially static. In *Don Quijote* different names and titles for the hero indicate some important aspects of his personality. Alonso Quijano el Bueno, for example, is the ultimate Quijote.

Don Quijote has a child-like fantasy, and, like a small boy, he imitates certain prototypes. In Part I he is malleable in regard to whom he identifies with. In Part II he seems to be trying to live up to an established conception of himself. Cervantes causes his hero to appear to be searching for self-realization, and this is made to appear to emanate from within the protagonist, not to be imposed from without. The hero is continually aware of himself and of his process of becoming. This presents a sort of moving-picture of individual experience in the making, filtered and viewed through the consciousness of the individual, while at the same time the experience is also seen from more than one vantage point outside. Thus the *Quijote* shows life as a process and not merely as a state of being.

The characters in Part II of the novel know of Don Quijote's earlier identity. But in this second part of the story the hero has changed; he is no longer so mad. Nevertheless, he is treated as if he were the same figure as in the earlier part. This, ironically, contributes to his disillusionment. Cervantes, in the *Quijote*, not only presents a protagonist aware of himself and of his continuing existence through time, a pre-requisite of the realistic modern novel, but also takes the characterization through to the enigmatic farther reaches of the personality, where personal identity disintegrates.

247. Riley, Edward C. "Episodio, novela y aventura en *Don Quijote*." *Anales Cervantinos*, V (1955-1956), 209-230.

The external or interpolated episodes in Cervantes' novel are those in which the Knight is not the origin and which move far along without the intervention of the two protagonists, so that the Don and his Squire could not be considered central figures of such episodes. In Part I the external episodes are: (1) Grisóstomo - Marcela; (2) Cardenio - Luscinda; (3) Fernando - Dorotea; (4) *El curioso impertinente;* (5) the captive captain - Zoraida; (6) Luis - Clara; and (7) Eugenio - Leandra - Vicente de la Roca. In order to understand the less obvious aspects of the *Quijote* we must switch our point-of-view and look at this so-called extraneous matter from the hero's viewpoint. What to us is extraneous is adventure to the Knight. We should also observe that in the interpolated episodes there is the same contrast between imagination and reality as there is between the hero's fictitious world and his "real" world. In addition, the interpolated episodes and tales make the principal action and the main characters stand out. Finally, one should note that only when the interpolated material resembles the matter of chivalry novels does the protagonist genuinely seek to take an active part.

In Part II Cervantes promises not to bring in extraneous matter, but he draws in several adventures that are not essential to the plot. However, in the 1615 *Quijote* all of these episodes could be considered adventures which befall the Knight.

248. Riley, E. C. *Cervantes' Theory of the Novel.* Oxford: Clarendon Press, 1964. Pp. ix + 244. (First published in 1962: Oxford, Oxford University Press.)

While Cervantes was a great novelist, he was not a highly original theorist. Nevertheless, there was no writer who vitalized critical problems as he did. His theory of prose fiction is predominantly neo-Aristotelian, in the manner of the major Italian and Spanish poetics of the late sixteenth and early seventeenth century though compounded with neo-Platonist doctrines and other ingredients. In his fiction Cervantes sought a confirmation of the validity of those principles, even though he was capable of exploiting their often mutually contradictory character.

The distinction between calculated and uncalculated absurdity is one of the most important concepts in Cervantes' theory. One weakness in the chivalry novel was that it was a genre that was absurd without any reason, and the author was not convinced of what he was doing. This *purposeful absurdity* concept makes his judgment against *Tirante el Blanco* understandable.

Formerly critics said that Cervantes was a careless, smiling genius. Now the danger is that we overemphasize his scrupulous percipience. Sometimes he will dodge a problem by having his characters discuss it in detail, and then, having lulled the inattentive reader into thinking the question has been resolved, pass on, leaving it exactly as it was. Detaching himself from what he writes, Cervantes puts mutually contradictory ideas together; neither affirming nor denying, he chooses both and chooses neither. Cervantes is not an innovator in critical method so much as a user of detached romantic irony as a novelistic technique.

The interaction of literature and life is a fundamental theme in *Don Quijote*. One purpose of this novel was to criticize books of chivalry. Cervantes' originality lies not in parodying them himself but in making the mad Knight parody them involuntarily in his efforts to bring them, by means of imitation, literally to life.

At the heart of Cervantes' literary theory lies the ancient dichotomy of art and nature. How can one make order (or a work of art) out of disorder (nature)? The idea that art imitates nature is not clear, nor is the concept that art perfects nature. Imitation of nature clearly did *not* mean realism, however. One great problem with Cervantes and other writers was how to reconcile verisimilitude with the need to arouse amazement *(admiratio)*. With Aristotle, style could arouse *admiratio,* but with Cervantes content is more important for this purpose. Another important question to Cervantes (and to sixteenth-century Italian estheticians) was how to achieve artistic unity if there were variety of incident. Cervantes has no solution to this problem and even tries three approaches: *Don Quijote* Part I, *Don Quijote* Part II, and the *Persiles*. Cervantes sees it generally as the novelist's duty to mould the variety of experience into a coherent artistic form that satisfies the intelligence without sacrificing the pleasures that variety produces.

Cervantes' principal contribution to the theory of the novel was a product, never properly formulated, of his imaginative method. The novel, he realized, must be rooted in the historical stuff of everyday experience, however much it might reach out to the marvelous heights of poetry. While the novelist does not have to be historically accurate, he still must take more cognizance of history than a poet. The modern novel owes more to Cervantes than to anyone else for the revised concept of the prose epic, even if it was for his example rather than for his precept, and even if he himself had no more than an intuition of the implications.

Truth versus fiction, reality versus illusion, were ideas that preoccupied the seventeenth century and Cervantes. The author of the *Quijote* put his imaginative grasp on their implications as a novelist, not as a theoretician. But his awareness of these problems made it possible for him to achieve in *Don Quijote* that extraordinary illusion of human experience which is not a shadow or distortion of human experience, but an illumination of its nature.

249. Río, Ángel del. "El equívoco del *Quijote*." *Hispanic Review*, XXVII (1959), 200-221.

The intimate law of the *Quijote* is a constant tension, or a balance magically maintained by the author, between radical oppositions: being versus seeming, reality versus fantasy, madness versus discretion, the sublime versus the grotesque. But the basic qualities of the author's mind are humor and an amazing artistic conscience. The true "equívoco" of the *Quijote*, one may say, is that when the author appears to be serious, he is joking; when he appears to be joking, he is serious. But though the *Quijote* appears to be non-transcendental and comic, it deals with the very meaning of existence.

The second part of the novel deals with a more problematical world. It is organized around three central and converging propositions: (1) the meaning of madness; (2) the truth in its double plane (literature and history) from the joining of which Cervantine truth emerges; (3) the evasive character of reality.

The *Quijote* was written at a time when man had just discovered his inner being and could not distinguish between reality and illusion. What is Cervantes' solution? To give none, to say with the prophesying ape and the enchanted head that part is true and part is not. The *Quijote* is thus a book of doubt — not rational Cartesian doubt, but existential doubt.

Cervantes is the midpoint between Rationalism and the Baroque. He sees that Rationalism does not answer life's questions but still does not completely accept the baroque idea that life is a dream. Instead, Cervantes suggests an affirmation of the individual life. What does the author mock? Everything, especially pretension to certainty. At the end of the novel the hero takes up the Bible and renounces his insane doings. The *equívoco* seems explained, but the renunciation should not be taken seriously, for the Squire immediately takes up the cry of idealism.

250. Río, Ángel del. "Quijotismo y cervantismo. El devenir de un símbolo." *Revista de Estudios Hispánicos (Puerto Rico)*, I (1928), 241-267.

There are two ways for an intelligent person to read the *Quijote*. One can treat it psychologically and sentimentally (the *quijotista* approach), or one can view it historically and intellectually (the *cervantista* approach).

The *quijotista* Unamuno, in his *Vida de Don Quijote y Sancho* (309), presents twelve basic ideas about Cervantes' masterpiece: (1) the hero's madness is of the imagination, not of the understanding; he understands reality and is aware of the jokes on him, but his imagination sees a better world; in honor of that better world he sacrificed his judgment; (2) the anxiety for glory and fame is the *espíritu íntimo del quijotismo,* and Dulcinea embodies these ideas of fame and immortality; (3) justice, truth and faith have their roots in eternity; (4) will is the basis of human life; (5) one should ignore the portions of the *Quijote* that do not relate to life: the literary criticism and interpolated *novelas;* (6) Sancho complements Don Quijote; he is not a contrast; (7) the windmills represent modern industry which crushes man's spirit; (8) Don Quijote has a procreative spiritual value; he can inspire the goatherds, even though they cannot understand him; (9) the world is what it seems to each person; (10) the will is the fountain of knowledge; (11) there are two circles of characters in the *Quijote*: (A) those around the hero, who are humble and ignorant; and (B) the circle of *vicio,* the *Duques,* the canon, Sansón, who are conscious enemies of heroism; and (12) mockery destroys heroism; we should return to the heroic, the only way to salvation.

Madariaga (182), also a *quijotista,* basically follows Unamuno, though the former modernizes the latter's ideas. Unamuno is a passionate individualist nourished in the nineteenth century. Madariaga belongs to our times; he is much more disciplined. His work is excellent in its study of the various characters from a modern psychological point of view.

Maeztu (184), a moralist and a positivist, observed that Spain was tired when Don Quijote went forth into the world. The moral of the *Quijote,* to Maeztu, was not to be a Quijote.

Ortega, in his *Meditaciones* (223), opens up new paths of criticism. He examines the literary problems which the *Quijote* plants, and is more interested in the ideas in that novel than in its characters. Ortega has several main ideas: (1) Cervantes is Mediterranean, impressionistic, and appeals to the senses; (2) the modern novel is realistic, ironic, and psychological and derives from Cervantes; and (3) Spain is ruled by its dead ancestors; Spain hates the new; it worships death.

Américo Castro, in his *Pensamiento* (63), seeks to place Cervantes in his proper epoch rather than trying to fit him into a later period. Castro criticizes those who believe Cervantes to be an unconscious writer as well as those who consider him a mere receptacle of what he had read. The attitudes of a writer, states Castro, are more important than his reading, and to understand his outlook it is best to study the epoch of the author first, then the author, for in that way one can discover what he chose from the culture of his times. In Cervantes' lifetime, Castro observes, medievalism clashed with new renaissance ideas. The author of the *Quijote* sought to resolve this conflict with reason, but found this to be of no avail. Therefore, he resorted to the double truth of reason and faith. Also, continues Castro, in Cervantes' days there was a dualism of truth among the preceptists: relative, historical truth and absolute truth. Cervantes' genius, Castro states, was in introducing into his heroes themselves this theoretical problem that disturbed the preceptists: Don Quijote represents poetic truth; Sancho symbolizes historical truth.

251. Ríos de Lampérez, Blanca de los. "Algunas observaciones sobre el *Quijote* de Avellaneda." *La España Moderna,* Año 9.°, núm. 101 (Mayo, 1897), pp. 37-89; Año 9.°, núm. 107 (Nov., 1897), pp. 84-145; Año 10.°, núm. 112 (Abril, 1898), pp. 103-140. [Based on summaries and comments kindly submitted by Paul M. Lloyd and María Scuderi.]

[Doña Blanca concludes that Tirso de Molina, a disciple of Lope, was the author of the false *Quijote.* She states, however, that Tirso was annoyed with Lope in 1614, and that the false *Quijote* made various attacks on Lope's extreme behavior. Doña Blanca further asserts that the chubby, talkative Tirso was the model for Cervantes' Sancho Panza and that the monstrously proud Lope inspired the figure Don Quijote. Doña Blanca reasserts her above views, in 1946, in the Aguilar edition of Tirso's works (Vol. I, pp. xxxvi-xxxvii and cxviii-cxxi). She is generally followed in her views by José López Navío (180) and Juan Millé y Giménez (203).]

252. Riquer, Martín de. *Aproximación al Quijote.* 2nd ed. rev. Barcelona: Teide, 1967. Pp. 236. [Appreciation is expressed to Patricia Pollock for her assistance in this summary.]

[In Chapter I Riquer discusses the origins of the chivalry novel, its rise and its decay. Chapter II deals with Cervantes' life. The third chapter examines the *Quijote,* its preparation and publication. The final chapter, entitled "Cervantismo," contains a short history of *Don Quijote* criticism from its inception to the 1960's. Whereas Menéndez y Pelayo (199) viewed Cervantes' novel as a purification of the chivalry genre, Riquer regards the *Quijote* as a satire throughout of episodes in chivalry novels. For that reason, a great deal of Chapter III of this work is devoted to an examination of the possible sources of the episodes in the *Quijote.* For example, the *cuerpo muerto* episode is said to be based on an incident in *Palmerín de Inglaterra,* the oxen cart adventure on an episode in *Lanzarote,* Montesinos' cave on an adventure in *Las sergas de Esplandián,* and Clavileño on *Cléomades* by Adenet li Rois. The advice to Sancho, Riquer concludes, is probably drawn from Juan de Castilla y Aguayo's *El perfecto regidor,* and the Altisidora episode based on happenings in *Tirante el Blanco.*]

253. Riquer, Martín de. "Estilo del *Quijote,*" in *El ingenioso hidalgo Don Quijote de la Mancha,* I. Barcelona: Editorial Labor, S. A., 1962, pp. lvi-lxviii.

There is a vast difference in style between the 1605 *Quijote* and that of 1615. Part I has interpolated stories to break the main plot, and the style and theme of the *Curioso impertinente* is quite different from the rest of Part I. In fact this tale could well have been omitted. The *cautivo's* story, moreover, is too close to the tale of *The Curious Impertinent,* and the former could also have been eliminated, since it is not especially interesting in spite of its autobiographical elements. It was simply a custom of Cervantes' times to insert tales that were different in style and content from the main plot. For example, Montemayor's *Diana* contains *El abencerraje* and Mateo Alemán's *Guzmán de Alfarache* incorporates the tale of *Ozmín y Daraja.*

In Part II, 1615, the style of the dialogue and narrative portions is unified, whereas the style of the 1605 *Quijote* contained many styles: the picaresque, the pastoral, the Moorish and the Italianate.

254. Riquer, Martín de. "El *Quijote* y los libros." *Papeles de Son Armadans,* Año XIV, tomo LIV, núm. CLX (Julio, 1969), 5-24.

Books play an extremely important role in the *Quijote,* and without them Cervantes' masterpiece would be unthinkable. Many characters in the story are intoxicated by books. For example, Basilio's cousin is a renaissance pedant full of false erudition. Don Quijote himself speaks like a book.

The background of fiction has enormous potential. It allows Cervantes to approach the reader. We feel he is on our side, pen in hand, translating and commenting along with us. When the false *Quijote* becomes part of Part II we are too close to the author to notice, at first blush, the impossibility of such a thing, for the false *Quijote* was published in 1614, and Cervantes' Part II is supposed to take place one month after the hero's return in a cage, in 1605 or earlier.

The *Quijote* is a work written on a double level. Cervantes may write one minute as Cide Hamete and another minute as himself. At times he appears to be the first reader of his novel, raising objections to the implausibility of certain events, such as Sancho's displaying wisdom beyond his normal ability.

255. Rivers, Elias L. "On the Prefatory Pages of *Don Quijote*, Part II." *Modern Language Notes*, LXXV (1960), 214-221.

Don Quijote establishes a literary form in which ironically shifting and balanced points of view provide a subtle complexity of shadings and perspectives; and the poetic characters of Cervantes' novel are not pseudo-classical types, either absolutely noble or absolutely base. Don Quijote, taken as a whole, is an irreducible complex of altruism and egoism, of nobility and absurdity, of self-aware inner freedom and compulsive slavery to a mechanical code. Despite its genuine implications of tragic anguish, the novel *Don Quijote* cannot be reduced to the pure and simple category of tragedy; nor, despite its undeniably comic aspects, demonstrated in Bergson's *Le Rire* (36) and Auerbach's *Mimesis* (14), is it pure satire or comedy.

256. Rivers, Elias L. "El grave defecto del *Quijote*." *Insula*, Año VI, núm. 64 (15 de abril de 1951), pp. 1-2.

The grave defect of Cervantes' novel is that there is a serious conflict between the author's conscious intention and the idealistic power of the hero. The disillusioned older Cervantes was not only against chivalry books but against idealism, and hence Ruskin was right about the author's intention. But the *Quijote* is not a "deadly" work, as Ruskin claimed, for the hero's idealism is a strong offset to the author's cynicism.

Yet the *Quijote* has one serious flaw: the renunciation by the hero of his ideals at the end of the novel. The Knight has been a symbol of faith, and we cannot accept his loss of faith. It is not a question of the hero's having a moment of truth before his death, as some argue. Nor is it a question of Cervantes' desire to prevent further exploitation of his hero, as others conclude, for death alone would have been sufficient. It is simply the fact that Cervantes the moralist here defeats Cervantes the novelist.

The philosophical interest in the *Quijote* lies in its dualism between the ideal and the real. It is not necessary that the reader accept the one to the exclusion of the other, though it may appear logical to do so. A wise artist leaves both possibilities open, regardless of his own personal beliefs.

257. Rodó, José Enrique. "El Cristo a la jineta," in *El mirador de Próspero. Obras completas.* Editadas con introducción y notas por Emir Rodríguez Monegal. Madrid: Aguilar, 1957, pp. 521-522. (Selection dated 1906.)

After the Christ of peace, human history required a warlike Christ, and then you were born, Don Quijote. A militant Christ, a Christ in armor, implies a contradiction, from whence derives, in part, the comicness of your figure, and also what is sublime in you.

As Christ broke up the tables of the money-changers, you likewise smashed the puppet show of Maese Pedro where the heroic had been reduced to charlatanry. People scorned and mocked both you and Christ, putting signs upon you in derison. You were both betrayed, Christ by Judas and you by Sansón Carrasco.

Both you and the Lord were part human, part divine. Your human part (Alonso Quijano) died. But your divine part (Don Quijote) will live on and continue to do good deeds.

258. Rodríguez Marín, Francisco. *Estudios cervantinos*. Prólogo de Agustín González de Amezúa y Mayo. Madrid: Ediciones Atlas, 1947. Pp. 656.

[The first article discusses Cervantes' references to the University of Osuna and seeks to fathom the author's apparent antipathy toward it. The second note deals with the question whether Cervantes studied in Seville. The third article concerns itself with whether the *Quijote* was written in a jail. Rodríguez Marín criticizes the traditions that Cervantes was imprisoned in Argamasilla de Alba and in El Toboso, and concludes that the *Quijote* was written in the royal jail at Seville where Cervantes was twice imprisoned. The following two articles discuss the influence of Andalusia on Cervantes and the shipment of the *Quijote* to America. Rodríguez Marín, in subsequent articles in this collection, deals with Córdoba, with the sonnet "Voto a Dios...," and the Arms and Letters speech. In one note (p. 373 *et seq.*) Rodríguez Marín discusses the origin of the names "Caballero de la Triste Figura" and "Caballero de los Espejos." The former, he concludes, comes from *Don Clarián de Landanís* and the latter from *Lidamán de Ganayl*. A somewhat longer article deals with the influence of Andalusia and Cordova on Cervantes' language. To Rodríguez Marín, Cervantes reveals his *andalucismo* in his hyperboles. The critic also concludes that Cervantes spoke like an Andalusian (from his frequent use of the *-ico* suffix). In the two following notes Rodríguez Marín discusses the expression "duelos y quebrantos" and the living models of Don Quijote. He concludes that Martín de Quijano, acting "veedor general de los galeras" was the most likely model for the Knight. In his note "¿se lee mucho a Cervantes?" Rodríguez Marín concludes that the *Quijote* is no longer widely read. In his following article the critic examines the authorship of the false *Quijote* and notes the numerous theories on the subject. Pages 495-559 contain a discussion of a picture of Cervantes supposedly painted by Jáuregui. Rodríguez Marín returns (at page 561) to the question of the most likely model for Don Quijote. Here he concludes that Martín de Quijano was only *one* model. Also the critic seems inclined to believe that Cervantes may have been drawing on an Alonso Quijada who was born prior to 1505. At page 621, et seq. the superstitions in the *Quijote* are discussed. At page 637, an article from 1933 entitled "El *Quijote*" is presented, in which Cervantes' life, his works, and their criticism are briefly dealt with. After a discussion of the centenaries of Cervantes, Rodríguez Marín studies the grammatical construction: "Ella, puesta las rodillas en el suelo."]

259. Romero, Francisco. "Don Quijote y Fichte." *Realidad, Revista de Ideas*, II, núm. 5 (Sept.-Oct., 1947), 220-233.

What an artist writes does not always correspond to his original plan, nor is the expressed, conscious intention of the author what is most important. In writing there is a law of internal consequence; once a thing is written by the author, the thing written suggests other matters to the writer, so that the material, in a sense, comes to collaborate with the author, inspire him, and even direct him to a certain extent.

The overflowing richness of the *Quijote* invites mythic interpretations. Though these may not be what Cervantes intended, they are justified. Thus, for example, the Don can legitimately be viewed as an idealized caricature of the Spain of his day.

Don Quijote has no fixed name nor past history. His story is that of his madness, and his tale ends when his sanity returns. Reading chivalry novels he becomes converted, in the manner of the sudden conversion of a social reformer. A conversion cannot cause a cowardly man to be brave. Alonso Quijano, however, was basically good. Madness awakes his true being; he decides to be openly what he already was secretly. Insanity makes him more true than he was.

Don Quijote and Fichte are symbols of liberty of the soul. For each of them the only true reality is his *yo y su conciencia*. Their *yo* is pure action, pure liberty. The *yo* is both act and agent. As Don Quijote pretends adversaries in order to show the strength of his arm, Fichte creates the world which will serve him to fulfill himself. For the Knight the only function of the *no-yo* is to offer motives and pretexts for the spirit to act and to be.

260. Romero Flores, Hipólito R. *Biografía de Sancho Panza filósofo de la sensatez*. Prólogo de Juan Marías. Barcelona: Editorial Aedos, 1969. Pp. 221. (First Edition, 1952.)

Sancho is basic to the *Quijote*, not secondary, not a mere counterfigure. Yet one should not go to the opposite extreme of making him a prima donna. At first the Knight and the Squire are opposites, but they later grow close through association and mutual tolerance. Most critics who have studied the Squire have been anti-Sancho, regarding him as a vulgar materialist. There are a few, such as P. Gatell, in 1793-1794, who treat him sympathetically. Unamuno (309), to be sure, looks favorably upon the Squire and treats him with understanding.

Sancho is more difficult to understand than his master. The Squire was not completely conceived at the beginning of the story, whereas the Knight was. Sancho grows more than his master. The humble *escudero* reflects the author's spiritual vacillations. The author becomes more and more absorbed with him, so that a process of *asimilación sanchocervantesca* takes place.

Sancho knows his inner and outer world. He is a thinker, though not a theoretical thinker. With his proverbs he is a true representative of Spanish philosophy. Don Quijote, dreaming and failing, and Sancho, living and reasoning things out, represent the synthesis of Spanish national history.

261. Rosales, Luis. *Cervantes y la libertad*. Madrid: Gráficas Valera, S. A., 1960. 2 vols.

Volume I

Liberty is the central and living nucleus of Cervantes' thought, and the origin of Don Quijote's disease is perhaps his concept of liberty. However, his madness is more a technical recourse than an illness. Don Quijote is actually more an adolescent than a madman. Like an adolescent, Don Quijote seeks to make the world over into his own image and views the real or familiar world as an obstacle. His disassociation of the social world from his personal world leads to *dolor*, the substance of *quijotismo*. In fact, the rupture with the social environment is undoubtedly one of the constant factors in Cervantes' works, and the confusion between the spirit of independence and the spirit of liberty is the connecting link between Cervantes' characters.

Volume II

In Part II of the Quijote the adventures change in tone and meaning. Adventures of attack in Part I become empty adventures in Part II (Montesinos, Clavileño, etc.). Nothing happens in these empty adventures except the probing of Don Quijote's bravery. In 1615 Cervantes opens up a new path — the cohesion of the hero's personality. To develop Don Quijote Cervantes moves him toward sanity. This could wreck the technical equilibrium of the story because the exemplarity of a sane Don Quijote perhaps has less artistic value than an arbitrary, insane hero. This switch toward sanity is the great technical problem of Part II, and Cervantes' solution of it is his greatest success. The function of the empty adventures of Part II is not to make us laugh but to show us the universal, human, pathetic depth of *quijotismo*. The *Duques'* palace places the hero in the vital situation that allows him to find himself. This episode is a contrived merger of fiction and reality that brings out the hero, that helps him make his dreams come true, and confirms the hero in his faith.

Montesinos' cave is an effort by Don Quijote to displace Sancho as the protagonist in the enchantment of Dulcinea. In addition, Montesinos is an attempt by the hero to reestablish his lost unity of vision in order to fix Dulcinea within the archetypal world of his ideas. This episode can be regarded as an effort by the hero to protect himself from *sanity* and to regain his former vision.

The relationship of Alonso Quijano to Don Quijote is quite complicated. They are not a contradiction. Don Quijote is the *proyecto vital* of Alonso Quijano, who, to a certain extent, becomes converted into Don Quijote — a slow process that is never completed. *Quijotismo* and *quijanismo* become integrated and influence each other. The most outstanding characteristic of *quijotismo* is considering *lo soñado* as if it were real. The most important feature of *quijanismo* is conquering *lo soñado*. *Quijotismo* transforms reality and considers a hallucinated vision of the world to be normal. *Quijanismo* sees reality but nevertheless continues to believe in the quixotic vision of life.

262. Rubin, Louis D. *The Teller of the Tale*. Seattle-London: University of Washington Press, 1967, pp. 3-23.

It has become an axiom today that the reader of a novel is supposed to be unaware of the author. This belief is of doubtful merit, for the *Quijote* seems the truest when we are *most* aware of Cervantes' presence, and when we are reminded by him that we are reading a work of fiction. One should realize that taking an author's presence for granted is quite different from forgetting about him altogether.

Storytelling, in the last analysis, consists of persuading the reader willingly to suspend his disbelief in the reality of the story being recounted. We always realize that we are witnessing *art,* and we should also be aware that we are witnessing an illusion. By slyly reminding us of the existence of this illusion Cervantes is able to intensify our conscious delight in our participation in the artistic process. He even pushes this process one step further by making his characters seem momentarily to be taking part in the illusion with us. At such a time, without losing for a moment their authority as characters, they seem to become even more life-like (and more illusory) than ever.

There is a definite distinction between the authorial personality and the biographical, real-life author. The authorial personality, whether dramatized as a first-person participant or existing only in the way the story is developed, *is* a part of the novel. The real-life author is outside the work and can be reached only through biographical investigation. At times the authorial personality and the real-life author seem very close. Yet no matter how closely the two authors may coincide, they are not the same person. Perhaps it was the sole purpose of the historical Cervantes to destroy chivalry novels, but this is not what the authorial personality accomplished. This authorial personality in the *Quijote* is the one who has the hero tell of what reading chivalry novels has done for him. That author pervades every page of the *Quijote*.

263. Rubio, David. *¿Hay una filosofía en el Quijote?* New York: Instituto de las Españas en los Estados Unidos, 1924. Pp. 166.

Cervantes' novel is eternally up-to-date because it penetrates into the depths of the human situation more than any other work. The author of the *Quijote* is a devout Catholic, and neither a hypocrite nor a follower of Erasmus. The Renaissance tried to destroy the true metaphysical meaning of the world. It split the world into inner and outer fragments. In the *Quijote,* the contrast between the real and the ideal does not cause the comedy and the tragedy. These are brought on by the contrast between the *fragmentismo* of the Renaissance and the *construccionismo* (unity) of the Middle Ages. Don Quijote is a medieval constructionist living during renaissance fragmentation.

Don Quijote's imperturbability reflects Cervantes' spirit, which is a product of Christian resignation, not of Stoicism. The Stoics did not understand the concept of sacrifice. Cervantes does not attack chivalry or chivalresque ideals such as loyalty and exaltation of women. He attacks only the exaggerations found in books of chivalry. Nevertheless, Cervantes sees that the Middle Ages are gone forever, and the anachronism of a medieval hero placed in modern times is one of the greatest charms of the book. The philosophy of *Don Quijote* is not systematic, but in that work there is a philosophy of faith in the ideal, in the value of effort, in the triumph of justice, and in the merit of sacrifice.

[Rubio's work, to a large extent, is written in anticipation of Américo Castro's *Pensamiento* (63), which appeared the following year, 1925. Rubio, throughout his work, criticizes Castro, without naming him, for his implication that Cervantes condemns those of his characters who do not follow their inner nature.]

264. Rüegg, August. *Miguel de Cervantes und sein Don Quijote.* Bern: A. Francke, 1949. Pp. 486.

The *Quijote* is not a gushy book of a youthful writer. It is a work by an idealist turned realist. Byron is correct to the extent that antiidealism is the starting point of the *Quijote*. However, Cervantes cannot stay away from the romantic, and, at the end, did not mean to satirize true chivalry. Historically *Don Quijote* is an outgrowth of Ariosto's *Orlando furioso*. Several episodes in Cervantes' novel are based on Ariosto's work, as is the ironic and satirical tone of the *Quijote* toward chivalry legends. But Ariosto's humor is subtle whereas Cervantes' humor is broad and deep. The Spaniard laughs outloud, yet he has a profound appreciation of the tragic source of humor. Ariosto is a skeptic; Cervantes is a believer. Ariosto's figures are puppets; Cervantes' characters are life-like. *Don Quijote* is, in part, a reaction against *Orlando furioso*, since Cervantes' novel reaffirms the values at which Ariosto scoffed.

The three germ cells of the *Quijote* are: (1) the parody of the chivalry novel in which chivalry is brought into daily life, producing a clash; (2) a psychological or pathological study in which is portrayed the tragedy of overexpectations (here are presented the eternal conflicts between youth and age, belief and skepticism, subjectivity and objectivity, poetic fantasy and prosaic sobriety);

and (3) the element of contrast to the central figure, the introduction of Sancho Panza.

Cervantes puts himself into both his main characters. He fluctuates between idealism and crass, cynical realism. In spite of his ironic attitude toward chivalry, Cervantes saw that there was something worthwhile in the extravagant idealism of his youth. This striving by the author for a new idealism in his later life is revealed in his handling of Sancho, who begins as a cynical materialist and attains a state of maturity. The contrast and antithesis between the Knight and the Squire springs from the author's attempt to portray and to work out his own inner conflict.

[At pages 484 through 486 Rüegg compares and contrasts Cervantes and Shakespeare. He concludes that the Spaniard's greatness lies in his being an innovator, a literary pioneer. He further observes that behind all the varied material of the *Quijote* there is a unified guiding spirit — the resolution of disappointment through humor.]

265. Rüegg, August. "Le réalisme de Cervantes." *Anales Cervantinos*, II (1952), 111-128.

It is better to approach *Don Quijote* from the point-of-view of realism than from that of romanticism. Cervantes is sincerely and naturally realistic, and the best parts of his novel are realistic. The figure of the hero is romantic, but the author is not. Cervantes, in essence, created the realistic European novel, writing *Don Quijote* in a spirit of disenchantment.

Don Quijote is a book of disillusion, but not of sarcasm. The author loved life with all its contradictions; he loved life because of its polarity. Cervantes cannot be called an absolute realist or an absolute romantic. Both moods alternate in his soul. The tension in *Don Quijote* and in the human soul (between the lofty and the earthly) is reflected not only in the dialogues between the hero and his Squire, but also in the very figure of Don Quijote — his high aims and his frail body.

266. Rüegg, August. "Lo erásmico en el *Don Quijote* de Cervantes." *Anales Cervantinos*, IV (1954), 1-40. (Read in 1942

at Basel, in German, and translated into Spanish by F. Maldonado de Guevara.)

Any direct influence of Erasmus on Cervantes is doubtful, though there is some trace of the spirit of the Dutchman in the *Quijote*. However, this Erasmian influence is not where Américo Castro [(63), (67)] and Marcel Bataillon (29) believe it to be (the *discursos*), but in the esthetic humorous, in the dialogues in the tradition of Lucian, Horace and Terence. And here Cervantes could possibly have been influenced directly by the classics. For example, the Glass Licentiate is similar to Lucian's character Demonax, and Sancho resembles the stock figure Micyll, the shoemaker. In addition, the adventures of Don Quijote have a certain connection with Lucian's *Vera Historia*.

The exterior course of Cervantes' novel is as follows: the hero is mad; what he believes in is an illusion, a chivalresque delirium; his ideas provoke conflicts; illusion leads to disillusion; both Knight and Squire are purged of their faults. The interior course of the story is this: the hero is not merely a madman, but a gentleman of noble elevation who gives of himself generously and tolerates calamities and scorn; he is wise in his own insanity, and is the only nonschemer, the only wise man in the novel.

Cervantes humanized the *figurón* Knight and showed the tragedy of the man of enthusiasm. The novel reflects the personal tragedy of the author. Cervantes, if influenced by Erasmus, was not influenced by the latter's desire to reform religion and morals, but by his tendency toward self-irony.

267. Russell, P. E. "*Don Quixote* as a Funny Book." *Hispanic Review*, LXIV (1969), 312-326.

For more than a century after the publication of the *Quijote* that novel was regarded as simply a funny book. The Romantic Sismondi, in 1813, is largely responsible for changing this view of Cervantes' masterpiece. That critic saw the *Quijote* as a sad book and felt that the reader should not laugh at the buffeted hero. But was the original interpretation of Cervantes' masterpiece so mistaken? No! The problem with the criticism of the *Quijote* since Sismondi is that it asks the reader to ignore large portions of the novel. Furthermore, one should realize that funny literature is not necessarily inferior literature.

The Romantics tended to view the Knight as a noble figure, insane only on the subject of chivalry. But seventeenth-century readers clearly did not consider the hero to be sane during his lucid intervals. The Romantics also set up dualities between the Knight and the Squire, the former being said, for example, to represent poetry, the latter, prose. Cervantes, however, apparently regarded his two protagonists as the twin faces of comic folly.

268. Salcedo, Emilio, "Cervantismo y quijotismo." *Anales Cervantinos*, III (1953), 309-328.

There are two deaths in *Don Quijote*, that of the Knight and that of Alonso Quijano. Cervantes kills them both and commits literary suicide because of Avellaneda's 1614 *Quijote*. The Knight actually dies on the beach at Barcelona, and it is Alonso Quijano who makes the trip back to the village. It is also Alonso Quijano who first fell in love with Aldonza Lorenzo. This shadowy figure Alonso is killed off by the author because Cervantes himself is dying. When he started Part II of the *Quijote*, the author was old and sick. He now saw that the story of his Knight was like his own. Though the author buffeted his Knight, he loved him, and could not tolerate others like Avellaneda mistreating his hero, for this was a buffeting of Cervantes himself.

In the *Quijote* Cervantes finds an authentic escape by giving a projection of his perishing existence in the eternal being of a myth. Some critics contend that Cervantes is Spain. This is not correct. Don Quijote is Cervantes, and Cervantes was a Spaniard, a good representative of Spain — but not the nation itself. It is foolish to search for the future of Spain in *Don Quijote*, but we should not overlook Cervantes' masterpiece. We need to know how Spain has been, and Cervantes and the Don are a major part of Spain's past.

269. Salillas, Rafael. *Un gran inspirador de Cervantes: El doctor Juan Huarte y su "Examen de Ingenios."* Madrid: Eduardo Arias, 1905. Pp. 162.

Juan Huarte's *Examen de Ingenios* had great influence on Cervantes' literary production, from *La Galatea* to *El Persiles*. It affected both the author's choice of the word *ingenioso* used in describing his hero as well as the description of the Knight's mental disorder. With Huarte, madness is always a state of the *ingenio*, and Cervantes' choice of the word *ingenioso* clearly refers to his madness.

Huarte's theory of *destemplanzas* held that mental stability (which to him was a fragile thing) depended upon the proper balance in the body among the four basic elements: heat, cold, dryness, humidity. If these elements should become out of balance, Huarte concluded, the *ingenio* would be disturbed in some manner, depending upon the new combination of elements. In picturing a man with a lesion in his imagination, though still of good *entendimiento*, Cervantes was particularly influenced by Huarte's case study of Demócrito Abderita who came to such power of *entendimiento* in his later years that his imaginative powers were damaged. As long as his doctor Hipócrates discussed only matters affecting his understanding Demócrito appeared perfectly sane, just as the Don appears normal when not affected by his chivalric illusion.

270. Sánchez, Alberto. "Historia y poesía en el *Quijote*." *Cuadernos de Literatura*, III, núms. 8-9 (Marzo-Junio, 1948), 139-160.

Cervantes does not give the reader any definite idea as to his conception of the word verisimilitude, the key to literature. The Don appears to follow Piccolomini's belief that verisimilitude is not an imperfection of the truth but something higher, the essential meaning of a thing. Although the Knight realizes the teaching function of historical truth, he prefers poetic truth as a stimulant and guide.

Cervantes sees the preceptist's problem in attempting to distinguish between poetic truth (verisimilitude) and historical truth. Yet he is not a preceptist but a writer who, though he has his own esthetic opinions, does not let himself be pinned down while he is composing. Is the *Quijote* literature (poetry) or history? It is more literature, though it takes place in a particular epoch and in a real geography. Cervantes reflected a great deal on the difference between historical truth and poetic (literary) truth, and his reflections achieved results. For in this border conflict between two forms of truth the conception of the *Quijote* was born.

In general the Don follows the line of poetic truth while the Squire pursues the line of historical truth. But Cervantes often mingles the two levels into a unitary and totalizing effect which encarnates the very reality of the world in all its dimensions, internal and external. In the *Quijote* history and poetry appear unified. Cervantes begins the modern epic, the modern realistic novel, by marvelously combining the experienced with the imagined.

271. Sánchez-Mariño, Rafael. "Un Alonso Quijano de carne y hueso." *Anales Cervantinos*, IX (1961-1962), 257-258.

[Sánchez-Mariño submits three documents dealing with one Alonso Quijano, "hombre de armas" of Felipe III and resident in Valladolid in 1604 and 1605, when Cervantes was also a resident there. An "hombre de armas," the critic explains, was the last vestige of chivalry just as Don Quijote is the last literary knight-errant.]

In Chapter I of Part I of the *Quijote* Cervantes refers to the hero's real name as being Quijada or Quesada. It is likely that the early part of the 1605 *Quijote* was written in Seville, and, as Rodríguez Marín (258) states, perhaps at this stage the author was satirizing an enemy of his family, one Alonso Quijada. In Part II the Knight's name turns out to be Alonso Quijano. It is possible that the Knight of Part II is based on the "hombre de armas" of Valladolid. This might well explain why the burlesque figure of Part I comes to be the human and noble figure of Part II.

272. Sánchez Rivero, Ángel. "Las ventas del *Quijote*." *Revista de Occidente*, XXVII (1927), 1-22.

Cervantes uses inns as an indispensable device, for in his inns all types of people can be brought together. At the first inn the hero's ideal world brusquely, even crudely, clashes with the picaresque world about him. But soon the hero and the world of sane people become less clashing; their differences become less precise. There is a movement from caricature toward humor. Sancho Panza is brought into the novel to accomplish this move, a move that was made largely by chance. Sancho is thus the true beginning of the *Quijote.*

273. Sánchez Rivero, Ángel. "Contestación" [to Américo Castro's "¿Cervantes, inconsciente?" (64)]. *Revista de Occidente,* XXVII (1927), 291-314.

The problem of ascertaining Cervantes' intentions in writing the *Quijote* arises from the confusion of the author's creative conscience and his critical conscience. Cervantes, actually, did not have a complete critical awareness of his novel, for it was too innovative, too audacious. He even appears to have preferred the *Persiles* to his masterpiece, since the former was more in line with the literary theories of his times, which theories stressed the heroic rather than the mundane. In fact, in view of Cervantes' respect for established literary concepts, it was a stroke of luck that he did not produce a mere imitation of Heliodorus instead of his masterpiece.

De Lollis (179) is wrong to think of Cervantes as a destructive reactionary and a product of the Counter Reformation. Instead he is renaissance, for his *Quijote* is joyous, biting, and mocking. His masterpiece is a descendant of Boccaccio, Ariosto, the *Celestina* and *Lazarillo.* Unlike the *Persiles,* the *Quijote* is not concerned with theories. It is free, a maximum adventure in liberty. In essence it is a total *bufonada* that becomes serious, to a large extent, by chance.

274. Sánchez y Escribano, Federico. "De la técnica realista en algunos cuentos pastoriles del *Quijote.*" *Anales Cervantinos,* IV (1954), 113-117.

After the *Galatea* Cervantes is constantly torn between neoplatonic idealism and baroque naturalism. In three pastoral episodes in the *Quijote* (Marcela, Leandra, and Quiteria) the author uses a conciliatory approach, a compromise between idealism and naturalism, a subtly conceived amalgam. In each of these three episodes Cervantes is careful to present, first of all, the realities of the lives of the minor protagonists. Later the author moves into the idyllic world of the pastoral.

In general, Cervantes, in his *Quijote,* shows a negative attitude toward the pastoral. He is no longer interested in neoplatonic idealism nor in the abstract idealization of man. He is more interested in the transcending or transcendental world in operation with the salvation of the soul.

Cervantes' realistic approach is a copy of Aristotle's (and Pinciano's) dictum that made-up stories are better and more delightful the more they resemble truth or the appearance of truth, and true stories are better the more they are true.

275. Sánchez y Escribano, Federico. "Dos notas cervantinas." *Anales Cervantinos,* VIII (1959-1960), 361-366.

[The first note studies the opening passages of *La Galatea,* the *Persiles,* and *Don Quijote.* Sánchez y Escribano states that whereas *La Galatea* and *El Persiles* have a neoplatonic or anguished Christian view of life, the *Quijote* has all of life. The two lesser works, the critic adds, have too much theory and lack the eternally human; *Don Quijote,* on the other hand, takes the essence of the human and real and makes it transcending and transcendental. In his masterpiece, Sánchez y Escribano states, Cervantes suppresses the overly poetic and the intellectual; through the whole novel runs a *dolor humano* that is humanizing and does not contain modern psychological tricks.

The second note deals with Casalduero's (56) assertion that the opening lines of the *Quijote* are a contrast to the opening lines of books of chivalry. Sánchez y Escribano agrees, concluding that the dry La Mancha was intended as a contrast to, and parody of, the green, lush scenes pictured in novels of chivalry. The critic concedes, however, that Cervantes may have been influenced by the lines in the ballad of *El amante apaleado,* cited by Martín de Riquer in his third edition of *Don Quijote* (Barcelona, 1955, p. 35, note 1).]

276. Santayana, George. "Cervantes," in *Essays in Literary Criticism.* Selected and edited, with an Introduction by Irving Singer. New York: Charles Scribner's Sons, 1956, pp. 112-119. (First published in 1897 in *Library of the World's Best Literature,* vol. VI, edited by Charles Dudley. New York: R. S. Pearle and J. A. Hill.)

Cervantes' natural tastes were for the chivalry novel, but events in his life plus his natural talent drove him to a very different sort of composition. The four factors which led to the writing of the *Quijote* were: (1) Cervantes' vast knowledge of chivalry novels; (2) his life of unrewarded endeavor; (3) his familiarity with the life of rogues; and (4) a spark of genius.

The hero Don Quijote at first appears to be insane, and probably seemed so to the author. But hero and author grow together, and soon there is disclosed the fund of intelligence and ideal passion which underlies the hero's superficial insanity. Sancho Panza is a contrast to his master, and the fact that Sancho becomes the squire of Don Quijote proves that a heroic and enthusiastic nature can gain ascendancy over the sluggish.

The *Quijote* has the quality of an improvisation. It is too strung together, and the episodes suggest themselves to the author as he proceeds. The interpolated material in Part I has no virtue. The *Quijote* is, in reality, a pre-novel, without dramatic structure, a private diary.

The intention of Cervantes' novel was to amuse, not to upbraid or discourage. In spite of all his disappointments Cervantes retained a healthy fondness for this naughty world. He is profoundly Christian. What would Cervantes probably have said the moral of his story was? That the force of idealism is wasted when it does not recognize the reality of things. However, the fact that the moral of the book is not perfectly clear is the greatest point in its favor.

277. Sarmiento, Edward. "On the Interpretation of *Don Quixote*." *Bulletin of Hispanic Studies*, XXXVII (1960), 146-153.

One of the basic problems in the interpretation of *Don Quijote* is the conflict between Cervantes' satirical intention and the right understanding of Don Quijote as a character. The satire in the novel does not preclude the presence in the author of a deep understanding and love for his hero, mistaken and wrong-headed though he be, nor the development in the reader of a similar sympathy and admiration for Don Quijote. There is no question that Cervantes was mocking the literary exaltation of chivalry; and it is also clear that he was condemning Don Quijote's tampering with truth. In spite of this, Don Quijote must be regarded as a hero.

The Montesinos' cave episode has been misinterpreted by a number of writers. The essence of this episode is that we do not know whether the hero is a plain liar or still the victim of an illusion. The true meaning of the adventure in Montesinos' cave is that Don Quijote cannot carry out his ideal in the outer world.

278. Savi-Lopez, Paolo. *Cervantes.* Translated from the Italian by Antonio G. Solalinde. Madrid: Calleja, 1917. Pp. 263. (First Italian edition published in 1913: Naples.)

Trying to discover the true intention of *Don Quijote* is impossible. It cannot be stated with certainty whether the hero is sane or insane, for we are all Don Quijotes at one time or other. The Knight is a hero of the internal life who lives his own truth. *Don Quijote* is not a symbolical work, and the hero's insanity has no transcendental meaning. Nevertheless, the novel presents the fluctuating mystery of life. Cervantes loves his Knight but can also make fun of him; the author can love chivalry as well as destroy it. The unity of the *Quijote* lies in its humor. Part I of the book is comic; Part II is grotesque, and the hero becomes a caricature of himself. This should make it clear to us that the author did not intend to make his hero the depository of a higher truth.

279. Schevill, Rudolph. "Three Centuries of *Don Quixote.*" *University of California Chronicle,* XV (1913), 181-206.

Cervantes' novel was probably intended at first to be only a short exemplary novel against the vogue of books of chivalry. But this purpose becomes crowded into the background as the story becomes a picture of society. *Don Quijote* was utterly without plan in construction. Cervantes no doubt put it aside from time to time as he composed it, and it is doubtful if he reread what he had already written. This accounts for the lapses of memory, the contradictions, and the repetitions found in his novel from time to time. The chief characteristic of the *Quijote* is its inexhaustible variety, the great inventiveness shown by the author. The very absence of plan goes hand in hand with the spontaneity and naturalness of the language in the story. If the *Quijote* has a fault, it is that it is carelessly written and lacking in polish at times.

Cervantes' humor is based largely on unforessen situations arising from violent contrasts and incongruities in the main theme (a medieval knight seeking adventures in an unromantic world). The real is offset by the ideal, the sane by the absurd, and the spirit of the impractical dreamer, who vainly tries to reconcile these contradictions, hovers over the whole. The perennial charm of the humor in Cervantes' novel lies in its ever bouyant tone and its lack of malice. The sympathetic presentation of human shortcomings in *Don Quijote* leads us to infer that in the great romancer's opinion the conditions of life are generally ridiculous rather than intolerable, that men are stupid and misguided rather than wicked, while the fantastic construction which the visionary Knight lays upon this unintelligible world suggests the importance of becoming squarely acquainted with it.

280. Schevill, Rudolph. *Cervantes*. New York: Frederick Ungar, 1966. Pp. iv. + 388. (Reprinted from the 1919 Edition, Duffield & Co.). [Appreciation is expressed to Angela Miller for her assistance in preparing this summary.]

The author of the *Quijote* was singularly aloof from the intellectual forces of his day and he cannot be identified with any specific philosophy. Cervantes' mind was not speculative, and he was uncritical of the political and religious tenets of his era. It is only when he deals with daily life and its realities that his intellect becomes singularly keen.

As Part I of the *Quijote* grew without any definite plan it may have occurred to the author to add variety to the main plot by introducing a number of formal elements. The interpolated episodes are generally serious and thus offset the comic scenes in the main plot. This offsetting was prompted by Cervantes' sense of harmony, by his desire not to overdo the scenes of humor and parody. Whatever may be the technical defects of these interpolations as suitable additions to the main plot they contain the noblest examples of Cervantes' prose and represent the highest level reached by the Castilian language in an age which for many reasons has been worthily styled the golden century.

It is in Part II of the *Quijote* that the hero's madness becomes, if not secondary, at least so greatly refined and restrained as to make logical the development of his saner nature. Don Quijote moves from a dreamer to a clear-headed reasoner on the character of human society. Sancho also changes and shows judgment and independence. It is fair to assert that in the development of Sancho's mind and character, far more than in the delineation of Don Quijote, Cervantes gave expression to a type of wisdom and eloquence and to a shrewd analysis of life which constitute the essence of his humanism.

Cervantes produced no disciples, no school of fiction, for works of such a caliber can be imitated only in isolated traits. He is an enchanter under whose hand an ever-changing series of impressions and pictures of human life succeed one another without any carefully premeditated framework or logical pursuit of the original theme. The rare inventor dominates the *Quijote*, while the conscious literary artist is in the ascendancy in the short stories. The *Quijote* is more universal, appealing to all nations; the *Novelas ejemplares* are more local, more intensely Spanish in the subtlest sense.

Although Cervantes is a writer who lacks the tragic instinct and is unaware of tragic depths, his masterpiece is more than merely a work of gaiety and wit; it is a fresh interpretation of life.

281. Schürr, Friedrich. Cervantes: *Leben und Werk des grossen Humoristen*. Bern-Munich: A. Francke, 1963. Pp. 161. (First edition 1947: Essen.)

The basic question in the *Quijote* is: if romantic irony destroys the illusion of the novel, how can the reader take the story seriously? The answer is that behind the outer parody there is an attitude of affirmation. The many obstacles and restrictions in Cervantes' life caused him to desire freedom. He fled to Italy as a young man, and the motif of flight often appears in his works. Both the author and his hero-knight fight for self-fulfillment without regard to outer reality. Cervantes does not consciously raise the identity and self-fulfillment problem, but the question does arise: can a man, in this circumscribed world full of restrictions, win his freedom in a flight into folly?

There are many fools in Cervantes' works, fools who are held prisoner by a fixed idea. But, in contrast to these confused figures, there are others who are not ruled by their emotions and who are free (Marcela). The fool motif is, in Cervantes' works, connected with the inner freedom of the personality. True freedom is an inner freedom, and this is the ruling idea in Cervantes' works. This inner freedom is achieved by way of humor, which is an inner release through an affirmation of one's personal fate and a reconciliation with it.

282. Schürr, Friedrich. "Romanticismo, realismo y humorismo de Cervantes." *Anales Cervantinos,* III (1953), 361-366.

From the *Galatea* to the *Persiles* Cervantes is dominated by the tension between reality and illusion. In *Don Quijote* only the hero lives in a world of illusion. In this respect Cervantes' novel differs from *Orlando furioso*. The reader of Ariosto's epic takes the magic of the poem seriously, at least as long as he is reading. In *Don Quijote,* however, the reader regards the magic with irony, just as Cervantes does.

Don Quijote flees from reality in order to fulfill his *yo,* and Cervantes ironizes this tendency, as well as the inevitable failure, with a benevolent smile and thus achieves his own inner self-liberation and catharsis. The self-realization of the author through humor is one of the aspects of symbolical meaning in the *Quijote,* and perhaps its outstanding feature.

283. Serrano-Plaja, Arturo. *Realismo "mágico" en Cervantes; Don Quijote visto desde Tom Sawyer y el idiota.* Madrid: Editorial Gredos, 1967. Pp. 236. (Translated into English as *"Magic" Realism in Cervantes; Don Quixote as seen through Tom Sawyer and The Idiot.* Berkeley, Los Angeles, and London: University of California Press, 1970. Pp. 216.)

The author of the *Quijote* constantly plays with the concept of the distinction between history and fiction. He tells the reader that there is doubt as to the hero's real name. This, oddly, has the effect of heightening historical reality, for if the novel were purely fictional (and, of course, it is), there would be no doubt as to the hero's name. Here Cervantes is showing us the front of the tapestry, while stating with apparent seriousness that it is the back side, and winking at us all the while.

Don Quijote does not mistake inns for castles; he is merely playing an elaborate child's game of pretending. Twain was perhaps the first to see this childlike quality in the *Quijote,* and therefore made his hero an imaginative boy, Tom Sawyer. Neither Don Quijote, Tom Sawyer, nor Myschkin (the idiot) have an immediate family, and therefore there are no outside restraints on them, no authority over them. All three are infants, and all three have a quest for justice on the fringe of the law.

Why did Don Quijote not test the helmet a second time? Because of magic. He merely held it to be good; and by this magic trick he caused it to be good. Tom Sawyer, similarly, uses a pick to dig a tunnel but insists that the pick is a case knife, as in adventure stories. In the first sally, why does the Don not leave by the front door? Because Cervantes omits to tell us that he is afraid of the housekeeper, just as Tom Sawyer is afraid of Aunt Polly.

Both Tom Sawyer and Don Quijote feel the need to do something difficult, Don Quijote to do penance and Tom to free Jim. Both want fame, in order to cause talk. In the episode in which the barber's beard falls off, Don Quijote clearly sees through the ruse. Why couldn't Cervantes say so specifically? The author is winking at us. We know deep down that the hero is aware of the truth but does not want to be cognizant of it. He wants to keep the illusion alive. Menéndez Pidal (196) is wrong to conclude that Don Quijote dies sadly because he concludes that the world is inferior to him. Instead, the hero is sad because he is dying and the game is over.

284. Shklovskii, Victor. "Kak sdelan Don-Kikhot," in *O Teorii Prozy.* Moscow: Izdatel'stvo "Federatsiya," 1929, pp. 91-124. (Reprinted in 1971 by Ardis, Ann Arbor, Michigan. (First printed in 1920 in *Zhizn' iskusstva,* No. 373, pp. 2-3; No. 375, pp. 1-13; No. 376, p. 1.) [Appreciation is expressed to Don Pruitt for his able assistance in preparing this summary. Appreciation is also expressed to Prof. Ludmilla B. Turkevich for the citation of the original version of this work.]

Don Quijote, as originally conceived by the author, was not to be intelligent, but brainless. Later, however, Cervantes needed his hero as a unifying thread for wise and largely unmotivated speeches, and thus the author decided to increase the mental capacity of his Knight. As the Don thus becomes more wise, the Squire goes through a curiously similar process. Sancho serves as a thread·on which is strung the folklore of the author's time, just as the Don becomes the mouthpiece of the booklearning of the day. Cervantes is well aware that there are inconsistencies in the portrayal of the Knight due to his having been loaded with wisdom. But having created a duality in the Knight, Cervantes begins to use this duality for his own purposes.

Part II of the *Quijote* is quite different from Part I in several respects: (1) Part II is more mosaic in structure, containing numerous small, hastily inserted scenes; (2) the Knight and the Squire become duped by others, rather than by the Don's illusions; (3) the hero becomes aware of himself in Part II, but only as a literary character.

There are several types of interpolations in the *Quijote*: poems, pastoral scenes, etc. The mechanism for joining these interpolations to the main plot varies. The author may use a messenger-narrator to motivate the introduction of extraneous matter. He then will have a character from the main plot interrupt the secondary narration by words or actions. The author may also cause a character from the interpolated episode to intervene in the main plot (Dorotea-Micomicona), or cause the Knight to struggle with a character from the inserted episode (Cardenio, Eugenio).

In the Arms and Letters discourse Cervantes specifically refers back to the hero's previous speech on the Age of Gold. This very curious technique of linking similar passages is somewhat like the repetition of a Wagnerian motif.

285. Shroder, Maurice Z. "The Novel as a Genre," in *The Theory of the Novel*. Edited by Philip Stevick. New York: The Free Press; London: Collier-MacMillan Limited, 1967, pp. 13-29. (Reprinted from *The Massachusetts Review*, 1963.) [Appreciation is expressed to Arthur Ramírez for his assistance in this summary.]

The *matter* of the novel — the theme that has informed the genre from *Don Quijote* onward — is relatively uncomplicated. The novel records the passage from a state of innocence to a state of experience, from that ignorance which is bliss to a mature recognition of the actual way of the world. Furthermore, the novel deals with a distinction between appearance and reality. It is not necessarily a question of ontological subtleties: the reality to which the novel appeals is that to which it is historically connected, the reality of bourgeois life, of business, and of the modern city. The basic distinction between the *romance* (forerunner of the novel) and the modern novel is in the protagonist. In the *romance* he is a hero; in the novel he is a perfectly ordinary man.

The sensibility that produces novels asks questions instead of making contrary statements. In what is perhaps the most thoroughly emblematic scene in Cervantes' novel, Don Quijote loudly proclaims that a group of windmills are giants. The adequate response to such a statement is not the contrary assertion, that giants are merely windmills. It is the question asked by the unwilling squire, Sancho Panza: "What giants?" But Sancho's question is not burlesque. It is the interrogative understatement that confounds Don Quijote's hyperbolic assertion. Sancho, in the episode of the windmills, does not initially reveal the truth of the situation directly and crudely. The peasant squire simply questions the romanesque premise, the highly-colored overstatement of his master. Without knowing it, Sancho is playing the *eiron* (self-depreciator) to the *alazon* (self-deceiver) Don Quijote. However, the irony of Cervantes' novel, and of later novels, arises less from the presence of an *alazon-eiron* pair like Don Quijote and Sancho Panza, than from the novelist's attitude toward the characters and the fictional world he creates. That is to say, the true heir to Socrates is not Sancho Panza but Cervantes, that the novelist is the *eiron,* while his protagonist (the "imaginist," the romance sensibility in a real world) is an *alazon* who learns, through disillusionment, that he is not a hero after all. Unlike the inflationary novelist, who advertises his characters (if not himself), the deflationary novelist, the ironic author, *appears* to allow his characters to magnify themselves, but is in reality subtly and silently reducing them to their actual stature. Irony, after all, modulates between comedy and tragedy. It is, according to J. A. K. Thompson's *Irony,* "the trembling equipoise between jest and earnest." Hence comedy often approximates tragedy. The comic fault of *alazoneia* is equivalent to tragic *hubris.* Thus Don

Quijote may be both a grotesque caricature and — for the Romantics — the martyred saint of the imagination.

286. Sletsjöe, Leif. *Sancho Panza hombre de bien*. Madrid: Insula, 1961. Pp. 136.

One must be skeptical about Madariaga's (182) theory of the *sanchificación* of Don Quijote, and even more cautious about Unamuno's (309) theory of the *quijotización* of Sancho Panza. The Squire's change is actually quite brusque, not continuous, and Cervantes is well aware that the change is not a smooth one.

Cervantes painted the Squire with certain obvious inconsistencies. He is too stupid one minute and too clever the next. Thus he is not, in a true sense, psychologically portrayed. Another problem is that there is a stage missing in Sancho's development, for the Squire, at the beginning of the 1615 *Quijote*, is quite different from what he had been in Part I. Thus there is no slow growth of the Squire's personality from the beginning of Part I to the end of Part II.

287. Snetkova, Nina. "Quelques particularités du style du roman *Don Quichotte* de Cervantes." *Beiträge zur Romanischen Philologie*, Sonderheft, c 1967, 1968. (Das literarische Werk von Miguel de Cervantes), pp. 85-91.

Cervantes makes use of the grotesque and the eccentric to show that absurd appearances conceal a wisdom deeper than common sense. The transformation of the *Quijote* from parody to the grotesque is accompanied by a change of attitude on the part of the author toward his hero. To put it another way, as the character of the Knight becomes deeper and more complex, Cervantes abandons the parody and begins to seek a new means, namely the grotesque, to reveal to us the rapport of the hero with the universe that surrounds him. Thus the author introduces into literature a grotesque figure who arouses, at one and the same time, our laughter and our sympathy.

Cervantes' Don and Charlie Chaplin's figure of the little tramp have much in common. Both struggle energetically to keep their dignity. Neither loses his interior "moi," regardless of the circumstances. Both are tragicomic. Both behave illogically and nonsensically, yet pursue a goal that is logical to them. Cervantes and Chaplin join two elements apparently contradictory: the tragic and the comic. But here these two elements do not clash, but fuse. Undoubtedly the grotesque of Cervantes and of Chaplin causes us to penetrate into the deepest recesses of the human soul so that we may have faith in its powers, in the grandeur of its aspirations and its ideal.

288. Spitzer, Leo. "Die Frage der Heuchelei des Cervantes." *Zeitschrift für Romanische Philologie*, LVI (1936), 138-178.

[In his *Pensamiento de Cervantes*, (63), 1925, Américo Castro had stated that Cervantes was often hypocritical in his remarks. Critics had attacked this view, but Castro, in 1931 (67), had defended his original assertion. Here Spitzer renews the polemic, stating that Cervantes is genuinely anti-Moor, that he is a medieval believer in a national religion, and that while the author's heart may go out to Ricote his mind remains with the Church. Spitzer also disagrees with Castro's (63) interpretation of *El curioso impertinente* (error and punishment). To Spitzer this interpolated *novela* reveals that lack of harmony leads to chaos. Another matter discussed here is Cervantes' use of the expression "de cuyo nombre no quiero acordarme." Here Spitzer views the phrase as a mere stylized negative. *See*, however, his later view in "Linguistic Perspectivism in the *Don Quijote*" (289).]

289. Spitzer, Leo. "Linguistic Perspectivism in the *Don Quijote*," in *Linguistics and Literary History: Essays in Stylistics*. Princeton, N. J.: Princeton University Press, 1948, pp. 41-85. [Appreciation is expressed to Arthur Ramírez for his assistance in this summary.]

The variety and instability in the names of Cervantes' characters (and the variety of etymological explanation offered for the names) reflects a deliberate refusal on the part of the author to make a final choice of one name (and one etymology): in other words, a desire to show the different aspects under which a character in question may appear to others. This relativistic attitude affects other linguistic details. Perspectivism, as Américo Castro (63) has noted, informs the structure of Cervantes' novel as a whole. Yet there is something unfluctuating behind all this — the novelist who assumes divine power in his mastery over the material and who takes a position of aloofness from the reader. The author of the *Quijote* sees that the world is susceptible to many explanations, just as names are susceptible to many etymologies. People can be deluded by their perspectives toward the world as well as by the etymological connections which they establish.

Cervantes was serious about attacking chivalry novels; he was also serious about attacking the bookish side of Humanism and the word-world of the Renaissance. For the baroque writer words are no longer depositories of truths nor an expansion of life, as they had been in the Middle Ages and the Renaissance, respectively. They are, like the books in which they are contained, sources of hesitation, error, deception — "dreams."

In writing the *Quijote* Cervantes at times breaks the illusion and lets us see the puppet strings, saying in effect: "see, reader, this is not life, but a stage, a book: art; recognize the life-giving power of the artist as a thing distinct from life!" Cervantes felt that his own being was split into a critical and illusionistic part (*desengaño* and *engaño*); but in this baroque Ego he made order, a precarious order, it is true, which was reached only once by Cervantes in all his works and which was reached in Spain only by Cervantes. And, indeed, only once in world literature has this precarious order come into being. Later thinkers and artists do not stop at proclaiming the inanity of the world; they go so far as to doubt the existence of any universal order and to deny a creator. Cervantes, however, is not trying to dethrone God to replace Him with the artist as superman. He bows to the teachings of the Church. As a moralist, Cervantes is not at all "perspectivistic." Nor is he a romantic rebelling against society. But as an artist he has, by the mere art of his narrative, extended the almost cosmic independence of the artist.

[Spitzer's essay contains a number of lengthy footnotes. Footnote 33, for example, discusses the opening line of the *Quijote*. To Spitzer, "de cuyo nombre no *quiero* acordarme" reflects the glorification of the artist's freedom, *qua* artist. He rejects the "silly" autobiographical explanation that Cervantes wanted to forget a particular town. Spitzer disagrees with Casalduero's (56) idea that

Cervantes opposes his novel to the romances of chivalry, which claimed to know exactly where the heroes were born. Also, the folkloric theory of María Rosa Lida (174), states Spitzer, fails to take into sufficient consideration the functional value, for the novel, of the attitude of the author expressed therein, the freedom of the artist.]

290. Spitzer, Leo. "On the Significance of *Don Quijote*." *Modern Language Notes*, LXXVII (1962), 113-129. (Reprinted in *Cervantes: A Collection of Critical Essays* (219), pp. 82-97. [Appreciation is expressed to Arthur Ramírez for his assistance in this summary.]

There are elements in *Don Quijote* which appeal to wisdom at the child stage: (1) a just world-order; (2) a fairy-tale world which builds up a second world on top of the real one in which the child moves; (3) the idea that man can master adverse situations; and (4) humor. A child feels superior to Don Quijote but sympathizes with his attempt to create a fanciful world. From an adult point of view (if we believe the author's statement) the book is an attack on chivalry-novel nonsense. We should not overlook this, as Unamuno (309) has done. Cervantes in fact poses the problem of the book and its influence on life — a permanent problem.

The novel is a hybrid genre; it arose in late Greek literature, later appeared in the Middle Ages, and again in modern times. The novel can blur the lines between reality and romance, and make the past seem the present. Both Cervantes and Flaubert are disillusionists who add criticism to the novel, an extra-poetic element. Cervantes creates the second variety of the novel, the critical novel which expands in the nineteenth century to a criticism not only of previous literature but of whole civilizations. But is the *Quijote* only destructive? Is there no striving back toward poetic beauty? There *is* such a striving: the poetry, the speeches, the stories. These lead us into an atmosphere of romantic nowhereness, where realism ceases and imagination holds sway. If Cervantes wanted to destroy chivalry novels, why did he let in so many stories written in the same spirit? Because he realized that the anti-novel in its pure form would result in disharmony in the reader's mind. The author sought, therefore, to balance the critical sense with the beauty of the fabulous. There are thus two aspects to the *Quijote:* (1) the criticism of imaginative beauty; and (2) the restoration of imaginative beauty in the face of all scepticism.

[The remainder of this article deals with matters discussed by Spitzer in the latter part of his "Linguistic Perspectivism in the *Don Quijote*" (289).]

291. Stagg, Geoffrey L. "Cervantes revisa su novela (*Don Quijote*, 1.ª Parte)." *Separata de los Anales de la Universidad de Chile*, Año CXXIV, núm. 140 (Oct.-Dic., 1966), pp. 5-27. (Translated by Mario Ferreccio Podestá from "Revision in *Don Quijote*, Part I," in *Hispanic Studies in Honour of Ignacio González Llubera*. Oxford, The Dolphin Book Co. Ltd., 1959, pp. 347-366.)

The original plan of the 1605 *Quijote* was quite different from the final version. Chapters, it seems, were an afterthought, and there are several possible explanations for the error in the heading to Chapter X (which states that Chapter X will deal *inter alia* with the *yangüeses*, who do not appear until Chapter XV). The most logical explanation is that originally Chapters X and XV were a *continuum* and that Chapters XI-XIV were later inserted after the conclusion of the *viscaíno* episode and before the beginning of that of the *yangüeses*. Originally Chapters XI-XIV (the friendly goatherds and the Marcela episode) were part of the Sierra Morena episode. This can be gleaned from the similarity in topography. Also, one should note that at the end of Chapter XIV Don Quijote rejects Vivaldo's invitation to go to Seville on the ground that he must clear the hills of thieves. This indicates that Chapters XI-XIV originally came shortly after the freeing of the *galeotes*, Chapter XXII.

The error about Sancho's ass has given rise to much comment. The donkey is a constant companion from Chapter VII to Chapter XXV where we are suddenly confronted with a reference to its loss. It remains lost until Chapter XLVI when it suddenly reappears without explanation. Originally the plan of the *Quijote* was that the loss of the donkey would take place during the stay with the friendly goatherds, which, as stated previously, originally came shortly after the *galeotes* had been freed.

The original draft of the 1605 *Quijote* contained twenty-two chapters of the adventures of Don Quijote and Sancho (and without the *escrutinio*), followed by thirty chapters of novelistic matter. Since there was too much disparity between the subject matter of the first and last portions of the original draft, Cervantes, in order to make the work more balanced, decided to mingle them. He did this quite hastily in his desire to get into print prior to the appearance of Part II of Alemán's *Guzmán de Alfarache*.

292. Stagg, Geoffrey L. "Sobre el plan primitivo del Quijote." *Tirada aparte de las Actas del primer Congreso Internacional de Hispanistas*. Oxford: The Dolphin Book Co. Ltd., 1964. Pp. 9.

There are a number of inconsistencies and repetitions in the *Quijote*, but it is wrong to accuse Cervantes of forgetfulness. It is more likely that he went back and hastily added certain parts to his earlier chapters and did not make later readjustments to prevent inconsistencies and repetition. There are six examples of later interpolations: (1) Cervantes appears to have gone back and added in Chapter I the name of the barber and of the priest and also the fact that they were well aware of the nature of the hero's mental illness. (The priest and barber, one should note, are named a second time, in the chapter in which the hero returns after his first sally, and the niece acts as if the priest and barber had no idea about her uncle's illness); (2) the inconsistencies about the hero's name indicate that the references to Quesada, Quijada, and Quejana were interpolated later; (3) the apparently superfluous explanation, at the beginning of the second sally, that the scene is Montiel, indicates that the reference in Chapter I to Montiel was placed there later; (4) the whole *escrutinio* appears to be an interpolation because: (A) the priest tells Don Quijote, who is having a dream adventure, that he is probably tired, although the story states that the Knight has slept twelve hours; (B) the library is walled up even though the books have been burned; (5) the innkeeper's advice to Don Quijote to get a squire (and the Knight's decision to return home to do so) appears to be an interpolation, since we later find the hero permitting Rocinante to choose the road to take; and (6) the remarks about the "autores desta historia" appear to have been added later. Cervantes started to write a *cuento* and only later hit upon the device of a true *historia* and of making Cide Hamete the historian. Hence he felt it necessary to add the matter about historians in the beginning chapters.

293. Stagg, Geoffrey. "La primera salida de Don Quijote: imitación de sí mismo." *Clavileño*, Año IV, núm. 22 (Julio-Agosto, 1953), pp. 4-10.

[Professor Stagg begins his article with a cogent summary of the varying opinions regarding the principal source of *Don Quijote:* the *Entremés de los romances* theory of Menéndez Pidal (196), the Camilote theory of Dámaso Alonso (3), the real-life model approach of Rodríguez Marín (258), the *Amadís* theory of José María Pemán (233), the *Orlando furioso* school of thought of Marco A. Garrone (124), the *Amadís-Orlando furioso* approach of Entwistle (100), and the *Esplandián* theory of Félix Olmedo (222). The major part of this article deals with the possible influence of Ariosto's *Orlando furioso* on the departure scene in Chapter II, Part I of the *Quijote*. Stagg concludes that the dawn description in that chapter is more a satire of Cervantes' own *La Galatea* than of *Orlando*.]

294. Stagg, Geoffrey. "Castro del Río, ¿cuna del *Quijote?*" *Clavileño*, Año VI, núm. 36 (Nov.-Dic., 1955), pp. 1-11.

There are several theories as to when the *Quijote* was begun. Fitzmaurice-Kelly [Ed. *Don Quijote*, 1901, Vol. I, p. xx] concluded that it was undertaken after 1591; Entwistle [(100), p. 105] concluded that the novel was begun in 1597 at Seville; Buchanan ["The Works of Cervantes and Their Dates of Composition," *Proc. and Trans. of the Royal Society of Canada*, XXXII (1938), 23-39] stated that Cervantes started his masterpiece in 1600; Rodríguez Marín [Ed. *Don Quijote*, 1927-1928, Vol. VII, p. 51] believed that the novel was begun in 1602 at the royal jail in Seville.

Américo Castro, in "The Prefaces to *Don Quixote*" (68), is incorrect in concluding that Cervantes is merely being metaphorical when he indicated that his book was conceived of in a jail, for the author of the true *Quijote* does not attempt to answer Avellaneda's jibe at him for his having been jailed. All in all, the most probable time and place for the beginning of the *Quijote* was in 1592 while the author was incarcerated at Castro del Río.

The latest book cited in the *escrutinio* was *El pastor de Iberia*, 1591. Although Cervantes uses *fue* when referring to the author of that work, Barahona de Soto (died 1595), the syntax does not indicate that Cervantes necessarily meant to state that Barahona de Soto was deceased. To those who state that the opening phrase of the *Quijote* is based on the ballad *Un lencero portugués*, published in 1597 or later, there are several possible answers. It is quite conceivable that Cervantes did not draw on that *romance*. Also, if he did, he could have heard the ballad prior to its publication.

295. Suarès, André. *Cervantes*. 2nd ed. Paris: Émile-Paul Frères, 1916. Pp. 121. (First edition also 1916, Paris, E. Paul. Translated into Spanish as *Don Quijote en Francia*, Madrid: Imp. Clásica Española, 1916.)

Don Quijote is the most noble and yet the most simple of men. He thinks like a child, and he is a marvel of good will. The Don has a madness for liberty, and Dulcinea represents this liberty. He thinks of an eternal victory, not and earthly one. The Knight is even Christ-like. He may be the Cross on horseback, both divine and humiliated.

Don Quijote did not willingly recant his high ideals on his deathbed. Perhaps his confessor forced him to do so. The last pages of his story should be ignored, for they are written neither by the Knight nor by Cervantes. Don Quijote is above his times. He believes in nobleness, in Christian friendship. The Knight is perhaps a Christian Socrates. Yet while Socrates believed that it was sufficient to think good, the Don believed that it was sufficient to desire good.

Cervantes has incomparable comic power. Like Rabelais and Flaubert his comic force lies more in his style than in his words, yet more in his words than in his thoughts.

296. Tarr, F. Courtney. "Recent Trends in Cervantes Studies: An Attempt at Survey and Prognosis." *Romanic Review*, XXI (1940), 16-28. [Appreciation is expressed to Arthur Ramírez for his assistance in this summary.]

Rodríguez Marín combines a *castizo* approach with a documentary approach, and emphasizes the picturesque and external realism of the subject matter and language in Cervantes' works. This reflects a cardinal phase of nineteenth-century criticism as a whole, which inspired the Taylorian lecture of Morel-Fatio (210) and *El Quijote y su época* (8) by José de Armas. The period of Romantic exaltation of Don Quijote reaches its peak in Rubén Darío's *Letania de Nuestro Señor Don Quijote* (89) and in Unamuno's *Vida de Don Quijote y Sancho* (309), both in 1905. In 1916 came the first direct and conscious combination of historical scholarship and critical insight, in the two articles devoted — in part — by Américo Castro to Cervantes' handling of the honor question. [*RFE*, III (1916), 1-50, 357-386; and *RFE*, IV (1917), 400.] These works were followed in 1920 (and 1924) by Menéndez Pidal's *Un aspecto en la elaboración del Quijote* (196), a study which takes some account of creative impulses, attitudes and processes, although concerned primarily with a problem of literary history — the relation of the *Entremés de los romances* to *Don Quijote*. Madariaga, in his *Guía del lector del Quijote* (182), 1926, continues the analysis of themes thus inaugurated by Castro and Menéndez Pidal, and studies the deliberate and subtle harmonies and contradictions between Don Quijote and Sancho. He also examines the significance of central episodes, such as the cave of Montesinos. But Madariaga was not the first critic to glimpse the complexity and profundity of Cervantes' literary art. Américo Castro, in his *El pensamiento de Cervantes* (63), had already done so. Castro, who showed Cervantes to be a conscious thinker and artist, drives out the concept of Cervantes as *genio inconsciente y vulgar*. The central theme of *El pensamiento* is Cervantes' relation to renaissance and counter reformation thought, an idea foreshadowed by Toffanin's *La fine dell'umanesimo* (300) in 1920. Savi-Lopez (278), even earlier, 1913, had stressed, in a superficial way, the influence of Italian culture on Cervantes. Another important feature of Professor Castro's book is the emphasis it lays on the totality of Cervantes' work in its ideological and — to a smaller but none the less real extent — its artistic unity. As much attention is paid to the "conventional" and "artificial" as to the "original" and "realistic" works. In recent years there has been an increased interest in the more conventional parts of *Don Quijote*.

The first writer to study Cervantes' esthetic principles and practice is Helmut Hatzfeld (141) in 1927. Mario Casella's *Il Chisciotte* (60), 1938, appears to be an esthetic study of Cervantes' masterpiece but is, in reality, a diffuse and tortuous attempt to claim Cervantes exclusively for the neo-Thomists or the Platonic-Augustinian school of thought. Casella correctly stresses the esthetic unity of the *Quijote*, but his analysis of that unity is not sound.

[At the end of his article Tarr briefly discusses the structure of the *Quijote*.] The symphonic motifs of *Don Quijote* are: *caballero, andante, enamorado, loco*, which are announced in the very first chapter and elaborated — consciously and spontaneously — throughout the rest of the book. Cervantes' choice and arrangement of material in the *Quijote* obeys the esthetic principles of harmony, variety, contrast and inversion. But the art of Cervantes goes even deeper. Not only does it show in Vossler's happy phrase, *die Literarisierung des Lebens (la literarización de la vida)* but also — and herein lies his unique gift — and to a far greater extent *la vitalización de lo literario*.

297. Terrero, José. "Las rutas de las tres salidas de Don Quijote de la Mancha." *Anales Cervantinos*, VIII (1959-1960), 1-49.

Although Fermín Caballero, in his *Pericia geográfica de Miguel de Cervantes* (Madrid: 1840), concludes that the author of the *Quijote* was an expert geographer, the three sallies of the Knight are imaginary, capricious, and completely ignore the map. Cervantes is vague about the name of the hero's village. Fermín Caballero and many others insist that it was Argamasilla de Alba, while Astrana Marín [(10), (11)] concludes that it was Esquivias. A number of other villages have been suggested, but neither they nor Esquivias lie in the region of Montiel where, Cervantes repeatedly states, the Knight had his home. [Terrero examines the principal episodes of the *Quijote* and seeks to fix their location.]

298. Terrero, José. "Itinerario del *Quijote* de Avellaneda y su influencia en el cervantino." *Anales Cervantinos*, II (1952), 159-191.

[Terrero furnishes several maps showing the itineraries of Cervantes' Don Quijote as well as Avellaneda's hero. The principal influence of Avellaneda on the geography of Part II of Cervantes' *Quijote,* the critic states, is when the author, instead of taking his hero into Zaragoza, lifts him through the air and places him near the Ebro in an impossible three-day journey. Terrero also notes that Cervantes' Knight takes another magic journey — from the palace of the *Duques* to his village in La Mancha, covered in four days, although the distance appears to be 342 kilometers measured in a straight line.]

299. Terterian, Ioana. "Sobre algunas interpretaciones del *Quijote* en la España del siglo XX." *Beiträge zur Romanischen Philologie,* Sonderheft, c 1967, 1968. (Das literarische Werk von Miguel de Cervantes), pp. 169-173.

Spanish interpretations of the *Quijote* are always interesting, though often arbitrary in their attempts to modernize the figure of Don Quijote. The Generation of '98 was fascinated by the figure of Don Quijote. Unamuno, in his *Vida de Don Quijote y Sancho* (309), formulated his conception of the tragic element in life long before he developed this idea systematically. Antonio Machado also meditated about the *Quijote* [*Obras Completas,* Mexico: Séneca, 1940, pp. 802-803]. He uses the concept of the monad taken from Leibnitz. A monad, to Machado, is the personality that contains an integral and absolute world within itself and pursues its own goal. But Machado does not conclude that man's solitary state is inevitable and incurable, contrary to many philosophies of the twentieth century. Yes, Machado states, each individual is an isolated and hermetic world, but each person feels the need of the other. Each is aware of the other monad. Thus, to Machado, both the Don and the Squire are completely convinced of the existence of the other. They converse with one another like two self-sufficient monads. Yet both desire to be complemented by the other.

Spaniards of the twentieth century do not agree, by any means, about the meaning of the *Quijote*. For example, to Unamuno Cervantes presents a tragic, agonizing world looking for a way out of a dead-end street, while to Azorín the world of the *Quijote* is a sleeping, immobile world.

A stage in the interpretation of the *Quijote* is reached in the years prior to the Spanish Civil War when several writers, such as Maeztu (184), begin to regard the hero as a typical example of "hispanidad," the Spanish affirmation of the monarchy and the Church and the rejection of all egalitarianism. This mystic-religious view becomes popular in the 1940's and 1950's.

In general, there are two principal attitudes toward the Knight. Some regard him as the picture of faith, the torch of mysticism, the eternal symbol of Spanish disregard for earthly life in favor of the divine. Others, the existentialists, view the Don's heroism in connection with the problem of the human personality, as the existentialists view it. A new view of the heroic element in the *Quijote* is needed, a view somewhere between the mystic and the existential.

300. Toffanin, Giuseppe. "Il Cervantes," in *La fine dell'umanesimo*. Torino: Fratelli Bocca, 1920, pp. 211-221.

The years of Cervantes' sojourn in Italy were the years in which the problem of history versus poetry was very much an issue. In face of this question Tasso despaired, yet Cervantes smiled. The core of the *Quijote* is this polemic over the distinction between fiction and history, the poetic universal versus the historical particular. The author of the *Quijote* takes this burning question and superbly integrates it into his story.

When in Part II, the hero hears of his previous history (i.e. Part I) an Aristotelian idea comes to him: the hero must be overstated or understated, better or worse than historical reality. He should be the poetic universal. Sancho is interested in the historical particular and thinks that all matters should have been included. If we bear in mind the critical-philosophical thought of the author's times, we realize that *Don Quijote* is more directly a literary and universal satire, not merely an attack on the waning popularity of chivalry novels. One should also note that Cervantes' novel is not a product of the full Renaissance, but of the Catholic reaction to it.

The present tendency is to praise the *Quijote* as an exaltation of literary creativity, to praise the Knight and to downgrade the Squire. But looking over the whole work, and the concluding scene, one feels that the hero is Sancho, symbol of our uncertain mortal destiny.

301. Togeby, Knud. *La composition du roman "Don Quijote."* Supplément de Orbis Litterarum. Copenhagen: Munksgaard, 1957. Pp. 63.

In *Don Quijote* and in the chivalry novel events follow one another arbitrarily, but in the *Quijote* there is a reason for the arbitrariness — the folly of the hero. Arbitrariness is the very principle of the action. Cervantes created the modern novel, but not out of whole cloth. He adds a certain concentration of time to the longer narration. Of the previous writers who have discussed the unity, or lack of it, in *Don Quijote,* Entwistle (100) claimed that the novel was medieval and without unity; Hatzfeld (141) saw a unity through a chain of motifs; Américo Castro ["La estructura del *Quijote*" (70)] saw unity through the central characters; and Casalduero (58) exaggerates the structural unity, for he sees a place for everything. Casalduero also concludes that the circular form of the *Quijote* symbolizes destiny, but the destiny of the novel is clearly brought about by the character of the hero. Rocinante's route is not the route of destiny but that of chivalresque folly, of the imagination; and the hero's return home is not the result of destiny but the result of a clash between reality and the imagination.

Part II, 1615, is more a work of genius than Part I. Cervantes goes out of his way not to imitate the 1605 edition, because Avellaneda had already done so. As a reaction against the false *Quijote* Sancho is made to cease being a glutton, and Dulcinea (who virtually disappeared in Avellaneda's version) becomes very important in Part II. The 1615 *Quijote* is not divided into arbitrary parts like the 1605 *Quijote* and like Avellaneda's version of 1614. The *Quijote* of 1615 is a book of recovery, a happy idea. The most important innovation in Part II is the equilibrium which is established between Don Quijote and Sancho. Master and Squire grow alike, as Madariaga (182) noted. Part II is a book of victories, especially of victory over oneself.

302. Trachman, Sadie Edith. *Cervantes' Women of Literary Tradition.* New York: Instituto de las Españas en los Estados Unidos, 1932. Pp. xiv + 177.

In general Cervantes' characters are either: (1) the poetic, novelistic type with a long literary tradition; or (2) realistic characters unmistakably from life (though at times they may have literary antecedents), whose chief merit lies in their individuality. People generally regard Cervantes as a realistic author, while his poetic creations are forgotten or considered inferior. Yet the poetical world is an essential factor in Cervantes. In his worst works the idealistic and the realistic worlds are separated, while in his best ones the two worlds are skillfully blended. The idealistic and the realistic formed a part of the profound unity of his soul and of his work; and both worlds must be studied in order to understand Cervantes' art in which each of these two worlds is necessary for the other. By reason of their coexistence, their fusion and harmony, they constitute Cervantes' supreme creation, the fundamental theme of his *Quijote.*

Cervantes' ideas on women are generally conventional. However, he is in advance of his times in both opposing the honor code of revenge and in recommending marriage for love. [Chapters II through XVIII of this work each deal with a type of female character, such as the Moorish type, the pastoral type, the chivalresque type, etc. In some chapters, subcategories are found. Under Moorish types (Chap. II), Zoraida is discussed, it being observed that female converts to Christianity were found in *La Chanson de Roland* and in *Tirant lo Blanch.* Miss Trachman notes, however, that, Cervantes' heroine, unlike prior models, is primarily moved by religion, not by physical love. Marcela is discussed under pastoral types (Chap. IV), and her likely models, states Miss Trachman, were Sylvia in Tasso's *Aminta* and Angelica in Ariosto's *Orlando furioso,* though Marcela's type was also found in mythology and in Heliodorus (Chariclea). Dorotea is discussed in Chapter VII, Ana Felix and Camila in Chapter X, and possible models are suggested for each. In her final chapter Miss Trachman briefly notes the appearance of Luscinda, Dorotea, and Camila in certain plays by Guillén de Castro, François Targa, and others.]

303. Trotter, G. D. *Cervantes and the Art of Fiction: inaugural Lecture of the Chair of Spanish in the University of Exeter delivered on 8 February, 1965.* Exeter, Devon: University of Exeter, 1965. Pp. 22.

Cervantes shows great control on several levels of fiction all at once. This control begins as early as the prologue to Part I, where the author refers to himself as the stepfather of Don Quijote. Vilanova, in his lecture at Exeter on May 5, 1964, stated that this was merely a stock technique used by Erasmus and others prior to Cervantes' time. But it is much more. Later we hear Cervantes refer to himself as the "second author." This is a step within the fiction to detach himself from the story. He shifts his position so that he is reading the novel along with us. This detachment is not a play-within-a-play device. To find anything like it we must wait until Unamuno, Pirandello or Cocteau. The strange thing with Cervantes is that as he detaches himself to obtain the objectivity of an ideal historian he contrives to move closer to his readers, and to establish with them as close a rapport as has ever been achieved by any author.

There was little in contemporary writing to help Cervantes find a new theory of prose fiction. What there was dealt with the distinction between poetry and history; but where he stands apart from his generation is in the detachment he brought to his art, and in the critical self-awareness and sense of purpose that went with it and were both its cause and its effect. This detachment appears to be due to his deep concern for the sacredness of objective, historical truth, a concern which was to lead Cervantes to the conclusion that the novel must be firmly founded on the truth of everyday experience. This is revolutionary and prophetic. It is on these terms that prose and poetry part company, and it is here, with Cervantes at the beginning of the seventeenth century, that the modern European novel is born.

304. Trueblood, Alan S. "Sobre la selección artística en el *Quijote:* '...lo que ha dejado de escribir' (II, 44)." *Nueva Revista de Filología Hispánica,* X (1956), 44-50.

While the conception of an ideal book of chivalry expressed by the Canon of Toledo is essentially Aristotelian, Cervantes does not equate the *Quijote* to such an ideal work. Actually, the canon conceived of a very broad frame where the pen could flow without hindrance. Cervantes-Cide Hamete, however, speaks of limiting himself, though he complains of limitations.

Cervantes' effort to eliminate what is artistically inoperative ties in with the neo-Aristotelian question of the distinction between history and literature, as Toffanin (300) noted. Following Toffanin, Américo Castro in his *Pensamiento* (63), made use of Robertelli's expression *relicta circumstantia* in order to explain Cervantes' artistic technique. Actually, Cervantes broadens the concept of *relicta circumstantia* for he eliminates not only details of daily life but also details of epic-novelesque material. Cervantes only goes into detail when a problematic vision of the world is involved, in order to reveal the inner world of his characters.

In the episode of Don Diego de Miranda the author omits details about that gentleman's household. He only points out the *silence*, which to the author is more important than details. Cervantes is here seeking to call forth a sensation or an experience. This is his authentic *poesis*.

In Part II of the *Quijote* Sansón Carrasco observes that many readers would have been happier if some of the beatings received by the Knight had been omitted. Sansón appears to be saying that too many drubbings adversely affect the verisimilitude of the story, since most readers considered the story to be fiction, not history. Don Quijote clearly equates *verdad* with *verosimilitud*, whereas Sancho equates *verdad* with the literal historical truth. Cervantes clearly takes Don Quijote's side in Part II, and though the drubbings of the hero do not cease altogether, they are sharply reduced. There is almost no physical violence upon the protagonists prior to their arrival at the palace of the *Duques*. The Knight's suffering becomes moral, not physical.

305. Trueblood, Alan S. "El silencio en el *Quijote*." *Nueva Revista de Filología Hispánica*, XII (1958), 160-180. [Appreciation is expressed to Shirley Weltman for her assistance in preparing this summary.]

The systematic use of silence is a comparatively new technique in literature, and *Don Quijote* is the only work by Cervantes where silence has a significant stylistic role. As a general rule, visual effects are more important in the *Quijote* than sounds, and sounds are more striking than silences. Yet silence may serve a variety of functions. For example, the silence of a character meeting Don Quijote may indicate amazement. Silence may also be used to arouse the curiosity of the reader.

Part II is a deeper work than Part I, and there are more silences in the *Quijote* of 1615. Here silence on the hero's part may indicate his confusion, as when he stares mutely at the peasant girl that Sancho has enchanted. Silence is also found at highpoints where lovers reunite. On certain occasions Cervantes appears to be imitating the episodes of silence in chivalry novels, as when he states that there is a great stillness at the inn, prior to the Maritornes bedside scene.

In the episode of the galley slaves Cervantes varies silence with talkativeness. Galley slaves one, three and five converse a great deal, whereas galley slaves two and four remain virtually silent. In Part II Sancho's silence on abdicating from his governorship marks a highpoint in the story. All in all, silence and sound are not handled routinely in the *Quijote*. The contrast between silence and sound strengthens the antithetical structure of the novel. Like other stylistic elements, the technique of silence and sound is consciously used.

306. Ullman, Pierre Lioni. "The Burlesque Poems Which Frame the *Quijote*." *Anales Cervantinos,* IX (1961-1962), 213-227. [Appreciation is expressed to Shirley Weltman for her assistance in preparing this summary.]

The burlesque poems at the beginning and at the end of the 1605 *Quijote* are not a collection of disconnected addenda. This frame of poems is linked intimately with the very structure of the novel, for it introduces the reader to Cervantes' perspectivistic technique of describing the reactions of different characters to the same situation. It is also a prelude to the intricate ways in which the author plays with the time dimension, especially the jumbling of the order of historical time. One idea that often appears in the *Quijote* is that of the past (the hero) judging the present. The same theme is found in the burlesque poems where, anachronistically, the heroes of the past judge Don Quijote. Again, the resurrection of the fictional heroes into the realm of reality, from which they may judge their own caricatures, anticipates in a way the incarnation of Don Quijote and Sancho within the historical present, effected by Cervantes in Part II of the novel, where these two fictional characters make an appearance before other fictional characters *(los Duques)* and real persons (Roque Guinart) who have read or heard of the Knight and Squire. The burlesque poems thus prepare the reader for the constant interplay of fiction and reality, past and present, seriousness and irony, truth and falsehood, which he will find throughout the pages of the book.

Outside the work, yet forming a "frame" between it and the reality of literary history, these burlesque poems are the key to the nest of tales-within-tales which is the *Quijote*.

[Each of the burlesque poems is studied by Ullman, who analyzes the perspective of the fictional author of the poem.]

307. Unamuno, Miguel de. "Don Quijote en la tragicomedia europea contemporánea," in *Del sentimiento trágico de la vida. Obras Completas,* VIII. Madrid: Escelicer, 1969, pp. 283-302. (First published in 1912.)

The Spaniards are not scientific, but mystic. The hero of Spanish thought is Don Quijote, who is more real than all the philosophers. He did not fight over idealism or ideas. He fought for spiritualism. The Knight made himself immortal by being ridiculous, and this is the highest form of heroism.

Speculative or meditative *quijotismo*, like practicing *quijotismo*, is madness, the mad daughter of the madness of the cross. Reason, therefore, despises *quijotismo*. Philosophy, at heart, hates Christianity.

308. Unamuno, Miguel de. "Sobre la lectura e interpretación del *Quijote*," in *Obras completas,* I. Madrid: Escelicer, 1966, pp. 1227-1238. (First published in *La España Moderna,* año XVII, núm. 196; April, 1905, pp. 5-22.)

What Cervantes' intention was in writing the *Quijote* is immaterial assuming that he was trying to say anything at all. Since when is the author of a book the one who understands it best?

Once published, the *Quijote* is no longer Cervantes' property; it belongs to those who read it.

Cervantes took Don Quijote from the soul of his people and from the soul of humanity, and in his book the author returned the hero to his people and to all humanity. Don Quijote actually lived and continues to live more intensely and more effectively than if he had existed historically in the usual sense. Each generation adds something to Don Quijote, so that he becomes transformed. He is what the reader thinks of him; he is a figure outside the book. Cervantes wrote his masterpiece at the beginning of the seventeenth century for the people of those times; but Don Quijote himself has traveled through all the countries of the world for three centuries. The fact that the figure Don Quijote is not the same person in nineteenth-century England that he was in seventeenth-century Spain proves the vitality of the figure Don Quijote.

Cervantes is enormously inferior to his masterpiece. Without the *Quijote* Cervantes might be a tenth-rate writer. His *Novelas ejemplares* are insipid. The *novelas* and other digressions in the *Quijote* do not deserve attention. Cervantes is also inferior to Don Quijote the man. If Cervantes was his father, Don Quijote's mother was the Spain in which he lived. And Don Quijote has more of his mother than of his father. Cervantes never understood the greatness of his novel. If he returned today, he would be a *cervantista* and not a *quijotista*. Sancho is also poorly understood. Cervantes misunderstood him too. If the author is malicious to the Knight, he is unfair to the Squire. Cervantes causes Sancho to say and do things the Squire could never have said or done. But Sancho changes from a materialist to one of the most disinterested creatures in the world.

309. Unamuno, Miguel de. *Vida de Don Quijote y Sancho, según Miguel de Cervantes Saavedra, explicada y comentada.* Madrid: Espasa-Calpe, S. A., 1958. Pp. 230. (First published in Madrid, 1905: F. Fe.)

[Unamuno gives a chapter by chapter analysis of the *Quijote*, omitting from time to time portions (especially the interpolated tales and episodes) which he does not deem to be pertinent to the heart of the story or to life in general. Many of the ideas contained in this work were summarized in the previous entry and will not be repeated here. Unamuno does point out in this work his belief that the mad Knight knows deepdown that inns are only inns. To Unamuno, a madman is a profound comedian who takes the play of life seriously without being deceived. Dulcinea is also discussed and declared to be the symbol of fame and immortality.

Throughout this work Unamuno notes parallels between Don Quijote and Ignatius Loyola whose biography had been published in 1583. Unamuno observes that the Knight and Loyola were of similar temperament, that they both loved chivalry novels, and that a number of the incidents in Don Quijote's career bear a striking resemblance to events in the life of Ignatius Loyola. Unamuno concedes, however, that Juan Huarte's *Examen de ingenios* was the probable source of the description of the Knight's personality.

For additional discussion of this work, see Paul M. Descouzis (90) and Ángel del Río (250).]

310. Valera y Alcalá Galiano, Juan. *Discurso escrito por encargo de la Real Academia Española para conmemorar el tercer centenario de la publicación de "El ingenioso hidalgo Don Quijote de la Mancha," leído por el excmo. sr. D. Alejandro Pidal y Mon.* Madrid: Imprenta Alemana, 1905. Pp. 46.

The *Quijote* is a pure book of entertainment, a literary satire, and it is amazing that it has had such an intellectual effect. Cervantes was not a reformer, though he criticized the vices of the clergy and other groups. He is a man of his era, a happy, active, and healthy conformist.

Sancho has been unjustly condemned. He is not a glutton, an egoist. Nor is he a contrast to the noble Don. Sancho is much more a complement to his idealistic master.

311. Van Doren, Mark. *Don Quixote's Profession.* New York: Columbia University Press, 1958. Pp. viii + 99. [Appreciation is expressed to Sonia de Lama for her assistance in this summary.]

Don Quijote suffered no delusion as to his identity. He formed, from his reading, a conception of life as he would henceforth lead it if he could, but he did not really think he was a knight. It is that he was first and last an actor, a skillfull and conscious actor who wrote his own play as he proceeded and, of course, kept the center of the stage. Does the Knight later forget he is an actor? This question is difficult to answer, but it is not impossible to say that he always knows what he is doing. He is that rare thing in literature, a completely created character. He is so real that we cannot be sure we understand him.

The *Quijote* is made up of a series of adventures or a series of conversations that become interwoven. The discussions often move the plot forward. Don Quijote is not only a doer but an eloquent speaker who can bring out the eloquence in others. At the end of the story the Knight decides to cease acting altogether, for he is weary of the hoax, of pretending that he does not know the world for what it is.

Cervantes never appears to be serious. Though his hero is lonely and absurd, the author is never sentimental in his defense. We must conclude that Don Quijote is the most perfect knight that ever lived, though Cervantes never asks us to come to that conclusion. As the book progresses, the author's satire ripens into comedy, his ridicule deepens into love. Cervantes does not, however, give adoration to the Knight and the Squire; he merely gives them life.

312. Varo, Carlos. *Génesis y evolución del Quijote*. Madrid: Ediciones Alcalá, 1968. Pp. 598.

[Varo's work consists of an introduction, twelve chapters, a lengthy bibliography and an index. Each chapter discusses a unit of the *Quijote* and contains a recapitulation at the end. The principal question in the interpretation of the *Quijote* is, to Varo, whether Cervantes is a resentful writer. This problem is traced from Juan Maruján in 1750. The critic concludes that the author of the *Quijote* was not bitter, that he loved mankind, that he was, like all his characters, a healthy optimist. Cervantes, Varo admits, at first created the Don as an anti-hero, but his "daimon" rebelled and during the Sierra Morena episode he began to picture his

Knight in a different light — as human and intelligent, not merely a fool.]

313. Vilanova, Antonio. *Erasmo y Cervantes*. Barcelona: C. S. I. C., 1949. Pp. 63.

[Vilanova first discusses prior works on the influence of Erasmus in Spain and on Cervantes, such as Menéndez Pelayo's "Cultura literaria de Cervantes" (198), Américo Castro's *Pensamiento de Cervantes* (63), and Marcel Bataillon's *Erasme et l'Espagne* (29). Next he presents his own approach to the true influence of the Dutchman on Cervantes' masterpiece.]

In his *Moriae Encomium* or *Stultitiae Laus* Erasmus sarcastically condemns the stupidity and madness of mankind. To make his irony more effective the author praises man's folly: his urge for fame, his cult of wisdom, his overemphasis on amorous passion, and even the madness of religious faith. But at the same time Erasmus sees madness as a vital impulse, a force for enthusiasm and progress. He further believes that the madman, who does not fear failure, is the truly happy man. Throughout his *Praise of Folly*, the Dutchman is ambiguous about reason and madness. All in all, however, we feel a need for insanity after reading his *Moriae Encomium*.

In the *Quijote* Cervantes injects the same imprecise duality of the sublime and ridiculous that Erasmus had pointed out as an essential characteristic of madness, and relegating to a secondary level his original intention to satirize books of chivalry, he illustrates his bitter awareness of failure by idealizing the sublime madness of his hero. Far from ridiculing the ideal madness of the Knight, Cervantes underlines with bitter discouragement the failure of the noble enterprise which the hero undertakes. The Cervantine conception of the *Quijote,* pregnant both with atrocious pessimism as well as with untamed enthusiasm, ridicules the chivalresque illusion because it is anachronistic in a world corrupted by wickedness and deceit. The author's true rancor thus is projected against the abject baseness of the real world, not against his foolish hero. In the figure of Don Quijote, Cervantes incarnates the most human personification of madness as the last refuge of justice, of truth, and of heroism.

Cervantes' conception of madness as a confusion of the senses has its source in Erasmus' *Moriae Encomium,* as does the Spaniard's belief that madness is necessary to happiness. It is also an Erasmian idea that the error of madness attributes more reality to the illusion of fantasy than to actual phenomena. This idea is seized upon by Cervantes with such force in the moment of elaborating the *Quijote* that almost all the episodes of Part I are based on this concept. From the moment in which the Don decides to become a knight, the hallucination of his madness replaces real life, and the world of fiction acquires a higher reality than the outer world. Also found in the *Moriae Encomium* and in the *Quijote* is the belief that excessive reading leads to madness.

Erasmus' case history of the poor man who thought himself Croesus is similar to the poor hidalgo's imagining himself a powerful knight-errant. Another case study by Erasmus, that of the man who swore that his average-looking wife was the most beautiful woman of all, is quite like the Don's idealization of prostitutes and his exaltation of Aldonza Lorenzo. As one can see, in Erasmus and Cervantes, there is an allusion to the same type of error which consists in the attribution of precious and non-existing qualities to the most gross and vulgar realities.

Although there are other important influences on the *Quijote,* such as *Orlando furioso* and possibly the *Entremés de los romances,* the illusion and reality concept of Erasmus is most significant, for Cervantes takes this concept and makes a story of it. The Knight is caused to have a madness of the imagination, not of the understanding (as was the case with Ariosto's Orlando). The madness of Orlando is an ironic joke, a grotesque ridicule of the hero. The insanity of the Don is a satire and at the same time an idealization of the illusions of glory of a madman who dreams heroic fantasies.

314. Villegas del Hoyo, Baldomero. *La revolución española: Estudio en que se descubre cuál y cómo fue el verdadero ingenio de D. Quijote y el pensamiento del simpar Cervantes.* Madrid: Imprenta de Fortanet, 1903. Pp. 623.

In seeking an esoteric interpretation of the *Quijote* three things should be borne in mind: (1) the Catholic Renaissance was a dismal thing for Spain, since it brought in the domination of the Church; (2) Cervantes was not a man in accord with his times, but a victim of his times; (3) the *Quijote* was not intended to ridicule books of chivalry, because they were of a truly primitive Christian nature, in opposition to the pagan authoritarianism of the Renaissance. Don Quijote and Sancho are a dualistic entity, spirit and matter, and represent the regenerative forces in Spanish society. They are opposed to the reactionary duo of the priest and the barber.

Part I of the novel is an abstract study of life, while Part II reveals the impurities of practical reality and gives rules for life and for governing. Sansón Carrasco represents the powers of reaction. The two names given him, Caballero de los *Espejos* and Caballero de la Blanca *Luna,* reveal objects (mirror and moon) which have no light of their own. Diego Miranda, El Caballero del Verde Gabán, is a possible redeeming force, for he is the best of the society of the times. Nevertheless, he is non-idealistic. He represents theocracy, while the Knight symbolizes democracy. The episode of Camacho's wedding reveals Cervantes' opposition to Church interference, at Trent, in marriages and to the assumption by the Church of the role of the parents in arranging marriages.

Montesinos' Cave is a criticism of the state of Christianity since it had been frozen by Charlemagne, who had unfortunately joined Church and State. The adventure of the enchanted boat, the boat without oars, reveals that society cannot be regenerated through the Church. The moral of the episode at the palace of the Duke and Duchess is that Spain can be redeemed only with the cooperation of the executive power.

Cervantes' four basic concepts are: (1) the Church should not intrude in non-religious matters; (2) the courts should be fair and independent; (3) the army should be small but exemplary in its bravery; (4) the executive power, whether a monarchy or a republic, should be temperate and should keep the courts, the army, and the Church in proper balance; the State should not impose its ideas on the people.

315. Wagner, Charles Philip. "The Sources of *El Caballero Cifar*." *Revue Hispanique*, X (1903), 5-104, at 59.

[While this work does not deal with the *Quijote* to any great extent, it is important because it appears to be the first comparison of Sancho Panza and the squire Ribaldo in *El Caballero Cifar,* a lengthy work written about 1300 and published prior to the *Quijote* only once, in 1512. Wagner states as follows:] Another agreable trait that clings to Ribaldo even after he has become the respected "Cauallero Amigo," counsellor of the king, is his fondness for proverbs. This habit, which he possesses in common with Sancho Panza, makes inevitable the comparison of the two characters. Both are of humble origin and are elected to serve the most serious of knights-errant. Both possess the same combination of simplicity, shrewdness and good-nature; and each has his fund of proverbial philosophy. This parallel is hardly a sufficient basis for the assumption that the *Quijote* owes one of its greatest charms to the humble *escudero* of the *Cifar;* but it is certain that Cervantes knew of more romances of chivalry than those sacrificed in the Curate's holocaust. If by some chance he was familiar with this obscure work, the literary influence of the *Cifar* is incalculable.

316. Wardropper, Bruce W. *"Don Quijote:* Story of History?" *Modern Philology,* LXIII (1965), 1-11.

The modern novel has its roots in historiography, in so-called "true" histories such as Lucian's *Vera Historia* and Heliodorus' *Historia Aethiopica.* The initial paradox of the *Quijote* is that it is a story (fiction) masquerading as true history. Aristotle sought to distinguish between history and fiction, but the distinction is not really clear. All history merely pretends to be true history, for historians often imagine motives. Cervantes is not sure of the distinction between literature and true history, and this awareness of the ill-defined frontier between the two genres, between truth and lie, is what constitutes the *Quijote,* what distinguishes the novel from the romance.

Cervantes uses a number of devices to make his hero seem true. For example, the questioning of the truth of his own work has the odd effect of adding the appearance of historical accuracy. Also the hero Knight of Part II standing up to face the false Don Quijote of Avellaneda adds great realness and trueness to Cervantes' Knight. Here, also, the author obliterates the dividing line between the actual and the potential, the historical and the fictional, the real and the imaginary.

Both the reader and Don Quijote lose their critical faculty; in fact, most of the characters in the story cannot distinguish between the fictional and the real. Thus it would seem that the chief butt of Cervantes' satire is man's guillibility, not books of chivalry.

317. Weinrich, Harald. *Das Ingenium Don Quijotes. Ein Beitrag zur literarischen Charakterkunde.* Münster, Westfallen: Aschendorff, 1956. Pp. 130.

[The word *ingenioso* has been translated in a variety of ways. The purpose of Weinrich's work is to examine the meaning of that word as used by Cervantes. Chapter I discusses the word *Ingenium* in general, and subsequent chapters seek to show its relation to insanity (Ch. II), to education (Ch. III), and to *Poesie* (Ch. IV).]

In Part I Cervantes uses the word *ingenioso* ironically. The hero's seeing windmills as giants is not a sign of true *ingenio*. *Ingenium* is somehow connected with *entendimiento*. Also, *ingenio* and *discreción* are related and occasionally used as synonyms. However, *ingenio* is a force without direction, whereas *discreción* deals with achieving a goal.

Don Quijote's madness becomes paradoxical as the story moves along, for Cervantes causes his hero to be a *cuerdo-loco*. It is wrong to condemn Cervantes for his attitude toward the Don's madness, for the author lifted his protagonist out of blind madness in sympathy for him, and based this uplifting on psychological principles known in his day.

There is a difference between *furor* (madness) and *stultitia* (folly), and this difference is one of the main themes of the *Quijote*. It is Sancho who is *stultus,* not the Don, for *stultitia* is related to a phlegmatic disposition. *Furor (locura)* can be positive (heroic) or negative (madness). Cervantes follows Aristotle's (not Plato's) concept of *furor divinus* (lofty madness), namely that it resulted from the good *ingenio* of the one possessed with madness, and did not result from the madness itself (Plato). Don Quijote is *amarillo,* or *palidus,* a sign of melancholy madness. Melancholy, in ancient literature, could lead to brilliance, *genio,* sharpness of mind.

Cervantes was wery much aware of the double nature of melancholy *furor*. Several kinds of *furor* were known to doctors of Cervantes' day, and earlier, and *furor propheticus* was one of these types. For that reason the hero is often pictured as a biblical prophet using language from the Scriptures.

Cervantes had two purposes in writing the *Quijote:* (1) to write a good novel of chivalry; (2) to parody the common-place wares of the existing chivalry novels. These two intentions are tied in with the two aspects of the hero's madness: (1) insanity; and (2) endowment with noble sentiments.

318. Willis, Raymond S. "Sancho Panza: Prototype for the Modern Novel." *Hispanic Review,* XXXVII (1969), 207-227.

Sancho is not just a sum of qualities opposite to those of his idealistic master. The Squire is not the epitome of common sense, nor is he completely sane. Sancho, though bedded in the earth, has a desire to mould his own destiny.

At the beginning of the story both protagonists have a tragic void; they lack a transcendental ideal, something that will galvanize them out of mere existence into actual living. But there is a difference between the two central figures. Don Quijote is not as "modern" as Sancho, because the Knight becomes insane and generates his own faith out of madness. He has a "self-starter" like the saints of earlier times.

Sancho has only a second-hand faith, and is functionally the prototype of the novelistic figures of today: creatures who are prey to doubt, discouragement and vacillation. Sancho is a modern man, and as such he is forced into a dilemma: he must both see *and* believe; he must see that the basin is a basin, yet believe that it is a helmet, if, logically, he is to be able to keep the harness. Like the modern man, Sancho blunderingly stands on the side of faith, while at the same time he unconsciously defines the equivocal nature of human truth with his ludicrous word "basi-helmet."

In a sense, Cervantes bequeathed to every modern novelist his central theme and preoccupation: the plight of modern man, the man of human dimensions, who is a stranger to himself, an exile in his own land, an alien to his own times, trying to forge an authentic existence within these impossible circumstances.

319. Willis, Raymond S., Jr. *The Phantom Chapters of the Quijote.* New York: Hispanic Institute in the United States, 1953. Pp. 128.

There are two types of textual linking in the Quijote: (1) at the end of a chapter the reader's attention is left not only suspended, but thrusting forward timewise into the future, textually into the next chapter; (2) at the beginning of a chapter, after the reader has been lulled into a false repose by the close of the previous chapter, and further deceived by the epigraph of the new chapter, there is a sudden provocation of the reader's recollection of not merely the substance but also the actual wording of the text that has preceded it.

An overall motif of the *Quijote* is the paradox of seeming and being, and Cervantes' stylistic paradoxes tie in with this overall motif: he appears to end an episode and then does not end it (as at the end of Chapter 34, Part I, where the author appears to be about to end the story of the *Curioso impertinente* but then has an interruption at the beginning of the next chapter).

The beginnings of many of Cervantes' chapters tie in with the overflow of the previous chapter, and hence, like his chapter closings, violate the logic of the chapter as a unity. But the situation in chapter openings is not simply the opposite of chapter closings. Since the reader has a memory of the previous chapter ending, the chapter opening is psychologically predetermined — depending on the type (end-stopped, overflowing, or restless) of the ending of the previous chapter. Cervantes capitalizes upon this predetermination of the structure of the chapter opening and uses the principle of "discord within concord," presenting a vast variety of chapter openings in spite of predetermination. He seeks ways to surprise and tantalize the reader by defrauding his expectations just sufficiently to maintain alive the awareness of stylistic liaison.

Viewed in the aggregate the Cervantine chapter is a self-contradiction, and not simply because it is stylistically annulled as a division of the text. The chapter is not congruent in any sense with the structure of the narrative, for the intervals may come at any point therein. Something is seriously, nor humorously, absurd about the chapter structure in the *Quijote*. In this novel there is no logical first nor last. There is, instead, a constant flux of doing and becoming. There are two antithetical entities in the *Quijote,* the *Historia* (adventures) and the *Novel* (the will acting on circumstances), and they are not simply co-existent within the same covers; they are interlocked. Hence the tension. And the tension is most evident where Cervantes effects formal division of the text. The text of the openings and the closings of the chapters in the *Quijote* is that which simultaneously destroys and recreates the textual movement. It is an expression and a synthesis of the Cervantine esthetic, a resolution of the difference between organic form and formal structure into a *furious statis.*

320. Woodberry, George Edward. *Great Writers.* New York: The MacMillan Company, 1912, pp. 1-36.

Don Quijote is a book that has all the dimensions of life: personal, geographical, historical, emotional, moral. It sweats Spain as an olive sweats oil. The novel is part life, part literature; and all varieties of literature used in Spain are to be found in it. Cervantes was double-natured, part realistic, part academic. His novel is like a watershed; it looks backward to chivalry and forward to realism. It is true that Ariosto had already viewed the world of chivalry with a certain irony, but Cervantes brings his irony into the living, actual world, the world of prose. Therefore, the Quijote is said to be the beginning of modern literature.

In his masterpiece Cervantes shows that both sense (Sancho) and soul-imagination (Don Quijote) are subject to error. The higher is betrayed by his own nobility; the lower is duped by his own baseness. Modern dismay begins with the realization that high aims may be ridiculous, that the soul in its exaltation, its gentleness and sacrifice, has no necessary wisdom and its own vision no warrant of reality. These are the truths that make the *Quijote* such sorry reading for the idealist. In essence, Cervantes concludes that the governing factor in human life is its mortal condition, not its spiritual motive. The peculiarity of the novel is that all this is set forth with loud laughter, with frank and overflowing sympathy with the world as it is. It is the acceptance of the lower element that reveals the victory of realism, of the positive spirit, and of the oncoming age.

ADDENDUM

321. *Revista de Filología Española,* XXXII (1948).

[This volume contains nine articles on Cervantes and his works, including the following six summarized in this bibliography: "Aportación de los hispanistas extranjeros al estudio de Cervantes" (232), by E. Allison Peers; "El concepto de la verdad en el *Quijote*" (230), by A. A. Parker; "Historia de la crítica e interpretación de la obra de Cervantes" (243), by César Real de la Riva; "La técnica narrativa de Cervantes" (93), by Guillermo Díaz-Plaja; "Arquitectura del *Quijote*" (212), by Enrique Moreno Baez; and "La significación doctrinal del *Quijote*" (227), by Leopoldo Eulogio Palacios.]

The Department of Romance Studies Digital Arts and Collaboration Lab at the University of North Carolina at Chapel Hill is proud to support the digitization of the North Carolina Studies in the Romance Languages and Literatures series.

www.ingramcontent.com/pod-product-compliance
Lightning Source LLC
Chambersburg PA
CBHW030615230426
43661CB00053B/2004